Music Library Association
Basic Manual Series

Jean Morrow, Series Editor

1. *Music Classification Systems*, by Mark McKnight, edited by Linda Barnhart, 2002.
2. *Binding and Care of Printed Music*, by Alice Carli, 2003.
3. *Music Library Instruction*, by Gregg S. Geary, Laura M. Snyder, and Kathleen A. Abromeit, edited by Deborah Campana, 2004.
4. *Library Acquisition of Music*, by R. Michael Fling, edited by Peter Munstedt, 2004.

Library Acquisition of Music

R. Michael Fling

Edited by
Peter Munstedt

Music Library Association
Basic Manual Series, No. 4

The Scarecrow Press, Inc.
Lanham, Maryland • Toronto • Oxford
and
Music Library Association
2004

SCARECROW PRESS, INC.

Published in the United States of America
by Scarecrow Press, Inc.
A wholly owned subsidiary of
The Rowman & Littlefield Publishing Group, Inc.
4501 Forbes Boulevard, Suite 200, Lanham, Maryland 20706
www.scarecrowpress.com

PO Box 317
Oxford
OX2 9RU, UK

British Library Cataloguing in Publication Information Available

Library of Congress Cataloging-in-Publication Data

Fling, Robert Michael, 1941–
  Library acquisition of music / R. Michael Fling.
    p. cm. — (Music Library Association basic manual series ; no. 4)
  Includes bibliographical references and index.
  ISBN 0-8108-5124-5 (pbk. : alk. paper)
  1. Acquisitions (Libraries) 2. Music librarianship. I. Title. II. Series.
ML111.F48 2004
025.2'88—dc22

                                                        2004007674

CONTENTS

Preface   vii

1 Introduction   1
2 Printed Music Publishing   11
3 Recorded Music Publishing   33
4 Music Publishers' Numbers   49
5 Vendors   63
6 Preorder Searching   81
7 Preorder Verification   95
8 The Ordering Process   115
9 Secondhand and Out-of-Print Music   133
10 Miscellanea   149

Glossary   179
Selected Bibliography   197
Index   215
About the Author   233

PREFACE

As many readers of this manual will already have learned, there are no library acquisitions rules for music comparable to those that music catalogers can consult; no standards as are applicable to binding, preservation, storage, statistics, and other library functions; nor is there any recognized canon of resources such as music reference librarians turn to. Much of what is described in this manual, therefore, reflects my personal experiences, accumulated largely through trial and error during more than two decades of selecting and acquiring scholarly and practical editions for a library serving the students and faculty at a large, academic school of music. It is inevitable, therefore, that some personal biases may have intruded, possibly to cause a few readers to wonder why this beloved vendor, or that favored verification tool, are not described in these pages. This manual cannot be all-inclusive, nor is it prescriptive. Readers are encouraged to investigate any promising music acquisitions resources available to them, whether or not described herein, particularly as new ones emerge.

There are several things that this manual does not attempt to do. It does not predict the future: inevitable mass extinctions of formats and evolving digital technology and applications will surely influence library collections and acquisitions practices of the future; the present discussion, however, focuses on music publishing models and formats prevalent in libraries in the early years of the twenty-first century. This manual does not reinvent the wheel: the reader can find excellent, broadly applicable advice elsewhere about such topics as automated acquisitions systems, acquiring serials, gifts and exchanges, the licensing of digital content, and professional ethics; the focus here, rather, is on procedures and practices peculiar to *music* acquisitions, to the exclusion (mostly) of other kinds of acquisitions. (Notable exceptions are the non-U.S. dissertations and the on-demand microfilms that are discussed among the miscellanea of the final chapter; although these formats are not specifically musical, they need to be acquired for many music collections, and they are largely ignored in the general acquisitions literature.) This manual does not discuss collection development, insofar as is feasible: the emphasis here is on *how* to acquire, not *what* to acquire.

In part because acquisitions work depends increasingly upon volatile online resources, it is inevitable that some of what is written here will soon become outdated, perhaps even before this manual reaches print: firms merge or cease operation, modify their business practices, and change addresses. (URLs for all websites identified in this manual were accessed and verified as of 15 March 2004.) Fortunately, powerful Internet search engines can often locate fugitive publishers and digital resources if they are still operating. When one is at an apparent dead end, however, no asset can be more valuable than the collective wisdom of colleagues: a query to the Music Library Association's electronic discussion group, MLA-L, has a good chance of eliciting current information about all manner of music library work, including acquisitions. Information about MLA-L and access to its searchable archive of messages dating back to 1990 are found among the "Useful Sources Online" at the association's website: www.musiclibraryassoc.org.

I wish to thank Peter Munstedt and Jean Morrow (of the MLA Basic Manual Series editorial board), who commissioned me to write this book, who indulged my need to postpone its writing for more than a year while I completed another project, and who offered editorial guidance along the way. Mary Wallace Davidson, head of the William & Gayle Cook Music Library at Indiana University, read several sections in draft versions, and her thoughtful suggestions have been incorporated into the text. I am particularly grateful to Christine Clark, president of Theodore Front Musical Literature in Van Nuys, California, who gave generously of her time and expertise in answering my many questions about the music business and how it relates to libraries, and for previewing draft versions of several chapters.

INTRODUCTION

Prior to the exponential growth in the output of library materials that began in the 1960s, and the concurrent emergence of the collection development librarian to manage them, "acquisitions" was commonly understood to include work that now is performed by selectors and bibliographers, as well as by ordering and receiving units. Writers routinely used "acquisition" as synonymous with "selection." In most libraries today there is a demarcation between the collection development process—the steps taken to determine what materials are needed for the collection—and acquisitions—the procurement of those materials. It is on the latter processes that this manual is focused.

Few librarians-in-training today are given meaningful instruction about the acquisitions process.[1] For those who go on to work in cataloging or reference, this shortfall appears to have little negative effect on job performance. Many librarians, however, are directly involved in acquisitions work, either in large libraries, where size justifies a separate acquisitions division, or in smaller ones, in which one librarian may be responsible for several functions—a familiar environment for many who work with music collections. These practitioners must learn their métier almost entirely on the job, by observation and osmosis, experimentation and error, serendipity and occasional epiphany. And there are no Anglo-American acquisitions rules.

While ordering, claiming, and receiving materials are the principal activities in acquisitions, there exists a wide range of associated procedures that, depending upon the organization of the library, may also fall under that rubric. Among these are preorder bibliographic searching and verification; vendor assignment; creation of purchase orders; online or paper order-file maintenance; canceling or claiming overdue orders; vendor correspondence to resolve shipping and billing problems; monitoring vendor performance; monitoring approval and blanket order plan performance; gathering and reporting statistics; notifying selectors and patron requestors of order status and new receipts; approving and processing invoices; and monitoring budgets.

Acquisitions was long the Cinderella of the library profession, toiling in her chimney corner while glamorous stepsisters Cataloging and Reference danced at the ball. Consequently the body of literature about library acquisitions was slow to develop and it still is relatively sparse compared with those of reference and cataloging. In the 1970s and 1980s, however, fairy godmother Automation arrived to wave her magic wand and redefine the role of the acquisitions librarian. Integrated library systems required that acquisitions work relate directly to collection development, cataloging, interlibrary loan, issues of access versus ownership, and the licensing of electronic resources. Acquisitions librarians became players in a broad range of management decisions, and their work the subject of increased discourse in the professional literature.

General Acquisitions Literature

Beginning in the early 1970s, the American Library Association (hereinafter ALA) recognized the need for some remedial literature about acquisitions and began publishing its monographic series *Acquisitions Guidelines*. Each of the brief handbooks in this series takes the reader through the basics of a discrete procedure, such as handling orders for in-print monographs, periodicals and serials, microforms, and software and other electronic publications. Additional titles in the series inform the novice acquisitions manager about statistics for acquisitions management, evaluating vendors, and managing approval plans.[2] Basics of these procedures also have been described more expansively in texts such as David Melcher's *Melcher on Acquisitions* (1971), Stephen Ford's *The Acquisition of Library Materials* (rev. ed., 1978), *Understanding the Business of Library Acquisitions*, edited by Karen Schmidt (2nd ed., 1999), Audrey Eaglen's *Buying Books: A How-to-Do-It Manual for Librarians* (2nd ed., 2000), and Wilkinson and Lewis's *The Complete Guide to Acquisitions Management* (2003).[3]

Acquisition of library materials has now become a rich enough topic to support its own body of periodical literature. *Library Acquisitions: Practice and Theory* (1977–1998) was the first journal to be devoted to acquisitions; in 1999 it expanded its scope (reflected by its new title, *Library Collections, Acquisitions, & Technical Services*) to provide a forum for the international exchange of ideas and experiences of members of the library technical services, collection management, vendor, and publishing communities. *The Acquisitions Librarian* (1989–) is an irregular publication that devotes each issue to a particular topic; each issue of the journal also is published simultaneously in a monographic series of the same title. *Against the Grain: Linking Publishers, Vendors and Librarians* (1989–) is a bimonthly practice-oriented acquisitions journal; in addition to feature articles, it has regular columns on legal issues, publishing, bookselling and vending, technology, and standards.

Other journals for librarians that include acquisitions as part of a broader palette of technical services concerns are two quarterlies: *Library Resources & Technical Services* from the Association of Library Collections and Technical Services (ALCTS) of ALA (1957–), and *Collection Management* (1976–).

ACQNET: The Acquisitions Librarians Electronic Network is a moderated discussion list where those "interested in acquisitions may exchange information and ideas, and find solutions to common problems."[4] During its first decade (1990–2000), ACQNET functioned as an electronic newsletter, with an International Standard Serial Number (ISSN) and volume and issue numberings. After the distribution of vol. 10, no. 17 (31 July 2000), it restructured to operate more like a typical electronic discussion list, though its focus remains unchanged, and its content continues to be moderated. Time-sensitive, single-issue postings, such as employment opportunities or conference announcements, are distributed by the editors as "ACQflashes," and the arrival of several per day in subscribers' e-mail is not unusual. ACQNET maintains an affiliation with AcqWeb, a website developed by Anna Belle Leiserson at Vanderbilt University, which provides links to publisher and vendor home pages, as well as links to a wealth of other resources of interest and value to library acquisitions personnel.[5]

Several bibliographies in the 1980s and 1990s chronicled the state of library acquisitions at the time. These contain citations, usually annotated, to literature on various classified subjects, including general works, approval plans, automation of acquisitions, out-of-print material, gifts and exchanges, vendor selection and evaluation, administration, publishing, and ethics. Among the more recent is Barbara Hall's "A Selected Bibliography for Library Acquisitions," 4th edition, compiled for ALCTS, posted at the association's website.[6] This listing recommends recent as well as "classic" books and articles that feature breadth and depth of coverage and broad applicability; it is partially annotated.

Music Acquisitions Literature

In contrast to this feast of readings to inform general library acquisitions, the plate set before music librarians holds thin gruel indeed. Most of the published guides to music librarianship are of such a vintage as to equate acquisitions with selection, and they do not venture into discussion of the methods and techniques of acquiring music materials.[7] These authors have set boldly forth to circumnavigate the globe of music librarianship, but seldom have they made acquisitions a port of call.[8] Similarly, articles and symposia that have assessed the state of music librarianship during a particular period, or have ventured to forecast the near future, have routinely had little to say about acquisitions.[9] This silence would be a puzzlement were it not for the fact that in few libraries are full-time, in-house music specialists involved in acquisitions. This activity usually takes place in a centralized acquisitions department, far removed from the music collection, though usually with the music bibliographer's advice. A common variation of the centralized model is for the music selector to be responsible for acquiring audio and other music nonprint media—a tacit admission that acquisition of music can require specialization, except, it seems, when it comes in a "traditional" format (print). Still, who among music librarians has not at some time been victimized by a central acquisitions department ignorant of the difference between a vocal score and a study score—much less between a *Taschenpartitur* and a *Spielpartitur*—and been forced to accept an unwanted edition. Having little direct contact with the acquisitions process, music librarians have had little opportunity to undertake empirical research about it, or develop theoretical underpinnings for it.

The paucity of writings about music acquisitions was documented in Don Phillips's 1974 classified listing of books and articles, *A Selected Bibliography of Music Librarianship*, which included only two articles about acquisitions procedures among the twenty-five in the section on "Selection and Order Work."[10] A few guides to music librarianship do cast at least a glance at acquisitions. *Manual of Music Librarianship* (1966), a collection of articles edited by Carol June Bradley, includes articles about acquisitions in the college library, and in the public library.[11] In addition to remarks about selection policies and tools, the authors make generalizations about the desirability of limiting the number of vendors used, ordering foreign editions from abroad to take advantage of favorable currency exchange rates, and the practicality of standing-order arrangements for certain types of publications.

Bradley's 1973 compilation, *Reader in Music Librarianship*, contains mostly reprints of earlier articles, and several of them tempt us with titles suggesting that practical acquisitions information will be coming our way.[12] Indeed, H. P. Dawson and B. R. Marks's "The Ordering and Supply of Sheet Music" gives tips about the essential information that should be included on a purchase order for music.[13] James B. Coover's "Selection Policies for a University Music Library" gives some guidelines for creating a blanket order for music scores and includes the profile established in 1968 with Otto Harrassowitz for the SUNY Buffalo Music Library.[14] For D. W. Krummel's "Observations on Library Acquisitions of Music," however, the compiler or publisher neglected to include the original subheading of the article— "Antiquarian Music Dealers: A Librarian Speaks"—which would have alerted readers to the article's rather more limited scope than the title itself implies.[15] In the same *Reader*, Vincent Duckles's "Book Buying in a University Music Library" focuses on the topic of collection policies, but also includes information about the structure of the materials budget at the University of California, Berkeley, Music Library at the time of its writing.[16] While the two volumes edited by Bradley provided useful advice in their day, the remarks about acquisitions in these articles are now far too dated to be of practical application in the wired library and music publishing environments of the twenty-first century.

The extent of Malcolm Jones's remarks about acquisitions in his *Music Librarianship* (1979) is to scold music librarians for taking money from the pockets of the few remaining music retailers by buying directly from publishers.[17] Ian Ledsham's recent *Comprehensive Guide to Music Librarianship* (2000) devotes a few pages to music acquisition methods and resources, but it has a British bias, and few of the sources named will be of much value to American users.[18] The collection of essays in *Music Librarianship in the United Kingdom* (2003), like its predecessors in a similar vein, steers clear of acquisitions.[19] Several guides to instrumental ensemble librarianship published between 1972 and 1995 offer little more than generalities about working closely with a local music dealer if possible, ordering well in advance of need, and providing full bibliographic information on purchase orders.[20]

Chapters about music, written by music librarians, in textbooks on collection building in the humanities often give good practical guidance to potential or new music selectors. Michael A. Keller's chapter in 1985's *Selection of Library Materials in the Humanities, Social Sciences, and Sciences* is a particularly fine discussion of the issues and sources for selection and acquisition of all kinds of music materials, and much of it remains valid nearly two decades after its appearance.[21]

Although the essence of Keller's chapter is collection development, he plants signposts, too, for the reader whose destination is acquisitions.

Finally, two publications from the early 1980s—one produced by a music vendor selling to libraries, and the other by the Music Library Association—give some real and practical information about music acquisition. Peter B. Brown's *Ordering and Claiming Music Materials: Tips from a Dealer*[22] is a concise presentation of useful tips for preparing music orders, and though now somewhat dated, much of it remains pertinent for librarians in the 2000s. Brown was an associate at Theodore Front Musical Literature, which published this booklet in response to the poor-quality purchase orders that libraries were sending. He gives guidelines for minimum information that dealers require to fill orders correctly, along with discussion of pricing practices, how to place antiquarian orders, music publisher edition numbers, and claiming procedures for orders believed to be overdue. *The Acquisition and Cataloging of Music and Sound Recordings: A Glossary*, compiled by Suzanne E. Thorin and Carole Franklin Vidali for publication as MLA Technical Reports no. 11,[23] is a useful handbook for nonspecialists who find themselves responsible for aspects of a music collection. Thorin compiled the "Music" chapter (that is, *printed* music), and Vidali the "Sound Recordings" chapter.[24] The glossary included terminology for the then-new compact disc, but users today will, of course, have to look elsewhere for definitions of more recent audio, video, and multimedia developments.

This brief recitation demonstrates how our forerunners in the music acquisitions game have mostly let chances slip by to transmit, in writing, the particular knowledge and skills they gained on the job. For the perspectives of a music librarian who is acquiring music in the 2000s, read on.

Notes

1. Karen A. Schmidt, "Education for Acquisitions: A History," *Library Resources & Technical Services* 34 (1990): 159–69.

2. A listing of all titles in the series is found in the present manual's bibliography. The earlier publications in this series are now out of print and due for updates, though still useful as concise checklists for basic procedures. A listing of all of ALA's in-print publications is found in the "Products and Publications" area of the organization's website: www.ala.org.

Notes (continued)

3. These are but a few of the available manuals on general library acquisitions; for more listings of monographs and articles on the subject, the reader is directed to the several bibliographies cited in the selected bibliography of the present manual, where full citations of all the general-literature monographs and series mentioned in this chapter will also be found.

4. Subscription information is found at http://acqweb.library.vanderbilt.edu/acqweb/acqnet.html. At this site there is also a link to the ACQNET archives.

5. http://acqweb.library.vanderbilt.edu. Among the features at AcqWeb is a selective directory of music publishers' and vendors' websites. AcqWeb provides links to ACQNET's backfiles and index, which are available also by anonymous FTP (file transfer protocol) from listserv.appstate.edu in the /pub/acqnet directory and related subdirectories. File-naming protocol for these backfiles is "ACQNET" followed by volume and issue number separated by a period (e.g., ACQNET2.50 contains vol. 2, no. 50). "ACQflashes" are not indexed, and are archived for only one calendar year.

6. ALCTS Bibliography, www.ala.org/Content/NavigationMenu/ALCTS/Publications6/Web_publication1/Web_publications.htm.

7. The following basic texts are essentially silent on the subject of music acquisitions: Lionel McColvin and Harold Reeves, *Music Libraries: Their Organization and Contents, with a Bibliography of Music and Musical Literature,* 2 vols. (London: Grafton, 1937–1938); rev. ed., *Music Libraries: Including a Comprehensive Bibliography of Music Literature and a Select Bibliography of Music Scores Published since 1957,* completely rewritten, revised, and extended by Jack Dove, 2 vols. (London: A. Deutsch, 1965). E. T. Bryant, *Music Librarianship: A Practical Guide* (London: J. Clarke; New York: Hafner, 1959); 2nd ed., with the assistance of Guy A. Marco (Metuchen, NJ: Scarecrow Press, 1985).

8. Note should be made of two French-language texts that address some of the topics covered in the present manual, but which focus on French resources, excluding many of those used by American librarians: *Guide d'acquisition de la musique imprimée à l'usage des bibliothèques musicales,* ed. by Michèle Lancelin, with Anne Catrice and Anna Guerrieri (Paris: Association Internationale des Bibliothèques, Archives, et Centres de Documentation Musicaux, 1993); and *Musique en bibliothèque,* nouv. éd., ed. by Yves Alix and Gilles Pierret, Collection Bibliothèques (Paris: Electre–Éditions du Cercle de la Librairie, 2002).

9. The absence of any discussion of music acquisitions in the following resources is notable: Jerrold Orne, "The Music Library in the College of the Future," in *Music and Libraries: Selected Papers of the Music Library Association Presented at Its 1942 Meetings,* ed. by Richard S. Hill (Washington, DC: MLA; ALA, 1943); Orne stated (p. 43) that "I am extremely grateful to you all for making it completely unnecessary for me to discuss the various phases of

Notes (continued)

processing the materials of music." Ruth Watanabe, "American Music Librarianship: An Overview in the Eighties," *Notes* 38 (1981): 239–56. *Modern Music Librarianship: Essays in Honor of Ruth Watanabe*, ed. by Alfred Mann, Festschrift Series 8 (Stuyvesant, NY: Pendragon; Kassel: Bärenreiter, 1989). *Music Librarianship in America*, ed. by Michael Ochs (Cambridge, MA: Harvard University, Eda Kuhn Loeb Music Library, 1991); originally published in *Harvard Library Bulletin* 2, no. 1 (Spring 1991). Mary Wallace Davidson, "American Music Libraries and Librarianship: Challenges for the Nineties," *Notes* 50 (1993): 13–22. *Music Librarianship at the Turn of the Century*, *Notes* 56 (March 2000), special issue; reprint, ed. by Richard Griscom with Amanda Maple, Music Library Association Technical Reports 27 (Lanham, MD: Scarecrow, 2000).

10. Don Phillips, "Selection and Order Work," in *A Selected Bibliography of Music Librarianship,* Occasional Papers 113 (Urbana, IL: University of Illinois, Graduate School of Library Science, 1974), 6–10. Phillips cites H. P. Dawson and B. R. Marks, "The Ordering and Supply of Sheet Music," *Brio* 2 (Spring 1965): 8–10, which is a primer on music acquisitions terminology, distinguishing among terms such as "full score," "vocal score," etc.; and Gordon B. Wright, "Music Literature and Its Dealers," *Notes* 23 (1966): 23–27, discusses the need for solid, friendly relations between librarians and vendors.

11. Walter Gerboth, "Acquisitions: College Library," and Irene Millen, "Acquisitions: Public Library," in *Manual of Music Librarianship* (Ann Arbor, MI: MLA, 1966), 14–21, 21–29.

12. *Reader in Music Librarianship*, ed. by Carol June Bradley (Washington, DC: Microcard Editions Books, 1973).

13. Ibid., 232–33; originally published in *Brio* 2 (Spring 1965): 8–10.

14. Ibid., 236–43; written specifically for the *Reader.*

15. Ibid., 225–31; originally published in *Notes* 23 (1966): 5–16.

16. Ibid., 234–35; originally published in *Notes: Supplement for Members* 8 (1949): 14–17.

17. Malcolm Jones, *Music Librarianship* (London: Clive Bingley; New York: K. G. Saur, 1979).

18. Ian Ledsham, "Music Acquisition Methods," and "Information Sources for Acquisition," in *The Comprehensive Guide to Music Librarianship: A Self Study Guide for Music Librarians*, 2 vols. and CD-ROM (Aberystwyth: Open Learning Unit, University of Wales, Llanbadarn Campus, 2000), vol. 2, unit 6, pp. 18–31; a supporting website is at www.aber.ac.uk/olu/muslib.

19. *Music Librarianship in the United Kingdom*, ed. by Richard Turbet (Burlington, VT: Ashgate, 2003).

20. Lawrence J. Intravaia, *Building a Superior School Band Library* (West Nyack, NY: Parker Publishing, 1972). Albert LeBlanc, *Organizing the Instrumental Music Library* (Evanston, IL: The Instrumentalist Co., 1974). Frank Byrne, *Practical Guide to the Music Library: Its Function, Organization and*

Notes (continued)

Maintenance (Cleveland: Ludwig Music, 1987). Christi Birch Blackley, "An Overview of Orchestra Librarianship" (M.S. thesis, University of North Carolina, Chapel Hill, 1995).

21. Michael A. Keller, "Music," in *Selection of Library Materials in the Humanities, Social Sciences, and Sciences*, ed. by Patricia A. McClung (Chicago: ALA, 1985), 139–63. See also Elisabeth Rebman, "Music," in *Humanities and the Library*, 2nd ed., ed. by Nena Couch and Nancy Allen (Chicago: ALA, 1993), 132–72.

22. Peter B. Brown, *Ordering and Claiming Music Materials: Tips from a Dealer*, Front Music Publications 4 (Beverly Hills, CA: Theodore Front Musical Literature, 1981).

23. Suzanne E. Thorin and Carole Franklin Vidali, *The Acquisition and Cataloging of Music and Sound Recordings: A Glossary* (n.p.: Music Library Association, 1984).

24. Obligatory full disclosure: I was editor of the MLA Technical Reports series when the *Glossary* was published, and my fingerprints are on many of the terms and definitions in it.

2

PRINTED MUSIC PUBLISHING

The development of printing technology in the fifteenth century, and its evolution thereafter, created a commercial market for intellectual works that brought about the establishment of publishing houses to produce works for distribution by booksellers. The term "publishing," therefore, became popularly associated with printing, an association that survives to this day. In time, publishers tended to concentrate on particular types of products, and by the nineteenth century, music publishing was well established as a separate mercantile enterprise. Until well into the twentieth century, the primary business of music publishers was to print copies of music and put them in shops for sale to the public.[1]

Today, music publishing, particularly in the realm of popular music, is generally more about copyrights than about printed products.[2] In fact, few pop songs are ever printed at all. Technological innovation and evolution have converted an industry that once created and marketed tangible products into a copyright industry that primarily licenses others to use its properties. Publishers' income now comes principally from the licensing of performance rights (radio play and live performances) and so-called mechanical rights (manufacture and sale of sound recordings); to a lesser extent, they also earn from synchronization rights (music used in timed synchronization with images in film, television, and advertising). Print today generates only about 10 to 12 percent of music publishers' income worldwide.[3] The heyday of inexpensive, mass-produced editions of songs in sheet form is over.[4]

Some popular-music publishers do oversee the preparation, production, and distribution of printed versions of their copyrighted works, but many others find it more expedient to license other companies (known as subpublishers, or selling agents) to print and distribute their music. These products typically are in the form of collections, called "folios," that feature works linked to a particular performing artist ("celebrity folios") or a particular album release ("matching folios"), are built around a theme such as *Great Songs of the Sixties* or *Favorites from Broadway and the Movies* ("concept folios"), or contain songs by diferent songwriters, popularized by different artists ("mixed folios"). Among the largest of these licensee–publishers are Hal Leonard Corporation, Music Sales Corporation, Warner Brothers Publications, and their affiliates (each subsumes many smaller imprints).

The functions of today's music publishers may be summarized as follows:[5]

Discovery and acquisition: publisher scouts for new composers by attending concerts and examining scores submitted for consideration; contracts with composers for rights to their works; may also acquire the catalogs of other publishers.

Promotion: advertises works to the public and to distributors; undertakes special campaigns, sponsorships, and other outreach, such as workshops for music educators.

Administration: manages copyrights, negotiates and licenses performance and recording rights, collects fees and disburses royalties.

Production: edits, arranges, prints, records, and distributes works for sale.

It is publishers who focus on the last named of these activities that have the attention of librarians, and luckily there are many music publishers, including some major ones, that still thrive by selling copies printed on paper.[6]

Types of Publishers

Most publishers of printed music limit their output to music (only a few book publishers have printed music departments, notably Oxford University Press, Faber, and Dover Publications). Depending upon the type of music they print and distribute, these publishers sometimes are categorized as concert music publishers, as educational music publishers, or as specialty publishers.

Concert music publishers (or publishers of "serious" music) print repertoire that is generally associated with the symphony orchestra, opera, ballet, chamber ensembles, instrumental and vocal soloists, and church music. Much of this music was written by pre-twentieth-century European composers, and is brought out in new editions tailored for today's school and amateur as well as professional performers. These publishers also typically produce study and instructional material for solo instruments and voice, and new works by composers of serious music. Some of the more ambitious concert music publishers also produce editions intended not for use in performance, but for the historical study of a composer or a repertoire—composer collected editions and historical sets (*Denkmäler*), for example. Editions by concert music publishers form the core of music collections in academic and research libraries. Representative concert music publishers include Theodore Presser, G. Schirmer, C. F. Peters, Boosey & Hawkes, Schott Musik International, G. Henle, Bärenreiter, Salabert, Ricordi, and Universal.

Educational music publishers print music intended primarily for use by students in schools, from elementary grades through college. Editions scored for concert and marching bands, choirs, and jazz groups, as well as solos and ensembles for school competitions are the main products of these publishers. Their editions are found in school band and choir libraries throughout America. Representative educational music publishers include Alfred Publishing, C. L. Barnhouse, Hal Leonard Corporation, and Southern Music Company.

Specialty publishers limit their catalogs to one kind of music. Specialties might be contemporary "serious" or avant-garde music (such as produced by Smith Publications), church music (GIA Publications), a particular instrument (Les productions d'OZ: guitar), a nationality (Edition Suecia: publishing arm of the Swedish Music Information Centre), or even a single composer (Dantalian, Inc.: works by American composer Donald Martino). Professional associations and institutes sometimes also function as publishers; they may publish a few works to meet some of the perceived needs, or to promote the interests, of the group (the Tuba–Euphonium Press of the International Tuba–Euphonium Association), while others exist solely to publish and promote a particular repertoire (the American Institute of Musicology: music of the Middle Ages and Renaissance). The possibilities for specialization are limited only by the founders' or publishers' interests or obsessions. In a subgenre of specialty publishers are composer collectives, such as Frog Peak Music (www.frogpeak.org), Master Musicians Collective (www.mmcproject.com), and the Association for the Promotion of New Music (www.subitomusic.com/APNM.htm). These artist-run organizations provide services that support performances and in some cases produce recorded and printed publications of their members' works.

The borders between these publishing categories are pliant, permeable, and partly artificial: there is no concert music publishers' guild to prevent educational music publishers from poaching their repertoire.[7] Specialty publishers, in fact, increasingly are the source for "new" concert music, particularly by American composers. Until recent decades, the mainstream concert music publishers sought out emerging composers of promise, printed their music, and actively promoted it through the sheet-music emporiums that once were found in every town. With the ascendance of the sound recording, however, and the attendant conversion of the public into passive listeners, market outlets and marketing opportunities for this music dried up, and the major concert-music publishers have shown an ever-decreasing interest in publishing it. If the continuity and supply of printed, newly composed music is to continue, it will be largely due to the activities of the many specialty publishers who have stepped into the gap.

U.S. Print Publishers and Their Distributors

Some music publishers are directly involved in the distribution of their editions, selling at wholesale to retailers and library vendors. Other publishers do not distribute their publications directly, but rely upon an intermediary—usually another, larger publisher—to deliver their goods to retailers. Examples of each are

> **Publisher only:** publishes music, and does only that; distribution is subcontracted; examples are Summy-Birchard Music, distributed by Warner Brothers Music; and Associated Music Publishers, distributed by the Hal Leonard Corporation.

> **Publisher and distributor:** publishes and distributes its own editions, as well as those of other publishers; examples are the aforementioned Warner Brothers Music and Hal Leonard Corporation, both of which claim at their websites to be the world's largest print music publisher.

Small publishers most likely enter into distribution agreements with larger publishers in hopes of increasing the visibility and sales of their editions. A publisher such as Hal Leonard Corporation, with its extensive network of more than 7,500 dealers and a large market share, certainly has the potential to enhance the success of the smaller catalogs that it represents. However, these arrangements can also fail, depending upon the quality of the smaller catalog and the larger publisher's interest in actually promoting the particular line of product. In these cases, the smaller publisher may seek a different distributor.

Foreign Print Publishers and Their U.S. Distributors

Several major music publishers have far-reaching international operations: Boosey & Hawkes has affiliates in the United Kingdom, the United States, Germany, and Australia, with agencies in nineteen other countries; Edition Peters operates in Frankfurt, Leipzig, London, and New York; Hal Leonard Corporation, headquartered in Milwaukee, Wisconsin, has offices in New York, Melbourne, Hong Kong, and London.

An alternative, or complementary, method of doing business abroad is for publishers to make arrangements with counterparts in other countries to distribute one another's editions. The venerable French publishing house Éditions Salabert, for example, makes its editions available in the United States through the Hal Leonard Corporation; Salabert, in turn, distributes Hal Leonard's publications in France. An advantage to the distributor of these foreign editions is that the U.S. retail prices can be set at the distributor's pleasure, usually at rates significantly higher than are charged for the same editions in their country of publication. Retailers typically are advised that the anointed distributor has the *sole* right to distribute this music in the United States. Such claims of exclusivity are often exaggerated—the domestic distributor may have obtained rights for only a portion of the foreign publisher's catalog—or are only part of the story. There is nothing to prevent the savvy vendor or librarian from bypassing the domestic agent's markup and ordering the publisher's editions from a distributor in the country of origin, where the original recommended list price is more likely to be honored.

In a perfect world, the U.S. distributor would keep in its warehouse plenty of copies of the complete catalog of the foreign publisher's editions, so that a library's order for one of those editions could be filled promptly. More often, the designated distributor keeps stock of only a small percentage of the foreign publisher's editions and may never intend to import titles that are judged to have limited appeal to American musicians.[8] Ordering from the publisher's U.S. distributor, therefore, is no guarantee that the order will be filled promptly—or at all. The distributor may simply declare the edition to be "not available" if it is not currently stocked in its warehouse. Once again, redirecting the order to a distributor abroad may produce a result that the U.S. distributor could not, or would not, match.

A directory of U.S. concert music publishers, with a listing of the domestic and foreign imprints they distribute, is maintained by the Music Publishers' Association (MPA) of the United States at www.mpa.

org (a reverse alphabetical index links the names of the distributed imprints to their distributors). These distribution agreements are reported by the publishers to the MPA, and are not authenticated by the association.

Print Publication Output

Collectively, print music publishers in 2001 produced worldwide approximately 3,200 to 3,500 new editions of the type of repertoire typically acquired by academic music libraries (about 1,800 to 2,000 of these editions were from American publishers).[9] And once scores are in print, some tend to remain available for appreciably longer periods of time than do books about music. Music editions of works still heard in recital and concert that were originally brought out a century ago by well-established music publishers remain in print today (though perhaps in updated guise) or they have been reprinted or re-edited by other publishers. Good music, it seems, is not as susceptible to changing times and tastes as is the written word.

On the other hand, publishers are allowing works by some seminal twentieth-century composers to go out of print. For example, many compositions by Lukas Foss and Norman Dello Joio, formerly published by Carl Fischer, are now described at the firm's website (www.carlfischer.com) as "permanently out of print"; perhaps a dozen works of Stravinsky and Prokofiev once available from Boosey & Hawkes also have been discontinued. Although it may not be economical for publishers to use traditional printing methods to produce the relatively large print runs required by economies of scale to keep these works in print, it is to be hoped that they will more aggressively adopt digital archiving and printing technologies that make possible the inexpensive, on-demand printing of even a single copy of a score, so that libraries and performers can continue to acquire this music. In theory, once a publisher's archive is digitized, none of its editions need ever be out of print again.

One observes, when perusing new-publication announcements from vendors and publishers, that much more newly composed music seems to be published in Europe, particularly in Germany, than in the United States. One possible explanation for this phenomenon is that American composers, reared in a culture that encourages, even worships, entrepreneurship, are more likely to self-publish than their European counterparts, and their works, therefore, simply may not achieve mainstream distribution. Another factor may be that music in Europe is subsidized by national and municipal governments; every town seems to have an orchestra, and even middling-size cities have thriving opera houses, where "house" divas are salaried as civil servants. The musicians who populate these institutions are always seeking new repertoire, and their audiences, perhaps, are culturally more receptive to hearing it. Publishers, therefore, may also be more likely to print it.

Reviews

New printed music editions are rarely reviewed. A commentator in the 1980s[10] estimated that "perhaps" 15 percent of published music ever gets reviewed at all; I suspect the number to be even smaller. Reviews may appear a few months after a work's publication, or even two or three years later, particularly if the edition is a scholarly one that requires careful consideration by an expert in the field. The decision to acquire a particular new edition for the library, therefore, rarely can wait for a review to appear, unless the edition is marginal to the library's collection in any case, since there is no guarantee that there will *be* a review.[11]

The principal journal reviewing new publications of serious music is the Music Library Association's (MLA's) quarterly journal *Notes*. Many other scholarly music journals contain at least occasional reviews of new printed-music editions, though none with the scope of coverage as is found in *Notes*. Reviews of new practical editions of music, intended for performers rather than scholars, can be found in several journals aimed at singers and players of particular instruments, such as *Classical Guitar* (www.classicalguitarmagazine.com) and the *Double Bassist* (www.doublebassist.com). These reviews are written by performers and teachers of the instruments involved.[12]

Bindings

Rarely is there a selection of bindings when acquiring music scores and parts. Composer collected editions and monumental sets—prestige projects for their publishers—customarily are hardbound during production, but most printed music is distributed only in paper covers. It is up to the library to bind it in some fashion, and it is a false economy not to do so.[13] Paperbound scores and parts are usually adequate for use by individual musicians and by ensembles that may rehearse and play from the printed parts of a particular work no more than once every few years. Printed music in libraries, though, needs strengthening if it is to have a reasonable life expectancy. Music editions as a rule are thinner than books—a score can be a single gathering or less, and a part is often no more than a single leaf—and they will not stand erect on library shelves without reinforcement. They are also subjected to repeated readings by successive users, all of whom will introduce dog-eared corners to facilitate page turns, and penciled—one hopes not penned—fingerings and rehearsal marks. Inadvertent rips also occur when breakneck page turns are required as the music moves relentlessly forward. While routine wear-and-tear resulting from normal use may not be significantly reduced by binding, every added protection given to the material will extend its usefulness.

Spiral Bindings

Wire spiral or plastic comb bindings (usually described by publishers as "spiral," whatever the actual makeup) are encountered in several circumstances. This inexpensive binding format is practical for some uses, because it allows the score to lie flat wherever it is opened. It is a popular format for liturgical organ music, and it seems to be de rigueur for the "fake books"—compilations of melodies with their chord symbols and lyrics—used by jazz and pop instrumentalists to improvise, or "fake," their own arrangements. Spiral bindings sometimes are used by composers who publish their own works, as well as by established publishers for scores that are expected to sell but a few copies. A spiral or comb can be threaded into a score by the publisher immediately before shipping—the score itself perhaps being freshly run off—thus saving warehouse space.

In a circulating library, it is inevitable that over time some of the perforated pages will become detached from the spiral, and that the spiral or comb itself will be broken or deformed from ordinary shelf wear. In recent years, music librarians have been working to raise the consciousness of publishers about the inappropriateness of spiral bindings for library collections, and a few publishers upon request now will produce and ship at least some of the scores in their catalogs in an unbound state. These are delivered as loose, printed sheets, without perforations, so that the library then can have them commercially bound in a way that is more suitable to circulating use. Scores that are designated "custom print edition" or by a similar phrase in a publisher's catalog are the most likely candidates for this treatment, since the publisher, presumably, has no stock on hand and must print each order from scratch. Similarly, rental scores that the publisher sells on special purchase sometimes can be sent unbound. In these circumstances, a request on the purchase order to "furnish unbound if possible" may produce the desired result.

Loose Sheets

Some editions are purposely delivered completely unbound, perhaps because the publisher has determined that there is no place in the music itself to include a page turn, or because the composer–publisher operating on a shoestring is simply delivering the goods in the most economical format. (In the latter case, one hopes, usually in vain, for double-sided printing, and sufficient margins to bind the material after it is received.) The publishers assume that performers will cobble the loose pages together, trimming and taping as needed, or will simply shuffle the separate pieces around on the music stand as required during rehearsal and performance. The former, of course, is not a suitable technique for a library to use. In many cases, simply protecting the loose parts in an envelope or portfolio may be the best course of action, with hopes that borrowers will return them in the same condition, without jury-rigged homemade "bindings."

Numerous other binding challenges face the librarian who manages a music collection, but few are susceptible to intervention by the library at the time the order is placed.[14] Editions with multiple performance parts, of course, are common, and most libraries have well-established procedures for dealing with them. Unanticipated anomalies can include parts that are printed on oblong single sheets folded accordion-style—known in the trade as "Leporello" binding, for the long list documenting his master's amorous conquests that the character Leporello dramatically unfolds during his act 1 aria "Madamina, il catalogo è questo" in Mozart's opera *Don Giovanni*. And sometimes parts are actually bound into the score—a remarkably impractical method of delivering scores and parts together. Staff who receive printed music acquisitions for the library should be alert for these and other unusual formats and bindings, and route them for appropriate treatment before they are sent out into the world.

Replacement Parts

Lost and missing parts are a plague upon printed music collections. When each of several performers in a chamber-music ensemble is responsible for one or more parts in a set, it is inevitable that, sooner or later, a part or parts will go missing. Unlike orchestral and choral parts, which are readily available from publishers in single copies, chamber music is usually sold only in complete sets. The odds are low, therefore, of being able to purchase only a clarinet part from a wind quintet. If the publisher will not provide single replacement parts, the library is arguably justified under section 108 (c) of the U.S. Copyright Act in replacing lost parts with photocopies. Although library photocopying in such cases may be perfectly legal, bear in mind that it can send a misleading message to individual borrowers—who may not understand the copying exemptions extended to libraries—that photocopying copyrighted music is an acceptable practice.

In some cases, the cost of acquiring an entire new set for the purpose of replacement may be low enough that doing so may be more economical and more convenient than borrowing from another library to copy the missing part, and then determining how best to format it so that it can be integrated with the remaining original parts. Replacement fees charged to borrowers for lost parts should, ideally, be set sufficiently high that full replacement is a viable option.[15] If the edition is out of print, however, the library may have no alternative to the copy machine.

Despite the caution about publishers' reluctance to sell individual parts, some, in fact, will do so if they have extras on hand, as can happen in the case of print overruns. It thus can be productive in some cases to e-mail an inquiry directly to the publisher about availability, particularly if the item is very expensive or oversize and not easily photocopied for a replacement part.[16]

Before acquiring replacements, whether photocopies or entire sets, a suitable waiting period is advisable in case absent parts should eventually find their way home. Some libraries harbor extensive collections of incomplete sets in hopes of happy reunions. Even if a replacement set is purchased, keeping the incomplete one on hand can be a good idea if space allows; returnees may appear months, even years, after the initial disappearance. If shelved in open stacks—even an incomplete set can be of use to some borrowers, as when, for example, a player can perform from an associated score in lieu of the missing part—they should be clearly marked as to which parts are missing, not only as warning to potential borrowers, but so that future borrowers are not incorrectly charged replacement fees.

Grade Levels (Difficulty)

Many educational music publishers, bibliographies, catalogs, reviewing sources, and some retailers use codes to indicate the level of difficulty of a musical work for the performer. The six grade-levels shown in figure 2.1 are used in the "New Music Reviews" column in the *Instrumentalist* magazine, and are widely adopted or imitated in the United States.

1—for beginners in their first year
2—easy music—for second- or third-year players
3—for intermediate students at the middle- or high-school level
4—for advanced high-school musicians
5—difficult—for college players
6—very difficult music—for advanced college players and professionals

Figure 2.1. Commonly Used Grading Levels

Sometimes a five-grade system is used that combines 1 and 2 of the six-grade system into a single "easy" category, reducing all the other grade-level numberings by one. Other systems use additional grade levels. Alphonse Leduc of Paris, for example, uses a nine-grade system, with 1–3 all designated as "facile" (easy), 4–6 as "moyenne force" (intermediate), and 7–9 as "difficile" (advanced). It is up to the user to interpret the finer shadings within each three-digit set.

Music for Large Ensembles

A symphony orchestra is a mutable ensemble. The wind and percussion instruments used in a work can vary depending upon the tonal coloration that the composer was seeking during composition. Publishers, dealers, and bibliographies of orchestral music use a standard numerical format to describe the instrumentation of an orchestral work in score order, beginning at the top: four digits represent the most commonly used woodwind instruments, four digits represent the most commonly used brass instruments; these are followed by abbreviations for percussion and strings. Thus,

2, 2, 2, 2—3, 2, 0, 0—timp, str

identifies a work for 2 flutes, 2 oboes, 2 clarinets, 2 bassoons—3 horns, 2 trumpets, 0 trombones, 0 tubas—timpani, and strings, which is the instrumentation required for Beethoven's Symphony no. 3 in E-flat, op. 55, the "Eroica."

Instruments that do not fall within the standard numbering code— saxophone, harpsichord, or a soloist, for example—are spelled out. Additional instruments within a group usually are indicated by a "+," and players who double on a second instrument—switch to it in midperformance—are indicated by a "d." Thus, woodwinds listed as

2+1, 2d1, 2+1, 2d1

indicate 2 flutes plus piccolo (3 players), 2 oboes with 1 doubling English horn (2 players), 2 clarinets plus 1 bass clarinet (3 players), and 2 bassoons with 1 doubling contrabassoon (2 players).

When ordering performance parts for orchestral music, specifying a "set" of parts normally means one of each part, including one of each string part. In most instances the number of woodwind, brass, and percussion parts is predetermined, since only one performer normally plays on a part. Beyond that, it is necessary to specify to the vendor or publisher the number of additional parts required for the string section, since the number of violins I, violins II, violas, cellos, and double basses will vary depending upon the size of the orchestra that will perform the work. Thus, if a total of 5 violin I, 5 violin II, 3 viola, 3 cello, and 3 double bass parts are needed, the order should specify the number of string parts, in score order:

1 set + added strings 4–4–2–2–2
or
1 wind set + total strings 5–5–3–3–3

"Wind set" means one of each instrument (including percussion, plectral, etc.) *except* for the strings. Bear in mind that one string part does not equal one player. A violin I section of ten players will require only five copies of the violin I part, since pairs of players in each string section, who play the same music, share a single music stand or "desk." On occasion it may also be necessary or desirable to order extra wind parts, to replace parts of an incomplete set or to circulate to students preparing for auditions; such needs should be spelled out. If the work is a concerto or otherwise features a soloist, a part for the soloist is not normally included in a set.

Some publishers distribute orchestra music in prepackaged sets, with common configurations shown in figure 2.2.

Set A = one of each part, including strings
Set B = score + 1 wind set + total strings 5–5–3–3–3
Set C = score + 1 wind set + total strings 8–8–5–5–5

Figure 2.2. Common Prepackaged Orchestral Sets

For the publisher Edwin F. Kalmus, who is a major publisher of orchestral music in the United States, a basic "set of parts" contains total strings 4–4–3–2–2.

Three companies in the United States specialize in the sale and rental of scores and parts for orchestral compositions—their own publications, or editions by other publishers:

Educational Music Service, 33 Elkay Drive, Chester, NY 10918. Tel: 845 469 5790; fax: 845 469 5817; web: www.emsmusic.com; e-mail: sales@emsmusic.com. Selected catalogs on the EMS website in PDF format include the Edwin F. Kalmus orchestra sales catalog and Mapleson rental library of orchestral music; full line of printed music from publishers worldwide also is available from EMS; annual CD-ROM database of "music-in-print" available to EMS customers; no online database.

Edwin F. Kalmus, PO Box 5011, Boca Raton, FL 33431. Tel: 561 241 6340; fax: 561 241 6347; web: www.kalmus-music.com; e-mail: efkalmus@aol.com. Kalmus distributes only its own publications, including reprints of much of the standard orchestral repertoire, and new editions; editions are available for purchase or rental; searchable online catalog.

Luck's Music Library, PO Box 71397, Madison Heights, MI 48071. Tel: 810 583 1820; fax: 810 583 1114; web: www.lucksmusic.net; e-mail: sales@lucksmusic.net. Distributes printed music of all publishers, as well as its own reprint editions; extensive catalog of works for rent; searchable online catalogs; PDF catalogs of solo and ensemble music of publishers worldwide.

For works that employ a chorus, the chorus music may be published in as many as three different formats (in addition to full and miniature orchestral scores if the work includes an orchestra): (1) vocal score, including the complete music for chorus and vocal soloists, if any, with the orchestral part reduced for piano; (2) chorus score, including only the sections of the work in which the chorus sings, printed in score format, with or without the instrumental music reduced for keyboard; and (3) chorus parts, including only the sections of the work in which the chorus sings, each choral line printed separately, that is, a separate part for sopranos, a distinct part for altos, etc. Each chorister normally will require either a vocal score, a chorus score, or a chorus part, though some ensembles may expect pairs of singers to read from a shared score or part.

Music for band is available in sets for jazz band, concert band, and marching band. Most sets, at least from the larger publishers, come with the number of parts predetermined by the publisher, so that an ensemble at a small school could receive more parts than needed for its clarinet section and others.

Rental Music

Library users often assume that if a work has been recorded or performed in concert, it must be available to buy in printed form. Even experienced musicians sometimes are surprised to learn that a great many copyrighted musical works cannot be purchased, but rather must be rented from their publishers. Music distribution by rental is not a modern development. In the late eighteenth and nineteenth centuries, engraving of music was a practical and relatively inexpensive alternative to letterpress printing with movable type, but it did not lend itself to the production of large editions, partly because the engraved pewter plates—a softer (and cheaper) metal than the copper plates commonly used before the mid-eighteenth century—were good for no more than about 200 to 500 impressions.[17] Thus, serious music typically was issued in initial press runs of only 130 to 500 copies—plates with some life left in them could be stored for reuse if the edition sold well—and some of the printed copies were made available at the music rental libraries that were active in most cities. Borrowers who liked a work well enough to want to own the music could pay an additional fee to have it copied out by hand.

Why Rental Today?

Today, musical works are disseminated by rental for a variety of reasons: the composer may want to restrict distribution for reasons known only to him- or herself; in many cases, a composer is simply reluctant to declare a composition "finished," and continues to revise the work while the publisher reproduces a small number of the latest version to meet the needs of the rental market. Printing a new edition suitable for wide distribution every time the composer had a change of mind would be economic folly. Furthermore, if a work has been commissioned, the commissioner may want to reserve rights of exclusivity. Rental also enables the publisher to license only performances that can be expected to transcend mediocrity; neither composers nor publishers want their creative commodity botched by hacks, and music that is rented to the consumer does not break free of the publisher's control, as do editions that are sold. The crux, however, is economics. New music that is expected to sell well—usually works by better-known composers—may still be engraved and sold commercially, at least in score format. Works with a less certain future in the concert hall are more economically distributed by rental.

Public-domain orchestral music can be rented for performance at about one-third the cost of purchase, and rental may be a more economical option for an ensemble that expects to perform a work infrequently. While a few libraries—usually at conservatories and universities—bear some responsibility for acquiring and preparing music for large ensembles in concert, more often the acquisition of music for bands, orchestras, and choirs is entrusted to discrete departments where specialists concentrate on the management of *only* such materials.[18] Nevertheless, in libraries where the selection and acquisition of printed music of any kind is a normal part of business, it is useful for librarians and staff to be aware of how such works make their appearances in publisher catalogs and bibliographies, and to know some basics about the rental process. Not only can staff avoid spinning their wheels when such a work is requested for addition to the collection, but they might be of some assistance in redirecting library users to appropriate resources to arrange their own rentals.

Applications for rental require that certain details about the planned performance(s) be revealed, such as name and status of the performing group (professional, semiprofessional, amateur), number of performances, name and seating capacity of each hall where performances will occur, names of conductors and soloists, and so forth (see the website of the music publisher G. Schirmer for an example of rental ordering instructions: www.schirmer.com/catalogs/ordeing_info.html). A rental fee is then quoted based on the information supplied to the publisher. Conductors still making up their minds can request that a copy of a rental score be sent for examination; in some cases a recorded performance can be sent as well. Rental requests should be made directly to the publisher rather than to a vendor, or to the publisher's U.S. agent if the publisher is not based in the United States.[19]

Rental Status in Catalogs

The status of a work—sale or rental—can be determined in many of the same sources used for verifying other publication details about scores: publishers' catalogs, the Music-in-Print Series, etc. Cataloging records in OCLC WorldCat and the RLG Union Catalog sometimes identify rental works either in a note field, or in the terms-of-availability area (MARC field 020).[20] An information source that concerns itself solely with rental music is the *Bonner Katalog*, which lists about sixty thousand copyrighted rental works that are marketed in Germany.[21] This catalog lists copyrighted editions of works by early composers, as well as contemporary art music. While intended for German users, the *Bonner Katalog* identifies the publisher of each work, and from this the user can derive from other sources the identity of the appropriate rental agent in the United States.

Publishers identify rental publications in their catalogs in a variety of ways. Often, rental works are segregated in a separately published catalog or area of the publisher's website (for example, the separate rental catalogs of Theodore Presser at www.presser.com and of G. Schirmer and Associated Music Publishers at www.schirmer.com). Other publishers mix rental and sale items in a single catalog and rely upon a coding system to identify terms of availability (for example the *Music of Our Time* catalog of Schott Musik International and the catalogs of Universal Edition provide a publisher number for each item on sale and omit publisher numbers for titles to rent); the *Kasseler Auslieferungskatalog* (the complete catalog of Bärenreiter-Verlag in Kassel, Germany), which is available online and for downloading at www. baerenreiter.com/html/index.htm, identifies rental items by substituting the letter "L"—*Leihwerk*, a work for rent—for a sale price. When working with a publisher's catalogs, whether printed or on the web, it is useful to become familiar with terms commonly seen in them. The following are some of the foreign-language terms used to identify sale and rental works in publishers' catalogs:

> *a noleggio*—*Ita.* For rent
> *Aufführungsmaterial*—*Ger.* Performance material
> *en location*—*Fre.* For rent
> *en vent*—*Fre.* For sale
> *Leihweise*—*Ger.* For rent
> *matérial*—*Fre.* Performance material
> *Mietmaterial*—*Ger.* Rental material
> *reversgebunden*—*Ger.* For rent

For scores published or otherwise copyrighted in the United States, an indication of rental-only status may be inferred from bibliographic records for them in OCLC WorldCat and the RLG Union Catalog. If the Library of Congress (LC) is the only library that reports holding a published score in those union catalogs, LC most probably has acquired it from the publisher through the deposit required for copyright registration. (Sometimes, one or two other libraries may have also acquired the edition, probably through some special arrangement with the publisher or composer.) These cataloging records often also have a note identifying the item as "rental material," and therefore not for sale.

Purchasing Rental Scores

"Rental material" does not necessarily mean not *ever* for sale. Some publishers, including Schott Musik International and Theodore Presser, have made it known that scores (but not parts for performance) of all of their rental titles are available for purchase as "special order editions." Others, like G. Schirmer and Carl Fischer, state that "selected" rental works for fewer than ten performers can be purchased. Whatever the publisher's stated policy, a personal contact with the publisher sometimes will result in agreement to sell a copy of a rental score to a library. A trusted music vendor may be the best intermediary between library and publisher in these cases. The vendor, after all, transacts business with the publisher, and the publisher depends upon the vendor for distribution of its regular sales items. The vendor may also have personal contacts there. An unheralded purchase order from the library for a rental score, on the other hand, is likely to be rebuffed.

New printing technologies are encouraging some publishers to move works from the rental to the sale category. Publishers can print and bind on demand in a matter of minutes a single copy of a score with parts for the occasional customer, and at a reasonable price. Chester Music, Novello & Co. Ltd., and Faber Music are among the publishers whose catalogs reflect this practice. Such works are usually identified in the catalogs as "printed to order" or with similar phraseology, and on the printed edition as "special order edition." Consequently, many more works by contemporary composers previously available only on hire can now be purchased.

Printed Directories of Print Music Publishers

Who are these publishers? Listed below are print directories of music publishers in the United States and abroad (online directories that have links to publishers' websites are listed in chapter 7, on preorder verification).

Directory of Music Publishers, New York: Music Publishers' Association of the United States; National Music Publishers' Association; Church Music Publishers' Association, 2001– . Annual. Earlier title: *Music Publishers' Sales Agency List.* Entries list foreign and domestic imprints distributed by the named U.S. publishers, and a reverse index is provided. The publisher–imprint relationships are stated as reported by the members of the three organizations, and claims of exclusive distributorship are not verified. The directory can be downloaded in plain text (.txt) and rich text (.rtf) formats at www.mpa.org/agency/pal.html, where links to many of the publishers also are found.

Music Publishers' International ISMN Directory, Munich: K. G. Saur; Berlin: International ISMN Agency, 1995– . Directory of publishers participating in the International Standard Music Number (ISMN) program, as well as those who do not; arguably the most comprehensive directory of music publishers currently available; new edition published about every three years.

Notes

1. For a more expansive survey of the history of music printing and publishing than is possible here, see Stanley Boorman, Eleanor Selfridge-Field, and D. W. Krummel, "Printing and Publishing of Music," *Grove Music Online* (2001), www.grovemusic.com. On the early days of music publishing, see also Hans Lenneberg, *On the Publishing and Dissemination of Music, 1500–1850* (Hillsdale, NY: Pendragon Press, 2003).

2. This is illustrated in *This Business of Music: The Definitive Guide to the Music Industry*, 9th ed., by M. William Krasilovsky and Sidney Shemel, with contributions by John M. Gross (New York: Billboard Books, 2003), which is widely regarded as a standard reference for music business practices; it devotes only 7 pages (pp. 283–90) of its 526 to printed music.

3. In the year 2001, print accounted for only 11.6 percent of music publishers' global income, according to the National Music Publishers' Association's NMPA International Survey of Music Publishing Revenues, 12th ed., www.nmpa.org/pr/NMPA_International_Survey_12th_Edition.pdf.

Notes (continued)

4. In 1910, which was "probably the apogee" of sheet music publishing, an estimated 50,000 printed music editions were published worldwide, according to D. W. Krummel, "Music Publishing," in *Music Printing and Publishing*, ed. D. W. Krummel and Stanley Sadie, Norton/Grove Handbooks in Music (New York: W. W. Norton, 1990), 129. The ensuing decline coincided with the beginning of wide distribution of commercial sound recordings.

5. Adapted from several sources, including Kent Underwood, "Archival Guidelines for the Music Publishing Industry," *Notes* 52 (1996): 1115–16; David Baskerville, *Music Business Handbook and Career Guide*, 7th ed. (Thousand Oaks, CA: Sage Publications, 2001), 51; and Tim Whitsett, *Music Publishing: The Real Road to Music Business Success*, 4th ed. (Emeryville, CA: MixBooks, 1997), 6.

6. For descriptions of the millennium-end state of print-music publishing, see "Music Publishing Today" in Krummel's article in note 1; and George Sturm, "Music Publishing," *Notes* 56 (2000): 628–34, one of several articles commissioned for a special issue titled *Music Librarianship at the Turn of the Century*.

7. There are, however, separate trade associations of music publishers in the United States: the Music Publishers' Association of the United States (MPA), with more than 55 publisher–members, addresses issues "pertaining to every area of music publishing with an emphasis on the issues relevant to the publishers of print music for concert and educational purposes" (from the association's website: www.mpa.org/scope.html); the National Music Publishers' Association (NMPA), with more than 800 publisher–members, is concerned primarily with the protection of copyrights in the popular-music domain (www.nmpa.org); and the Church Music Publishers Association (CMPA) serves a similar function for about 50 publishers of Christian music (www.cmpamusic.org). Some publishers are members of all three associations.

8. This can be illustrated by examining Salabert's online percussion catalog (www.salabert.fr): in April 2003, that catalog listed 136 percussion editions for sale. By contrast, Hal Leonard Corporation, Salabert's designated U.S. distributor, at the same time listed only five Salabert percussion editions in its online catalog (www.halleonard.com).

9. These estimates are by Christine Clark, president of Theodore Front Musical Literature, a firm that supplies music in all formats to libraries around the world. Clark estimates the annual output of serious books about music at about 1,500 to 1,800 worldwide. The European vendor Otto Harrassowitz, at www.harrassowitz.de/mus_approval_plan.html, estimates that it adds about 5,000 records for new scores annually to its database (principally from European publishers).

10. Michael Keller, "Music," in *Selection of Library Materials in the Humanities, Social Sciences, and Sciences*, ed. by Patricia A. McClung (Chicago: ALA, 1985), 142.

Notes (continued)

11. The situation is similar for scholarly books about music. See Michael Ochs, "What Music Scholars Should Know about Publishers," *Notes* 59 (2002): 288–300, esp. 291–92.

12. For a snapshot, circa 1989, of available music journals, with descriptions of the types and numbers of reviews they contained, see Ann P. Basart's *Writing about Music: A Guide to Publishing Opportunities for Authors and Reviewers*, Fallen Leaf Reference Books in Music 11 (Berkeley, CA: Fallen Leaf Press, 1989), which gives detailed information on over 430 periodicals from 21 countries that were then publishing articles and reviews in English.

13. Binding extends the shelf life of a score by a factor of four or five, according to Joan O. Falconer, "A Handguide to Do-It-Yourself Music Binding," *Wilson Library Bulletin* 48 (1973): 335.

14. For full discussion of standard music-binding formats and the issues related to them, see Alice Carli, *Binding and Care of Printed Music*, Music Library Association Basic Manual Series 2 (Lanham, MD: Scarecrow Press, for the Music Library Association, 2003).

15. A recurring topic on MLA's electronic discussion list, MLA-L, is how to manage multipart editions (links to the MLA-L archive and instructions for joining are found with the "Useful Resources Online" at the MLA website, www.musiclibraryassoc.org). Some libraries lend a set of parts as a unit, making one individual player responsible for the entire set; others circulate parts individually. Discussion of the pros and cons of each procedure is beyond the scope of this manual.

16. However, it is unlikely that vendors would want to intervene in these cases, unless your library is a *very* good customer, as there cannot be much in it for them.

17. Lenneberg, 105. The variability depended upon the alloy (cheaper compounds wore out more quickly).

18. For a brief overview of the duties of a librarian for a performing organization, see the Major Orchestra Librarians' Association's "The Orchestra Librarian: A Career Introduction," www.mola-inc.org. A more discursive presentation is by Frank P. Byrne, *A Practical Guide to the Music Library: Its Function, Organization, and Maintenance* (Cleveland: Ludwig Music, 1987); by "music library," Byrne means an orchestra or band library.

19. Publishers' addresses, and links to their agents, are found at the Music Publishers' Association's *MPA Directory of Music Publishers*, www.mpa.org/agency/pal.html.

20. The Online Computer Library Center (OCLC, www.oclc.org), and the Research Libraries Group (RLG, www.rlg.org/toc.html) are the world's two largest shared cataloging utilities. Their online catalogs are known as OCLC WorldCat and the RLG Union Catalog. MARC is the acronym for MAchine-Readable Cataloging, which defines a data format for the representation and communication of bibliographic and related information in machine-readable form. It provides the mechanism by which computers

Notes (continued)

exchange, use, and interpret bibliographic information, and its data elements make up the foundation of most library catalogs used today. Additional information about MARC is found at http://lcweb.loc.gov/marc/.

21. *Bonner Katalog: Verzeichnis reversgebundener musikalischer Aufführungsmateriale*, 4th ed., ed. by Deutsches Musikarchiv of the Deutsche Bibliothek and Deutscher Musikverleger-Verband, 2 vols. (Munich: K. G. Saur, 2000); 6th ed. (2003) on interactive CD-ROM.

3

RECORDED MUSIC PUBLISHING

The history of recorded sound is a chronicle of format change. Ever since Thomas Edison first recorded the human voice (reciting "Mary Had a Little Lamb") in 1877 on a piece of tinfoil wrapped around a brass cylinder, new technologies have revolutionized sound recording with near-metronomic regularity.[1] In 1885 Charles Sumner Tainter and Chichester Bell patented the "graphophone," which essentially was Edison's device with wax substituted for tinfoil so that sound could be recorded more permanently. Edison retaliated in 1888 with the "improved phonograph" cylinder player. A year earlier, Emile Berliner had patented the "gramophone," which recorded sounds on flat discs that could be duplicated more efficiently than cylinders by stamping. By the turn of the century, the recording industry was well established, and within a few years, most companies had given up cylinders in favor of the more durable discs, although cylinders continued to be produced into the 1920s. During the first three decades of the twentieth century, perforated paper rolls for player pianos ("Pianolas") were found in millions of homes, until the market for the instruments collapsed during the Depression years.

The first magnetic wire and tape recorders were developed in the 1930s, and by the end of the 1940s tape recorders were being widely used. In 1948 Columbia introduced the first twelve-inch 33⅓ rpm LPs, and a year later RCA Victor came out with the seven-inch 45 rpm record. The first stereophonic LPs were sold in 1958. Within five years the compact cassette tape was introduced, and in 1979 Sony brought out the Walkman portable audiocassette player. Homes and libraries entered the digital audio age in 1982 with the introduction of compact discs, and in 1996 the first DVD players were sold.

In the early years of the twenty-first century, Super Audio Compact Discs (SACDs) and DVD-Audio recordings[2] competed to supplant the original compact disc, while peer-to-peer sharing of digital audio files over the Internet tested the boundaries of copyright and the nerves of the recording industry. In 2003, albums and individual tracks downloaded over the Internet to local hard drives and to home-burned CDs became a commercially viable enterprise when Apple Computer opened its online iTunes Music Store, while companies like Classical.com streamed licensed audio into libraries and homes as supplements to, or as substitutes for, recordings sold as physical objects. And post-2003 libraries face additional audio choices and challenges.

Major Labels

As of the end of 2003, five multinational companies controlled more than 80 percent of the world's recorded music production.[3] All of these companies have extensive classical music catalogs; all market their own labels and distribute recordings of smaller companies as well. Three of these five (BMG, Sony, Universal) maintain full online catalogs of the products they distribute, and visitors to their websites can shop online.

BMG Entertainment (a division of the Bertelsmann Group), more than 200 labels, including Arista, Bad Boy, BMG Label Group, RCA Label Group, and Windham Hill (there is no list of component labels at www.bmgmusic.com, though online shopping is enabled through a membership/record club arrangement).

EMI Music Group, more than seventy labels, including Abbey Road, Angel, Blue Note, Capitol, EMI, Mosaic, Parlophone, Reflexe, and Virgin (complete listing at www.emigroup.com). The database of each EMI Music Group label must be searched separately; some labels allow direct purchase online, while others redirect buyers to the selected recording at the Amazon.com website.

Sony Music Entertainment (formerly CBS/Sony), includes Columbia Records Group, Epic Records Group, Legacy Recordings, Sony Classical, Sony Nashville, and Sony Wonder (online shopping is enabled at www.sonymusic.com).

Universal Music Group (a division of Vivendi Universal), includes Decca, Deutsche Grammophon, Geffen, MCA, Mercury, Motown, Philips, Polydor, Universal Records, and Verve (complete listing of about fifty labels is at www.umusic.com, where online shopping is enabled).

Warner Music Group (a division of Time Warner, often abbreviated WEA, for Warner, Electra, and Atlantic), includes Atlantic Group, Elektra Entertainment Group, London-Sire Records, Rhino Entertainment, and Warner Brothers Records (no label listing, recording database, or online shopping are available at www.wmg.com).

Independent Labels

In addition to the major labels, there are hundreds of domestic and foreign labels that market their products directly, or through independent distributors that account for the extensive catalogs of a number of important classical music labels. Most of the independents deal in specialized product—classical, jazz, folk, Latin, and so forth—and their founders and owners often got into the business because of a love for the music, rather than as a way to wealth.

The most important of the independent distributors, which also happen to be labels in their own right, are Albany, Allegro, Harmonia Mundi, Koch International, Naxos, and Qualiton.

Albany, more than one hundred classical labels, including Albany Records, Bridge, Camerata, Gasparo, Hänssler Classic, Music & Arts, New World, Olympia, and Preiser (complete listing at www.arkivmusic.com, where online shopping is enabled).

Allegro, hundreds of labels, including Arabesque, GM Recordings, Nimbus, and Summit (complete listing at www.allegro-music.com, where online shopping is enabled after customer registration).

Harmonia Mundi, more than fifty labels, including Black Box, Channel Classics, Chant du Monde, Gimmel, Hyperion, Naïve, Opera Rara, Opus 111, Testament, and Wergo (complete listing at www.harmoniamundi.com, where online shopping is enabled).

Koch International, more than 130 labels, including ASV, BBC Music, Berlin Classics, Chandos, Koch International Classics, Koch Schwann, MD&G, Mode Records, New Albion, Nightingale Classics, Ondine, and Pearl (complete listing at www.kochint.com); no direct sales to consumers from the home site, though links are provided to individual labels distributed by Koch, where purchases often can be made.

Naxos, about twelve labels, including Amadis, Dacapo, and Marco Polo, in addition to the Naxos label (complete listing at www.naxos.com); no direct sales to consumers.

Qualiton Imports, more than 200 labels, including Bis, Bongio-vanni, Cedille, and Hungaroton (complete listing at www.qualiton. com, where online shopping is enabled).

The listings of labels and affiliates in this manual, both of major labels and of independents, should be regarded as provisional. Frequent merg-ers and takeovers in the recorded music industry mean that no such list-ing can be accurate for long. There is intense competition for labels among distributors, and it is not unusual for a label to bounce around two or three distributors in a single year.[4] When one of the "majors" acquires a label, it may fold it into the larger operation, or the label may continue to operate much as it did as an independent, often with the original management, but with surer financial support. For the most current information, readers should consult the companies' websites.

Private Labels

The declining fortunes of the recording industry in the 1990s and into the 2000s, and the shrinking market for all but established superstars and new artists with some commercially exploitable allure, has had a chilling effect on the major labels' ability to nurture emerging talent and finance costly new recording projects. Instead, they have rum-maged through their archives for classics that could be "digitally re-mastered" for reissue on the cheap to a new generation of listeners, while new repertoire and artists have become ever more marginal commodities. But digital technology has made it increasingly easy for today's composers and artists to edit recorded performances of their works, and to burn and distribute discs directly to buyers from their websites and at concert engagements, allowing them to retain complete artistic control, and to reap the full profits from their sales. Several of the composer collectives mentioned in chapter 2 in the category of spe-cialty publishers, including Frog Peak Music and Master Musicians Collective, sponsor private labels that produce and distribute recordings of their members' works—repertoire that is unlikely to sell in sufficient quantities as to interest the traditional labels.

Some major ensembles now emulate these individual composers and collectives. In recent years, orchestras in New York, Philadelphia, Boston, and Chicago have issued large retrospective box sets that cull gems from their archives; these are sold through the orchestras' web-sites. Other ensembles, rebelling against the subversion of artistic choices by their labels' bean counters, have taken bolder initiatives. In

2000, for example, the London Symphony Orchestra—reputedly the most recorded orchestra in the world—launched its own label, LSO Live; the San Francisco Symphony followed suit in 2002 with the SFS Media label; and in 2003, both the Orchestra of St. Luke's and the Budapest Philharmonic established their own private labels (St. Luke's Collection and BPO Live, respectively).[5] These orchestras' labels document *new* rather than archived performances, and their recordings are available through normal retail outlets, as well as at the ensembles' websites. This kind of activity is not limited to orchestras; the vocal ensemble the Sixteen, for example, has been releasing new recordings and reissues on its Coro label since 2001.

International Distribution

The multinational nature of the recording industry—a major label may have offices and distribution in dozens of countries—means that not all recordings released by a label are available in all markets. While companies such as EMI Classics and Deutsche Grammophon maintain catalogs of their complete *international* output on their websites, these recordings are marketed and distributed in various regions of the world by company subsidiaries that, at their discretion and within certain limits, can pick and choose from the label's total output only those titles that they judge will sell best in their local markets. This means that not all recordings listed in the complete online catalogs, or that are advertised or reviewed in print journals, will necessarily be readily available in all territories. For similar reasons, a recording may be distributed in some marketing territories earlier than it is made available in others. Thus, a library selector who is seduced by a review in *Gramophone* or *International Record Review*—both are British journals—may never see the coveted recording advertised or reviewed in an American journal and may never see it in a local music shop, nor find a cataloging record for it in OCLC WorldCat or the RLG Union Catalog, the world's two largest shared cataloging utilities.

Recordings that *are* released in multiple territories will typically exhibit distinct characteristics. A disc marketed to French consumers, for example, can be expected to have program notes and title in French, while the same recording released in the United States will be offered with English-language notes. There also will likely be variants in the publisher's number for the recording (a different prefix in each territory, for example), and there may even be slightly different content, as in the case of a song recital with one or two songs substituted on the French release for others on the American release.

Absence of official distribution in a local market no longer means that a recording can be acquired only with some difficulty. Improved communications and the Internet mean that libraries and individuals now can more readily order direct from vendors or retailers in the country of origin. Vendors and retailers in the United States who specialize in imports also routinely claim to be able to acquire virtually any in-print recording from anywhere in the world.

Recorded Music Publication Output

In the United States, 33,443 audio albums were released in 2002: 7,306 by the major labels and 26,137 by the independents. Sales averaged 7,871 units per title (31,296 units per title from the major labels, though a release by a major pop artist can sell in the millions).[6] Global sales of prerecorded music in 2002 totaled about $32 billion.[7]

The persistence of a recording in its label's catalog is impossible to predict with any accuracy; a recording may be deleted within a matter of months, while another containing similar repertoire performed by the same artists might remain available for years.[8] Major-label manufacturers produce initial runs based on the demand expected for the particular repertoire or performer, coupled with how long they expect the product to command space in retailers' bins before being pushed out by the next new thing. A few independent labels aim to keep their entire catalogs continually available. For best order fulfillment of recordings, regardless of label, repertoire, or artists, orders should be placed as soon as possible after new releases are advertised or reviewed.

Some labels are emulating the original just-in-time manufacturing philosophy developed by Toyota in the 1970s and famously copied in the United States in the 1990s by Dell Computers: produce goods to meet exactly the customer demand in time, quality, and quantity. In other words, manufacture only goods for which orders are already in hand. Since 1996, Smithsonian Folkways Recordings has honored a commitment to keep every title in print by distributing the obscure ones as burned-to-order compact discs.[9] Nimbus Records in 2002 began to make its back catalog of deleted recordings available as on-demand compact discs, with digitally printed booklets.[10] Likewise, the nonprofit New World Records is digitally archiving its own recordings, as well as those of defunct Composers Recordings Inc. (CRI) and Albany Records in order to keep each album available as a custom-made compact disc, burned to order and delivered to the customer with the original liner notes.[11]

Reviews

Compared with the number of published reviews of printed music editions (see chapter 2), the number for sound recordings is significantly larger. Although a 1989 study[12] concluded that only 11.7 percent of popular-music recordings were reviewed (3.25 months after the release of a recording, on average), data published in a study four years later determined that an impressive 59 percent of the classical music recordings surveyed were reviewed.[13]

Reviews of sound recordings of classical music differ from those of books in a significant respect: because the reviews often are not about works newly created, but rather works newly performed, they are not so much concerned with musical content as with the quality of the performance and the technical aspects of the recording. Comparisons with other recordings of the same music are common in reviews.

Among the journals that contain substantive reviews of significant numbers of new recordings of classical music are the American bimonthlies *Fanfare* (www.fanfaremag.com) and the *American Record Guide* (no website), and the three British monthlies *International Record Review* (www.recordreview.co.uk), *BBC Music Magazine* (www.bbcmagazines.com/music), and *Gramophone* (www.gramophone.co.uk, which includes a link to "Gramofile," the free online archive of all CD reviews published in the journal back to 1983).

Popular-music genres are reviewed in the many magazines directed to the consumers of this music, including *Spin* (www.spin.com) and *New Music Monthly* (www.cmj.com/newmm); recordings of jazz and blues are reviewed in *Downbeat* (www.downbeat.com), and folk and world music in *Dirty Linen* (www.dirtylinen.com). The trade journal *Billboard: The International Weekly of Music, Video and Home Entertainment* (www.billboard.com), and the popular-culture biweekly *Rolling Stone* (www.rollingstone.com) both contain in each issue, in addition to reviews, "charts" that rank recordings according to numbers of copies sold. Several of these journals' websites post full texts of a selection of reviews from their current issues.

Printed Directories of Recording Labels

Listed below are print directories of publishers of sound recordings in the United States and abroad (online directories with links to labels' websites are listed in chapter 7).

> ***Billboard International Buyer's Guide***, New York: Billboard Pubs., 1970– . Annual; separate listings of major and independent labels, including web and e-mail addresses; also lists major "sheet music" publishers and video companies; a separate international section is arranged by country.

> ***Musical America: International Directory of the Performing Arts***, Great Barrington, MA: ABC Leisure Magazines, 1974– . Annual; separate listings of American and international recording companies; online version (www.musicalamerica.com) is available to paid subscribers as a searchable database.

> ***Recording Industry Sourcebook***, Los Angeles: Ascona Communications, 1990– . Annual; separate listings of major and independent labels, with web and e-mail addresses.

SPARS Codes

The three-letter "D" (digital) and "A" (analog) designations often seen on compact discs and in reviewing media are SPARS codes—for the Society of Professional Audio Recording Studios, which devised the codes—which attempt to convey whether analog or digital procedures were used in the sequential stages of the recording process. The first letter indicates how the album was originally recorded; the second, how it was mixed (the process of combining a number of separate audio tracks into, usually, two channels for stereo sound); the third, how it was mastered (transferred from tape to disc for the purpose of pressing or manufacturing recordings). The meanings of these SPARS codes, therefore, are:

> **DDD**—digital tape recorder used during session recording, mixing, and mastering.

> **ADD**—analog tape recorder used during session recording; digital tape recorder used during subsequent mixing and mastering.

> **AAD**—analog tape recorder used during session recording and subsequent mixing; digital tape recorder used during mastering.

As to which is best, the code—taken by itself—does not indicate recording quality in any specific sense. Although utilization of digital technology might be said to have the potential to result in wider dynamic range, low noise and distortion, and so forth, the technology is only as good as the application. Terrible recordings have been made using the latest digital technology.

Since compact discs are digital, by definition the master tape from which the discs are made must be digital as well. Therefore, all recordings that were originally analog are remastered to digital for the compact disc medium. Phrases such as "digitally remastered from the original analog tape," therefore, may mean nothing more than that a necessary step was followed to get the music into the digital domain and ready for encoding on the CD. Though an analog recording may be remixed and edited digitally as well, this is not automatically implied.

As technology has advanced, the distinctions between the recording stages have become blurred. A compact disc carrying a code of "DDD" may actually have had its sound manipulated in analog form several times during the recording process, so that now the codes are largely meaningless. For classical music recordings, which have a long history of fine engineering, and whose qualities depend greatly upon musicianship and interpretation, the SPARS codes should not be a prime factor in choosing one recording over another.

Video Recordings

International Video Standards

Recordings in the two audiovisual media dominant in libraries at the time of this writing—VHS cassettes and DVDs—have geographical restrictions: a VHS video produced in the United States cannot be played everywhere else in the world, and vice versa.[14] Worldwide, there are three main television and recording standards for commercially released video, and each is unique and incompatible with the others because of differing rates of frame-per-second delivery:

NTSC (National Television Standards Committee): used in North America, Central America, parts of South America, Korea, the Philippines, Japan.

PAL (Phase Alternation Line): Europe (except France), Argentina, Australia, China, India, much of Africa.

SECAM (Séquential couleur avec mémoire): France, the countries of the former Soviet Union, the Middle East, North Africa.

A television set bought in PAL territory will not receive broadcast signals if hooked up in NTSC territory. Similarly, videocassettes intended for playback on PAL televisions cannot be viewed in NTSC territories. Many websites provide detailed country-by-country listings of the video standards used worldwide, some with color-coded maps of the world for an easy overview.[15]

DVDs

DVDs also have geographical restrictions, but for a different reason than do VHS cassettes. Motion pictures are not released simultaneously worldwide; that is, a film may be released in Europe and elsewhere months after its release in the United States. A movie may, therefore, come out on DVD in the United States just as it is hitting screens in Japan. Furthermore, studios sell distribution rights to different foreign distributors and would like to guarantee an exclusive market in each territory. Thus, when the DVD standard was developed, the United States motion picture industry lobbied for the inclusion of codes to prevent playback of certain discs in certain geographical regions. DVD players, therefore, are given a code for the region in which they are sold, and will play only discs that are coded for that region. There are code-free players that will play DVDs from around the world and that can be used with televisions using any broadcast standard. These players are not generally available from the major electronics chain stores, but they are offered for sale by many Internet retailers. The codes on the DVDs are not an encryption system, but merely a byte of information that the player checks before it launches the program. And they are a permanent part of the disc; they do not "unlock" after a period of time.

Regional codes are optional for the disc manufacturers, and discs without region locks will play on any player in any country (these are usually described as "0 region" discs). Because the sequential releases characteristic of feature films are seldom relevant for concert, opera, and ballet recordings, many classical music DVDs are coded for region 0. Regional codes do not apply to recordable DVDs: a DVD that is made on a PC or a DVD video recorder will play in all regions. The world's DVD region codes are shown in figure 3.1.

Region 1: United States and its territories, Canada
Region 2: Europe, Japan, South Africa, Middle East
Region 3: Southeast & East Asia (except China & North Korea)
Region 4: Central & South America, Australia, New Zealand, Pacific
Islands
Region 5: Russia, Eastern Europe, North Korea, Africa, Indian Sub-
continent
Region 6: China
Region 7: Reserved
Region 8: International venues (airplanes, cruise ships, etc.)

Figure 3.1. DVD Region Codes

On a practical level, all this means is that care must be taken if purchasing imported videos, either domestically or from abroad, to verify that
the products are compatible with U.S. playback standards; recordings
purchased from North American vendors and retailers are unlikely to
be coded other than DVD regions 1 or 0, or to be in other than the
NTSC cassette format. Responsible vendors who serve an international
clientele will identify the DVD region codes and the VHS formats of
the recordings that they sell.[16]

Laser Discs

DVDs should not be confused with 12-inch "laser discs" (often
identified by a "LD" symbol), another video format found in many libraries. Unlike DVDs, laser discs are an analog medium, though the
signals encoded on the discs are read by a laser. Laser discs became
available commercially in 1978, and gained favor with opera and film
buffs because of sound and picture quality that were far superior to
VHS. Production of laser discs declined after the 1998 introduction of
the DVD (which essentially is a refinement of the laser disc), and they
have not been manufactured in the United States since about 2000.
They are still seen, however, in listings from secondhand dealers.

Video Performance Rights

In the acquiring of commercially printed music and recorded
sound, copyright rarely raises its hydra head. Audiovisual works, on the
other hand, including musical video recordings as well as theatrical
films, embody a cluster of rights related to their acquisition and use that
are reserved exclusively to the copyright owner. The sole reason for
acquiring a VHS or DVD recording is to "perform" all or part of the

intellectual property contained in it—in private homes, classrooms, meeting rooms and auditoriums, and library carrels—and one of the exclusive rights reserved to copyright owners "in the case of literary, musical, dramatic, and choreographic works, pantomimes, and motion pictures and other audiovisual works, [is] to perform the copyrighted work publicly."[17]

Interpreted strictly, the copyright law designates most uses of video outside of the home as public performances.[18] Libraries that acquire videos exclusively to be circulated for home use, as would be the case with many public libraries, would have no need to be concerned with securing public-performance rights for those videos. If, on the other hand, the library wants to show a documentary or concert video featuring a musical luminary who is to present a forthcoming lecture or recital, or intends to include video as part of an exhibit, it is the library's responsibility to acquire public-performance rights for it.

Usually, public performance of a video falls into one of three categories: theatrical (admission is charged), nontheatrical (no admission charged, nor donations solicited, typically by nonprofit agencies), and educational. In the last-named category, provisions in the law allow for the use of copyrighted videos in "face-to-face" classroom teaching and in other educational contexts, though these apply only to schools and academic institutions—public libraries, by law, are not considered to be educational institutions.[19]

More difficult is the issue of in-library viewing of a video by an individual at a carrel. Whether or not such viewing constitutes public performance is controversial, with informed and strong opinions lined up on both sides. In the case of educational institutions, much of the individual viewing is directly related to scholarship, research, and teaching, and these are among the activities specifically named in section 107 of the U.S. Copyright Act as subject to interpretation as "fair" uses. In addition, some posit that individual viewing of copyrighted material in connection with specific curricula can be interpreted as an extension of the face-to-face teaching exemption. Thus the case for individual viewing can reasonably be argued on terms of both the educational exemption and fair use.[20] Whatever the future resolution, if any, of this point, single-viewer use of videos in libraries without the sanction of public-performance rights is an almost universal practice in academic libraries, and in many public libraries as well. The results of a survey of academic libraries undertaken in 1995 showed that nearly a quarter of the fifty-nine respondents did not even *know* the licensing arrangements of the video recordings in their libraries.[21] In this survey, 54 percent of the libraries allowed users to watch home-use videos in the library; 33

percent of respondents allowed it under certain conditions; only 13 percent did not allow in-library viewing at all.[22]

How is a library to know if a video in its collection has public performance rights? Feature films and most nontheatrical home-use videos—including the opera, concert, and dance titles found in a typical music collection—almost never include performance rights in the purchase price.[23] On the other hand, producers and distributors of educational videos—music history surveys, composer biographies, and documentaries, for example—are far more likely to include public-performance rights with their products, and this often is reflected in a higher per-unit cost than typically is asked for home-use-only videos (price, however, is not necessarily a reliable indicator). Videos with public-performance rights will often declare these rights on the container or in the copyright statement that appears on the screen before the title frame, but these statements sometimes are vaguely phrased, and the absence of any such statement does not necessarily mean the video is for home use only. If the publisher or the distributor has a website or a printed catalog, its licensing and pricing policies may be spelled out there.[24]

Complicating this issue is that large, second-party distributors of nontheatrical videos—Facets Multimedia, DVD Planet, and Amazon.com, for example—are rarely the copyright owners and cannot grant performance rights for most of the videos they sell. Furthermore, some nontheatrical videos are sold both with and without performance rights, meaning that a title can be purchased for home use from a retailer at one price, and with public-performance rights from an educational video specialist at a different, almost surely higher, price. If a video's performance-rights status is not stated clearly on the item itself and cannot be determined for certain from the library's internal records or the publisher's literature, the best practice probably should be to identify who is the copyright owner—itself a sometimes daunting task—and seek such rights prior to any public showing.

Notes

1. For a compact and readable account of these developments to 2003, with emphasis on their cultural influences, see journalist Mark Coleman's *Playback: From the Victrola to MP3; 100 Years of Music, Machines, and Money* (New York: Da Capo, 2003). For a more extended history to about 1990, see Pekka Gronow and Ilpo Saunio, *An International History of the Recording Industry*, trans. by Christopher Moseley (New York: Cassell, 1998).

Notes (continued)

2. See this manual's glossary for descriptions of these formats.

3. In late 2003, two of the five (BMG and Sony) made a "handshake deal" to merge their recorded-music divisions to become Sony/BMG, subject to regulatory approval in the United States and the European Union. See "Merger Merry-Go-Round" [opinion], *Billboard* 115 (13 December 2003): 14.

4. Readers will find these mergers and acquisitions tracked in the weekly trade journal *Billboard* (Cincinnati: Billboard, 1894– ; title and imprint vary).

5. The London Symphony Orchestra's "most recorded" reputation has been noted by, among others, John Fleming, "A Word from the Brits: Can They Teach Us a Thing or Two?" *American Record Guide* 66 (November–December 2003): 6.

6. Ed Christman, "Average Sale of Albums Dropped in '02 as Labels Released More, Sold Less," *Billboard* 115 (26 April 2003): 9.

7. Gordon Masson, "IFPI: Global Sales Down 7.6% in '02," *Billboard* 115 (19 April 2003): 1, quoting figures compiled by the International Federation of the Phonographic Industry, www.ifpi.org. The decline in sales documented in this article, and in the article cited in n. 6, is blamed by the authors primarily on piracy of compact discs, and peer-to-peer exchange of audio files on the Internet.

8. The recording industry refers to recordings in release less than 18 months as "current catalog"; recordings in release 18–36 months are "recent catalog," except for classical and jazz, which are designated recent catalog after 12 months; recordings in release more than 36 months are "deep catalog." These definitions are according to Chris Morris, "Biz Seeks Boost for Ailing Catalog Sales," *Billboard* 115 (26 April 2003): 1.

9. Chris Nelson, "Thriving on Musical Obscurity," *New York Times*, 17 February 2003.

10. Nimbus Records, www.wyastone.co.uk/nrl.

11. Anthony Tommasini, "CRI Is Dead. Long Live CRI!" *New York Times,* 27 April 2003, national edition, Arts and Leisure section. It is to be hoped that these efforts will be emulated by other labels.

12. Virgil L. P. Blake, "Picking the Hits: The Reviewing of Popular Music Recordings," *Collection Management* 11, no. 3/4 (1989): 23–58.

13. Donna Mendell, Roslyn Dlugin Mylroie, and Judith Lynn Stern, "The Role of Reviewing Media in the Selection of Classical Recordings," *Collection Management* 18, no. 1/2 (1993): 71–88. The study did not address timeliness of the reviews. It compared a random sample of 200 titles among the 3,269 included in the "New Listings" section for classical releases in the 1989 *Schwann CD Catalog* with entries in the "Index to CD Reviews" column in the Music Library Association's quarterly *Notes*. The Schwann catalog and the *Notes* index to reviews are no longer published.

14. "Video," in popular usage, has come to be equated with the VHS cassette format (VHS is the abbreviation for "video home system"), and "DVD" with the DVD-Video format. There are several DVD formats, including DVD-

Notes (continued)

Audio, which is a new-generation improved version of the audio compact disc. Because of the multiplicity of DVD formats, the abbreviation usually is interpreted to be mean "digital versatile disc" (its original meaning was "digital video disc"). In this manual, "DVD" is used for the digital video format; "video" is used collectively for all video formats.

15. A more detailed explanation of these systems can be found at "Worldwide TV Standards: A Web Guide," www.ee.surrey.ac.uk/Contrib/WorldTV/index.html.

16. If a library finds that it has inadvertently acquired a video in an incompatible format, services can be found on the web and in many communities for converting from one format to another. Note, however, that the result could be considered a reproduction or an adaptation of the original, or both, and the right of creation of either is reserved in the U.S. copyright law exclusively for the copyright owner: http://www.copyright.gov/title17/chapter01.pdf.

17. Copyright Act of the United States, sect. 101, www.copyright.gov/title17/chapter01.pdf. The public-performance right reserved to copyright owners in *sound* recordings is limited in section 107 to performance "by means of a digital audio transmission," as in Internet broadcasts and cable music subscription services. Note, however, that the underlying music *on* the recording may be copyrighted and require permission of its publisher.

18. "To perform or display a work 'publicly' means (1) to perform or display it at a place open to the public or at any place where a substantial number of persons outside of a normal circle of a family and its social acquaintances is gathered; or (2) to transmit or otherwise communicate a performance or display of the work to a place specified by clause (1) or to the public, by means of any device or process, whether the members of the public capable of receiving the performance or display receive it in the same place or in separate places and at the same time or at different times." Ibid, sect. 101.

19. These provisions are spelled out in the U.S. Copyright Act, sect. 110.

20. For a more detailed examination of these and other issues related to copyright in videos in libraries, see Gary P. Handman, "The Rights Stuff: Video Copyright and Collection Development," in *Video Collection Development in Multi-Type Libraries: A Handbook*, 2nd ed., ed. by Gary P. Handman (Westport, CT: Greenwood Press, 2002), 287–305; and James C. Scholtz, "Copyright Issues within the Acquisitions Process," in *Video Acquisitions and Cataloging: A Handbook*, Greenwood Library Management Collection (Westport, CT: Greenwood Press, 1995), 97–119.

21. Kristine R. Brancolini and Rick E. Provine, *Video Collections and Multimedia in ARL Libraries: Changing Technologies*, ed. by Laura A. Rounds, OMS Occasional Paper 19 (Washington, DC: Association of Research Libraries, Office of Management Services, 1997), 13.

22. Ibid., 14.

23. Handman, 290.

Notes (continued)

24. For example, Films for the Humanities & Sciences, producer of a number of educational music videos, states in the FAQ at its website (www.films.com) that "the prices for all programs listed on this website include full public performance rights." Instructional Video—a retailer rather than a producer—acquires public-performance rights for the products it distributes and identifies at its website (www.insvideo.com) and in its publications the type of performance rights that are included with each title that it sells.

4

MUSIC PUBLISHERS' NUMBERS

The number that is assigned by the publisher to a score, a recording, or a music book is a critical element to include on the purchase order. For some publications, this number, together with the publisher's name, may be the single most important piece of information the library can provide on the order. Many kinds of musical works are published in multiple printed formats. An opera, for example, may be available as a full or conductor's score that includes the music for all the participants; as the same in a reduced size for study purposes; as a vocal score that includes the music for all the singers, with the instrumental parts arranged for one piano for rehearsal purposes; as parts containing only music for the chorus, with or without a piano accompaniment; or as parts for the orchestral players. Sometimes, the wording on the title pages of some or all of these variant versions may be inadequate to distinguish clearly among them. Each, however, is likely to have a distinct number assigned by the publisher. Bärenreiter's publication of the conductor's score of George Frideric Handel's opera *Tamerlano*, for example, carries no statement on the title page of its exact format; its publisher's number is BA 4052. The title-page of Bärenreiter's vocal-score edition for this opera does identify itself as a "Klavierauszug" (piano reduction), though in a position far enough along in the title transcription to fall victim to truncation on a printed purchase order; Bärenreiter's number for it is BA 4052a. The supplementary "a" in the publisher's number for the vocal score helps the vendor to identify the exact version of this work that is being ordered.

Although publishers typically assign unique numbers to each of their editions, at least two publishers—G. Henle and Bärenreiter of Germany—have adopted the practice of reusing an edition's number for newly revised versions of the same work, even though details as significant as pagination and the editor's name may distinguish the new version from the old.[1]

Nonstandard Publishers' Numbers and Plate Numbers

Publishers' Numbers

Several kinds of numbers may be used by publishers for music, and one or more numbers or types of numbers may be associated with a single edition. Most common is a number that is printed on the title page, cover, and/or first page of music of a printed edition or embossed on the label side of a compact disc and printed on its container. Sometimes each disc in a multidisc set will have a distinctive number, and a different number representing the set as a whole will be printed on the container. Such a number can be of any length and format—though each publisher tends to pick a style and stick with it—and can include alphabetic elements, spaces, and hyphens or dashes. It can be a simple number that represents a sequence in the publisher's total output (for example, "12 679" for a publication from Schott Musik International), or it may represent a subdivision or subseries of the publisher's output (such as "FTR 148" for a volume in Schott's *Il flauto traverso* series of editions for the flute). On some editions, both types of number are present. A few publishers use no publishers' numbers of any kind, including, for example, Seesaw Music Corporation and Hildegard Publishing Company.

Plate Numbers

Printed scores also can include "plate" numbers, which originally were assigned to the engraved printing plates by the publisher or engraver as a way to keep all the plates for an edition together during production, and probably to store them afterward in numerical order. Some publishers assigned sequentially higher plate numbers to each new edition, so that the numbers provided a chronology of the publisher's output.[2] Each plate for an edition, and therefore each page printed by it, bears the plate number(s) for that edition, usually centered at the bottom of each page. Often, an alphabetic abbreviation for the name of the firm constitutes a part of the plate number. Sometimes plate numbers are derived from the publisher's number, or they may be identical to it. As a general rule, if a number is placed *only* on the title page and/or first page of music, it is designated a publisher's number; plate numbers appear on *every* page of an edition, though the plate number can also serve the added role of publisher number. Although plate numbers came into being to manage engraved editions, the term currently is used generically for similar numbers, regardless of whether engraved plates actually are used for printing.[3]

MARC Coding of Plate and Publishers' Numbers

Publishers' numbers, rather than plate numbers, are the "public" identification numbers for score editions. These are the identification numbers that usually appear in bibliographies and publishers' catalogs, and often they will be the only such number known by library staff at the time of placing an order. In MARC records, both plate and publishers' numbers for scores are recorded in the repeatable 028 field (presupposing a conscious and conscientious cataloger). Plate numbers are distinguished from publishers' numbers in the MARC field by the first indicator, that is, the first digit following the "028" field number (the first digit after the first colon in figure 4.1): publishers' numbers for scores use a first indicator of "3"; plate numbers use a first indicator of "2." Publishers' numbers for audio and music video recordings are also encoded in the 028 field: sound recordings are coded with a first indicator of "0"; numbers assigned by publishers to music video recordings, as opposed to numbers that may be assigned by distributors, should be encoded with a first indicator of "4" (see figure 4.1).

The second indicator (the second digit following the "028" field number) determines whether the publisher's and plate numbers display in the online public catalog as a formatted note: "Publisher's no.: 49 023 Schott," and "Plate no.: Z 13 048 Schott," for example. Notes are generated if the second indicator is "1" or "2." In automated acquisitions systems, the second indicator also can determine whether the numbers print on a purchase order.

MARC 028:02:	recording issue (label) number (displays note)
MARC 028:0 :	recording issue (label) number (no display)
MARC 028:22:	score plate number (displays note)
MARC 028:2 :	score plate number (no display)
MARC 028:32:	score publisher number (displays note)
MARC 028:3 :	score publisher number (no display)
MARC 028:42:	video publisher number (displays note)
MARC 028:4 :	video publisher number (no display)

Figure. 4.1. Coding of Music Publisher, Issue, and Plate Numbers

When faced with a choice between disparate plate and publisher's numbers for an edition, acquisitions staff normally should use the publisher's number (including any alphabetic components) to convey to the vendor the identity of the desired edition. If only a plate number is available, usually it serves also as the edition's publisher's number.

Internal Production Numbers

A renegade sort of music publisher's number is the internal production or manufacture number printed at the bottom of the final page of scores published by Schott Musik International. Although assigned by Schott solely to facilitate internal operations—they appear in very small typeface, and can easily be overlooked by the casual user—many music catalogers are encoding them as publishers' numbers in MARC records. While these numbers may prove to be important to future music bibliographers in establishing the publishing history of a work or edition (much as plate numbers have done for early engraved editions), they do not appear in Schott's printed or online catalogs, and they are irrelevant to music acquisitions procedures. Nevertheless, many of them lurk in MARC cataloging records for Schott editions, indistinguishable there from their legitimate and essential siblings, the true publishers' numbers assigned by Schott. If unsure of the status of multiple "publisher's" numbers when using a MARC record to order a score, the only bulletproof option is to transcribe them *all* on the purchase order, and trust the vendor to sort them out.

Standard Publishers' Numbers

Several types of "standard" numbers have been adopted internationally for use on publications, including printed music, and on books, journals, and monographic series about music. Publishers who use these numbering schemes are providing precise, numerically encoded identification of themselves and of each of their publications.

International Standard Book Number

The International Standard Book Number (ISBN) was adopted in 1969 by the International Organization for Standardization (ISO), and has since become ubiquitous in the international book trade. The ten-digit code consists of four elements that identify (1) a national, geographic, or language group; (2) a specific publisher or producer; (3) a particular title produced by that publisher; and (4) a checkdigit that is computer generated by algorithmic calculation to determine the validity of the entire number. The four parts of the ISBN are normally printed separated by hyphens or spaces. In the example "ISBN 0-02-872415-1," the initial "0" is the group identifier (anglophone countries, including the United States, Australia, part of Canada, Gibraltar, Ireland, New Zealand, South Africa, Swaziland, the United Kingdom, and Zimbabwe use group identifiers "0" and "1"; "2" is used by francophone areas; "3" by German-language areas; and so forth; smaller areas or language groups are assigned multiple digits, so that Italy is "88," Iceland is "9979"); "02" in the example identifies the book publisher Macmillan, Inc.; "872415" identifies the title *Baker's Biographical Dictionary of Musicians*, 8th edition, published by Macmillan subsidiary Schirmer Books; and "1" is the checkdigit. The size of each field is not fixed, excepting the checkdigit, so that a very small publisher will have a long number for the publisher identifier, leaving fewer digits to enumerate its publications; conversely, a very productive publisher will be assigned a short identifying number, leaving more space for book numbers.[4] Publishers of printed music are not prohibited from using ISBNs, but few have opted to do so. Most of the ones that do use ISBNs are publishers whose principal activity is the publication of books, such as Oxford University Press; carryover of the ISBN system into its music catalog is, therefore, a natural extension of Oxford's established practice for books. Oxford also uses on its music editions, in tandem, the type of nonstandard publisher's number described above.

International Standard Music Number

Similar to the ISBN is the International Standard Music Number (ISMN), which was adopted in late 1993 by the International Organization for Standards. The ISMN also consists of ten characters, but there is no initial geographic or language-group number, on the grounds that music is an "international" language. The first digit is replaced by the constant "M," followed (as in the ISBN) by two variable-length elements for publisher identifier and item identifier, and the ISMN concludes with a checkdigit.[5] In the example "ISMN M-051-21239-2," "051" represents the publisher Boosey & Hawkes, "21239" the Boosey title *Music for 18 Musicians* by Steve Reich, and the calculated checkdigit is "2." The ISMN is not used for books *about* music, or for sound or video recordings, except when they are material accompanying a printed edition.[6]

Many of the publishers that have adopted the ISMN also have retained their traditional, nonstandard edition-numbering systems, with both kinds of numbers being associated with individual publications. Not unexpectedly, the "traditional" numbers often are recycled to do double duty as the item identifiers in the ISMNs (see figure 4.2). It also would not be unexpected for music publishers that adopt the ISMN to begin to phase out their older forms of publishers' numbers. Boosey & Hawkes has done so: the older numbers may still appear on the printed products, but they are vanishing from Boosey's catalogs.

The ISMN has experienced increasing acceptance and application in Europe since its adoption in 1993, but as of 2003 it had scarcely penetrated the United States music trade, except where used by publishers that are multinational (Boosey & Hawkes, for example). This lag can be attributed in part to the extended negotiations that were involved in identifying an agency in the United States to administer the system (R. R. Bowker, which administers ISBNs, began overseeing ISMNs as well in the United States in 2002).[7]

International Standard Serials Number

The International Standard Serials Number (ISSN) is the numerical identifier for serial publications, which, in addition to journals, encompasses monographic series, including those of published scores. It takes the form of two sets of four digits, separated by a hyphen. An example is A-R Editions series *Recent Researches in the Music of the Nineteenth and Twentieth Centuries*, each volume of which carries the ISSN 0193-5364, as well as its unique ISBN number. Unlike ISBN and ISMN, which encode identifiable publisher prefixes and title information, the ISSN is an "idiot" number whose digits carry no inherent meaning at all; the only "smart" part of the ISSN is the final checkdigit.[8] In MARC records, the ISSN is encoded in field 022. The ISSN is administered in the United States by the National Serials Data Program, which is a part of the Library of Congress's Serial Record Division.

An ISBN, ISMN, or ISSN is like an edition's fingerprint. Unlike a nonstandard music publisher's number, which exists at the publisher's caprice, these standard numbers adhere to rules that are not subject to variation. The ISBN and ISMN systems are administered by international agencies, which in turn contract with national or regional ones that liaise with publishers in their geographic areas. The national agencies assign the publishers' identifiers.

The hyphens normally imbedded in ISBNs and ISMNs are omitted in encoded MARC records (ISBN is MARC field 020; ISMN is MARC 024 with first indicator "2"). Out-of-the-box automated acquisitions systems normally print ISBNs and ISSNs on purchase orders as a matter of course if they are present in a MARC record being used for ordering purposes. They normally do not print ISMNs and nonstandard music publishers' numbers.[9] Often, however, acquisitions modules can be customized locally to do so, and it is a modification well worth pursuing with local technicians and systems administrators so as to avoid the necessity of adding the numbers manually to music purchase orders. They are essential.

Bar Codes for Music Products

Product bar codes—developed in the early 1970s for supermarkets to track inventory and sales, and affixed to just about everything we buy today—have no particular library applications as of this writing, but their relationship to publishers' numbers is due to change in the year 2007 (see the "ISBN-13" section, below).

There are several bar-coding systems in use that vary according to the environment.

Universal Product Code

Sound and video recordings normally employ the Universal Product Code (UPC), which is the same type of twelve-digit bar code as used on other nonbook merchandise. The first six digits of the twelve are a permanent company code that is obtained from the Uniform Code Council and the next five digits are assigned by the company to identify a particular product. The fifth of these five—the penultimate number represented on the bar code—is a standard-configuration code that identifies the medium of the product: CD, audiocassette, videocassette, etc. The familiar "–2" at the end of many publishers' numbers on compact discs identifies the product's format. A checkdigit completes the code. Most recording companies incorporate all or part of the publisher number that is embossed on the face of a CD and printed on its container into the bar code numbering, while other companies use completely different numbering systems for the two functions. When encoded in MARC records, the UPCs for recordings appear in field 024, with a first indicator of "1." Figure 4.2 shows examples of publishers' numbers and UPCs for compact discs. Shared numerals are displayed in bold type.

Bach, Johann Christian. *Complete opera overtures* [sound recording].
Georgsmarienhütte: CPO, 2003.

UPC:	761203**996327**
Publisher no.:	cpo **999 963-2** (set)
Publisher no.:	cpo 999 129-2 (disc 1)
Publisher no.:	cpo 999 488-2 (disc 2)
Publisher no.:	cpo 999 753-2 (disc 3)

Donizetti, Gaetano. *Anna Bolena* [sound recording]. New York:
Deutsche Grammophon, 2000.

UPC:	028946595725
Publisher no.:	**289 465 957-2**

Gibbons, Orlando. *The woods so wild* [sound recording]: *keyboard works*. Glasgow: Linn Records, 2002.

UPC:	691062012522
Publisher no.:	CKD **125**

Glass, Philip. *Philip on film* [sound recording]: *filmworks by Philip Glass*. New York: Nonesuch, 2001.

UPC:	075597**966022**
Publisher no.:	**79660-2**

Holliger, Heinz. *Schneewittchen* [sound recording]. Munich: ECM
Records, 2000.

UPC:	028946528723
Publisher no.:	ECM1715–ECM 1716 (discs)
Publisher no.:	**465 287-2** (container)

Figure 4.2. Publishers' Numbers and UPCs Used on Selected
Compact Discs (Shared Elements in Bold)

European Article Number

Bar-coded books, scores, and serials use a different system: a thirteen-digit array conforming to the European Article Numbering (EAN)
system.[10] EAN bar codes begin with a national identifier (00 through
09 are used for the United States). Because ISBNs already indicate
country of origin, or at least a language, the EAN Authority in 1980
conceived the mythical country "Bookland" (honest) whence come all
books. Bookland was assigned the country code 978, and these numbers introduce the bar codes for all books. These three digits are followed by the first nine digits of the ISBN, with a new checkdigit calculated thereafter (in the United States, a five-digit supplemental bar code
can be used for added data, usually price information).[11] For ISMNs,

the "M" is replaced by "0" and preceded by the constant "979" (Musicland?), and the remainder of the ISMN carries over unchanged, including the *original* checkdigit. (Because the checkdigit is not recalculated, the ISMN can easily be reconstructed from the numbers on the bar code.) ISSNs are preceded by "977," the original checkdigit is replaced by a two-digit price code—almost always "00"—and a new checkdigit is calculated thereafter to make up the requisite thirteen digits. Figure 4.3 shows examples of publishers' numbers and EANs for printed music (note the exception in the Cerha entry, where UPC replaces EAN). Shared numerals are displayed in bold type.

Abe, Keiko. *Marimba d'amore: for marimba solo.* Tokyo: Schott Japan, 2001.

Publisher no.:	SJ-**051**
ISBN:	4-89066-**051**-8
ISMN:	M-65001-**177**-8
EAN:	9790650011**778**

Beethoven, Ludwig van. *Streichquintette.* Herausgegeben von Sabine Kurth. München: Henle, 2001.

Publisher no.:	HN **9267**
ISMN:	M-2018-**9267**-2
EAN:	9790201892672

Busoni, Ferruccio. *Drei Stücke für Violoncello und Klavier = Three pieces for violoncello and piano.* Wiesbaden: Breitkopf & Härtel, 2000. [no carryover from publisher number to ISMN]

ISMN:	M004181003
Publisher no.:	**8712**
Plate no.:	EB **8712**

Cerha, Friedrich. *Netzwerk-Fantasie für Klavier (1988).* Vienna: Universal, 1989. [no carryover between any of the numbers]

Publisher no.:	UE 31 435
ISBN:	3-7024-0483-X
ISMN:	M-008-06379-4
UPC:	803452002390

Egk, Werner. *Allegro für 3 Violinen (1923).* Mainz: Schott, 2001.

ISMN:	M-001-**12932**-9
EAN:	97900011**129329**
Internal prod. no.:	50 153

Figure 4.3. Publishers' Numbers and EANs Used on Selected Scores (Shared Elements in Bold)

Conversion of Publisher's Number to Bar Code

Converting ISBNs, ISMNs, or publishers' numbers to EAN or UPC bar code numbers is not mandatory, though most publishers seem to do so. Notable exceptions include the music publisher Hal Leonard, whose bar code numbers bear no relation to the items' ISBNs, and Universal Edition, which assigns traditional nonstandard publisher numbers, as well as ISMNs *and* ISBNs, many of which bear no relation to the EANs or UPCs used on their editions (see, for example, the Cerha entry in figure 4.3; this edition bears a UPC rather than the usual EAN).

ISBN-13

When the ten-digit ISBN system was created in the 1960s, it had the capacity, theoretically, to assign one billion numbers. The hierarchical allocation of blocks of numbers to groups and publishers, however, limits the system's overall capacity. If the ISBN were a "dumb" number like the ISSN, that is, if it did not contain any meaningful internal elements, then the nine digits aside from the checkdigit could be used in any combination, and the capacity would truly be a billion. As a result of the proliferation of new publishing formats and other changes in the publishing industry, the available numbers are being consumed at a much faster rate than was originally anticipated. The world is running out of ISBN numbers.

On 1 January 2007, the ISBN system is scheduled to change from ten digits to thirteen (called "ISBN-13"). The new ISBN numbers will simply be the Bookland EANs already used on bar codes for books, incorporating the 978 prefix: it no longer should be necessary to assign two numbers—the thirteen-digit EAN product code and the ten-digit ISBN—to any book. The existing capacity will be doubled, because book publishers also will begin using the 979 prefix, which was reserved long ago for use by publishers, and which already has been used for several years as the prefix on bar codes for music publications that carry ISMNs (see above).

In the same time frame as the move to ISBN-13, U.S. manufacturers and retailers of other types of products also are to begin moving from twelve-digit UPCs to thirteen-digit EAN codes. The European Article Number (EAN) and the ISBN-13 (an EAN-13) will be totally compatible. A box of Cheerios will have the same kind of bar code as Schirmer's edition of Beethoven's Piano Sonatas and the music books published by Macmillan.

Additional information about ISBN-13 can be found at the website of the ISBN organization (www.isbn.org); FAQs about the revised standard are at www.nlc-bnc.ca/iso/tc46sc9/isbn.htm.

Vendors' Catalog Numbers

In addition to the numbers assigned by publishers to their editions, some music vendors devise their own numbering systems, which may be used in lieu of the publishers' numbers when ordering from them. Music vendor J. W. Pepper & Son, for example, assigns seven- or ten-digit numbers to the titles it sells, and excludes the actual publishers' numbers from its catalogs and new-publication announcements. Unfortunately, this omission can impede the preorder searching process, particularly if the bibliographic description is also abbreviated, or has been translated to English from another language, as often is the case with some vendors' information. The searcher must sometimes make a leap of faith when judging whether the title being advertised matches a full bibliographic record found in OCLC WorldCat or the RLG Union Catalog. European library vendor Otto Harrassowitz also assigns a unique ID number (nine digits) to each title it offers, as does the Italian firm Casalini Libri (eight-digit "card" numbers), but both also provide users of their data with ISMNs, ISBNs, and any other numbers associated with a publication. Obviously, Pepper, Harrassowitz, or Casalini catalog numbers on purchase orders sent to other vendors would be meaningless to them, and could, in fact, cause them confusion.

Searching by Music Publishers' Numbers

It should be apparent from the variety of numeric and alphanumeric formats in the examples in figures 4.2 and 4.3 that nonstandard music publishers' numbers and plate numbers are far from uniform. Furthermore, their encoding in the 028 fields of MARC cataloging records can vary depending upon choices made by individual catalogers or cataloging agencies. Alphabetic prefixes may be omitted, or may—or not—be separated from numeric elements by spaces; punctuation may be omitted; 028s may be repeated with the "same" number displayed in multiple configurations, such as once with an alphabetic prefix and once without; or they may be missing from a record entirely. Music publishers' numbers are reliable identifiers when used in tandem with composer and performer names, publisher and record label names, publication dates, and formats, and they should be used with those elements when ordering music printed editions and recordings. Unlike the standard formats of the ISBNs and ISMNs used on some music editions, however, they are unreliable access points, and should not be depended upon in keyword and Boolean searches of online resources.

Notes

1. See, for example, Henle's 2003 edition of Robert Schumann's Fantasy in C Major for Piano, op. 17, edited by Ernst Herttrich (46 p. of music); the 1979 Henle edition of this work was edited by Wolfgang Boetticher (39 p. of music); both versions have Henle's number 276. See also Bärenreiter's 2003 edition of Mozart's Concerto for Horn and Orchestra, K. 495, in E-flat major, piano reduction by Martin Schelhaas, which has the same number (BA 5313a) as the 1990 edition of this concerto, with piano reduction by Douglas Woodfull-Harris.

2. More about this is found in *Guide for Dating Early Published Music: A Manual of Bibliographical Practices*, compiled by D. W. Krummel for the International Association of Music Libraries, Commission for Bibliographical Research (Hackensack, NJ: Joseph Boonin, 1974), 53–64.

3. For a more extended explanation of plate numbers and music publishers' numbers, see the entries for those terms in the glossary included in *Music Printing and Publishing*, ed. by D. W. Krummel and Stanley Sadie (New York: W. W. Norton, 1990), 526–27, 532–34.

4. For a fuller explanation of ISBNs, see the introduction to any edition of *The Publishers' International ISBN Directory*, Handbook of International Documentation and Information 7 (Munich: K. G. Saur; New York: R. R. Bowker, 1989–); or any recent volume of *The Bowker Annual: Library and Book Trade Almanac* (New York: R. R. Bowker, 1961–).

5. Note should be made of at least one publisher that does not play by these rules: Éditions du Centre de musique baroque de Versailles uses bogus ISMNs. See, for example, the six trio sonatas opus 9 by François Joseph Gossec published by the Centre in 2003 as vols. 102–7 in its series Cahiers de musique: The "ISMN" printed in each volume is identical to the other five, except for the "checkdigit," which increments by one number through the series of six trios. These numbers can be seen at the Centre's website, www.cmbv.com/fr/index.html.

6. For a fuller introduction to ISMNs, see Hartmut Walravens, "ISMN: The International Standard Music Number," *Fontes Artis Musicae* 42 (1995): 164–71; or the introduction to any edition of the International ISMN Agency's *Music Publishers' International ISMN Directory* (Munich: K. G. Saur; Berlin: International ISMN Agency, 1995–), which includes music publishers regardless of whether they use ISMNs (the ISMN prefix is given in the directory for

Notes (continued)

each publisher that does). More detailed explanation is found in the English-language ISMN users' manual, available as downloadable PDF and HTML documents at the website of the International ISMN Agency located in Berlin: *ISMN Users' Manual*, 3rd ed. (1998), www.ismn-international.org/manual. html.

7. Launch of the ISMN in the United States was announced by Bowker on 15 August 2002 (see www.bowker.com/bowkerweb/Press_Releases/ISMN%20Launch.htm). Publishers of printed music can apply online for an ISMN publisher prefix at the agency's website (www.isbn.org/standards/home/isbn/us/ismn/index.asp).

8. The U.S. agency that issues ISSNs has occasionally given meaning to these numbers, as when it assigned one incorporating four digits matching the year of the Byzantine empire's end for an appropriate publication, and on another occasion allowed a numerologist to choose an auspicious number, according to Regina Reynolds, "ISSN: It's Still Some Number!" *Against the Grain* 8 (June 1996): 26.

9. That these two MARC fields are below the radar of the general community of library professionals is illustrated by the fact that neither the 024 nor the 028 appear among the thirty-eight MARC fields surveyed by Allyson Carlyle and Traci E. Timmons in "Default Record Displays in Web-Based Catalogs," *Library Quarterly* 72 (2002): 179–204.

10. An exception is Universal Edition, which uses EANs on some of its printed editions and UPCs on others. See the Cerha example in figure 4.3.

11. Readers interested in a more thorough explanation of how these standard numbers are converted to Bookland EAN codes are referred to the Book Industry Advisory Committee's *Machine-Readable Coding Guidelines for the U.S. Book Industry: Recommendations to the Publishing Industry* (New York: Book Industry Study Group, 1997). A shorter explanation is found in *The Bowker Annual of Library and Book Trade Information*.

5

VENDORS

Libraries can order music directly from many publishers, and there are sometimes benefits in doing so. As a rule, however, using music dealers (or "vendors") as go-betweens results in more efficient and economical service than publishers can hope to match.[1] When working with one or more vendors who distribute the editions of many publishers, a library reduces the number of separate orders that it must dispatch, of packages to receive and unpack, of invoices to check, of payments to remit, and of points to contact when something goes awry. All of this reduces time and costs at the library's end. It is also easier to monitor the performance of a few vendors than of dozens or even hundreds of individual publishers. Each publisher, furthermore, will have its own policies for distributing books and scores to libraries, and of charging for them, making it impossible when dealing with many direct orders to anticipate how much the library will actually pay, how the order will be shipped, whether the invoice will include all the information required by the library, and how difficult it will be to return damaged or incorrect shipments. Vendors can also provide services not normally available from publishers: responsible vendors provide invaluable information on the status of newly published and available material of interest to libraries; they can claim and report on titles not shipped promptly; efficiently handle standing orders for sets and series; tailor invoices to suit the library's needs; prepare reports on the library's purchasing activity; and offer discounts on the cost of some materials. A few music vendors can also service approval plans. A vendor that handles a significant volume of orders for a library also will be more responsive to the library's needs than will a publisher for which the library may represent only a few orders a year. For publishers, too, it is more practical and efficient to distribute goods through a cadre of vendors and retailers than to work with many libraries directly.

Librarians often assume that ordering direct from a publisher will produce the fastest result in a "rush" ordering situation. Maybe. But a responsive vendor, fully informed of the library's needs in a particular situation, usually can have a musical edition delivered to the library as expeditiously as can its publisher (expect there to be extra charges for rush orders).

Another reason to place orders with vendors is the plurality of attitudes that music publishers have about direct orders; some welcome them, but many do not. In the latter camp, Alfred Publishing Company, Carl Fischer, Hal Leonard, Kendor Music, and Mel Bay, to name a few, have put statements on their websites in strong support of music retailers, and they provide links to online and brick-and-mortar stores where users are directed to purchase their editions. Other publishers—Dover Publications, G. Henle USA, Edwin F. Kalmus, and Southern Music, for example—offer the full online shopping experience. Presumably, they also would accept a library's purchase orders. As these examples illustrate, publishers have no unified position on direct orders. Ordering from a vendor will yield more consistent results for the library than will second-guessing the practices of multiple publishers.

And then there is the matter of discounts: dealers purchase from publishers in quantity, and they thereby qualify for wholesale trade discounts that are not normally available to libraries.[2] It is these trade discounts that allow vendors, in turn, to sell some editions to libraries at below list price, although some vendors give no discounts at all. Score vendors that also sell books may not be able to offer such discounts for books as well as scores, simply because they typically purchase books in lesser quantities, and therefore may not qualify for the best wholesale discounts from those publishers.

More important than discounts, many would agree, are the benefits the library gains from the vendor's expertise. Vendors work with publishers daily and are usually the first to know if an edition has changed price or distributor, or has gone out of print. Few libraries have the resources to track these day-to-day changes in the music publishing business that for vendors are required knowledge for efficient operation.

One of the ways that vendors learn of new score publications for their clients is through new-issue subscription plans with publishers: a vendor agrees to accept automatic shipment from a publisher of a predetermined number of copies (as few as one) of its new editions (either *all* new editions, or some agreed upon subcategory of them) in exchange for a one-time deeper-than-normal discount on them. The vendor then can actually have the new scores in hand from which to describe them to clients, perhaps in fuller detail than would be possible if working with only the publisher's catalog descriptions. These new-issue plans can involve some risk for vendors, since almost no publisher of printed music will allow vendors to return unsold scores for credit, whether they were acquired as new issues or by normal stock-order procedures. The vendor could find itself stuck with a couple of hot-off-the-press concertina concertos, when in the history of the firm not one concertina work has ever been sold.

The policies of publishers of printed music prohibiting returns of unsold stock are in marked contrast to the generous return policies of publishers of books, which allow bookstores to return unsold stock for full credit up to two years after being acquired from the publisher.[3] This explains, at least in part, why bookstores can stock thousands of the most marginal imaginable titles, while the music vendor and the local music shop must often special-order all but the best-known regular sellers.

Some categories of materials may be—or may *appear* to be—available *only* from their publishers, notably the following:

Self-published works. One learns of these particularly from direct mailings by the "publisher" and from reviews or advertisements in journals that are targeted to a particular caste of musicians—a clutch of new double-bass quartets, for example, reviewed in the quarterly *Double Bassist*, with the composer's postal or e-mail address supplied for ordering. Ordering direct from the composer may involve some back-and-forth to establish terms and usually will require pre-payment. Public-spirited music acquisitions staff may want to consider putting a vendor on the case (be sure to include relevant source and publisher-contact information on the order that is sent to the vendor): the vendor may thus learn about new repertoire and editions to inform its other customers about, and the composer might appreciate the opportunity to have a professional distributing his works. Potentially, everybody wins.

Works published by societies and associations, or similar organizations that are not primarily in the publishing business. These editions may be available through vendors, but often at a premium, since the dealer may have to add a service charge if the publisher does not allow a trade discount. On the other hand, the small savings realized by ordering direct may not be worth the inconvenience of establishing a new vendor account in the library's online system to facilitate check writing and paying in advance, which is a common requirement. Some professional associations contract with trade publishers to distribute their editions—monographic publications of the Music Library Association, for example, currently are printed and sold by Scarecrow Press—and these editions can be purchased in the normal way. Some organizations also offer library memberships, which may allow the library to acquire its publications at a discount. Details of these arrangements, if they exist, can usually be found in a society's journal or on its website.

Microforms. These are often distributed only by their producers, particularly in the case of large, multipart filming projects like the *Music Manuscript Collection of the British Library* published by Primary Source Microfilm, and *Music Manuscripts of the Classical and Romantic Eras* published by Adam Matthew Publications. Whenever the library anticipates adding parts of a set that is being acquired in installments, look for the "gap" sales offered annually by some microform publishers; discounts can be steep.

Dissertations from the UMI Dissertations Services division of ProQuest Information and Learning. No trade discounts are allowed to dealers on dissertations, though academic institutions and individuals associated with them who order from UMI are eligible for discounts of more than 30 percent.

Works distributed by national music information centers. The main purpose of these centers, most of which are subsidized by their national governments, is to document and promote at home and abroad their national music, principally contemporary art music. Some of these centers have their own imprints, such as Edition Suecia of the Swedish Music Information Center, and CeBeDeM of the Belgian Centre for Music Documentation. These editions can be purchased through music retailers and vendors. Typically, these centers also have archives of unpublished compositions that they will copy on demand for sale or rental to individuals and institutions. A directory of these centers, with links to its members, is found at the website of the International Association of Music Information Centres (www.iamic.net).

Prepublication discount offers, usually on expensive items. Librarians often suspect that these offers are testing the market and that publication plans could change if insufficient interest is shown. Ordering deadlines usually are far enough in the future to bide your time; vendors often come forward with the same terms, and placing the order with a vendor rather than the publisher may be preferable.

Clearance sales, when a publisher needs to reduce warehouse inventory or has lost the distribution rights for another publisher's editions.

Out-of-print works. A publisher may have a few remaining copies of an edition that is described as out of print; if a shelf-worn copy from the publisher's dwindling stock is acceptable, say so on the order. Some publishers also offer on-demand or "special order" reprints of editions from their archives that they no longer consider to be commercially viable, and therefore are not widely advertised. Calling ahead to determine the status in each case is a good idea; an inquiry by your cooperative vendor will likely produce the best result.[4]

For many libraries, an important exception to the "use a vendor" mantra will be subscriptions to the several Recent Researches in the Music of . . . series of musicological editions published by A-R Editions of Middleton, Wisconsin. Patrons of libraries that have standing orders *direct* with A-R for any of these series qualify for permission to reproduce for study or performance any part of an edition in that series.[5] Subscriptions *can* be placed through an intermediary, but without reaping the benefits of A-R's copyright sharing policy. Although this generous and intelligent policy may not aid the library directly, the library's users who want to perform from these editions can do so without imposing undue wear and tear on the library's copies, or undue stress on the "fair use" section of the copyright law of the United States.[6]

At least two major North American vendors that supply U.S. trade, professional, and scholarly books to libraries also can supply music audio and video recordings: Ambassador Book Service and Baker & Taylor.[7] No major North American library book vendors, however, supply a full range of printed music. The book and music publishing industries in the United States seldom intersect and their avenues of distribution are largely different.[8] This demarcation is manifest by the general absence from printed music editions of ISBN numbers (see chapter 4), which, when imbedded in books' bar code symbols, enable publishers, vendors, and bookstores to track inventory and sales by computer, and which are obligatory if trade and scholarly books are to be marketed successfully. Few publishers of printed music participate in the ISBN program. Those that do—Alfred, Amsco, Dover, Mel Bay, Hal Leonard, and Warner Brothers, for example—are the publishers whose editions will be found under the "Music" signs at local Barnes & Noble and Borders Books and Music chain stores. But lacking this basic tool to manage distribution of the majority of music scores—and no doubt noting also their miniscule share of the publishing marketplace—U.S. library book and media vendors eschew scores.

Several publications are available to guide acquisitions librarians in selecting and evaluating library vendors.[9] The detailed guidelines given in those guides, however, are intended for application to full-line wholesalers of English-language *books*, published by a well-organized and cohesive industry and subject to excellent bibliographic control. Typically, the only clients of these vendors are libraries. Music vendors, on the other hand, deal in editions that originate on several continents, where variable trade practices and qualities of music bibliographic control are in play. The music vendor's customers normally include schools, professional and amateur ensembles, churches, and individual musicians, as well as libraries. Still, some general principles apply, and the following brief list of some components of vendor characteristics may be useful to keep in mind during the vendor selection process (some of these questions may be answered by vendors' websites).

Fulfillment Capability

What are the vendor's specialties ("art" music, world music, geographic area, other)?

What formats can be supplied (scores, audio and video recordings, books, serials, other)?

What purchase plans are available (firm orders, standing orders, approval plans, subscriptions, search for obscure publishers and titles, search for out-of-print editions, other)?

What inventory is on hand?

Is there a cyclical claim system for outstanding orders? At what frequency?

How long are titles that are temporarily out-of-print or temporarily out of stock at the publisher or distributor kept on backorder?

Who are the primary library clientele (academic, research, public, school)?

What are typical delivery times for U.S. and foreign editions?

Customer Services

Are new publications announced to clients? How (catalogs, newsletters, U.S. mail, e-mail, frequency)?

What are the communication options (mail, phone, toll-free, fax, e-mail, web)?

Are there customization options (invoices, status reports, shipping frequency)?

What are the policies and procedures for rush orders, claims, cancellations, returns?

Can drop-shipment direct from publishers be arranged if speed requires?

For non-U.S. vendors, is correspondence in English?

Is the staff musically knowledgeable? This is important.

Pricing

> Are discounts offered on some or all sales? How are they calculated (flat percentage, sliding scale based on quantity, different discounts for approval and standing orders)?
> How are shipping and handling fees calculated (postage, postage plus handling, percent of invoice total, other)?
> What are payment terms (designated time period, late payment fee, supplemental fees, other)?
> For non-U.S. vendors, is payment accepted in dollars; is there a currency exchange fee?

Automation

> Searchable database of material for sale? What information is included in a typical entry? Inventory status stated online?
> Orders accepted electronically? In what format(s)?
> Order status available online?

Music vendors tend to specialize. Some sell only recordings—usually video as well as audio—while others concentrate on printed music, perhaps including music books as well. Some non-U.S. vendors sell only publications originating in their own geographic areas. Though a few music vendors offer the full range of published formats, libraries typically opt to allot their orders among several vendors to take advantage of the particular expertise that each has to offer, and also to take advantage of geographical pricing advantages. Often, a book or score purchased from its country of publication will cost the library less than the same publication purchased from another country; a music score published in Italy and acquired from an Italian vendor, for example, typically will cost a bit less—sometimes significantly less—than the same edition purchased from, say, a German, British, or U.S. vendor. A few minutes spent comparing prices of non-U.S. editions in publishers' and vendors' web catalogs will reveal this to be a generally reliable, though not foolproof, rule of thumb.[10] Just as one knows not to shop for shoes at Safeway, the music acquisitions specialist soon learns which music vendors sell this or that format and where to send orders to obtain the best results.

U.S. Vendors of Printed Music

The vendors listed below are some of those in the United States that are experienced in obtaining and providing in-print music to libraries from publishers worldwide (out-of-print music and its dealers are discussed in chapter 9). These are not the only vendors who can fill library music orders, but they are among those who have maintained visibility in the music library community through exhibits at MLA and other music association conferences, corporate membership in MLA and financial support of its programs, or advertisements in MLA's quarterly journal *Notes*. Some distribute catalogs or regular announcements about new music publications, delivered in print or electronically. Some also perform out-of-print searches, as indicated in the notes following the contact information for each. Theodore Front, alone among these, also distributes sound and video recordings. Note that OMI's specialty is published facsimiles of early-music manuscripts and editions.

Broude Brothers Limited, PO Box 547, 141 White Oaks Road, Williamstown, MA 01267. Tel: 413 458 8131; fax: 413 458 5242; e-mail: broude@sover.net. Printed music of all publishers; publishes occasional specialty catalogs; publishes its own line of scholarly score editions; no online database.

Educational Music Service, 33 Elkay Drive, Chester, NY 10918. Tel: 845 469 5790; fax: 845 469 5817; web: www.emsmusic.com; e-mail: sales@emsmusic.com. Printed music of all types by all publishers (specializes in orchestral literature); no online database; maintains an in-house music-in-print database that it licenses as an annual CD-ROM to customers, with the fee based on amount of purchases made in the previous year (in 2002, $60 annual license fee for purchases exceeding $2,000, $750 fee for purchases less than $2,000); several specialty catalogs and brochures are mounted as PDF files on the website.

J. W. Pepper & Son, 2480 Industrial Boulevard, Paoli, PA 19301. Tel: 610 648 0500, 800 345 6296; fax: 610 993 0563, 800 260 1482; web: www.jwpepper.com; e-mail: satisfaction@jwpepper.com. Printed music of all types by all publishers, selected books about music; searchable database with truncated bibliographic descriptions (online ordering enabled); new-issue listings in three-month groupings available via a "Library Editions" link; publishes occasional printed catalogs of new issues; approval plans for North American score editions available.

Luck's Music Library, PO Box 71397, Madison Heights, MI 48071. Tel: 248 583 1820; fax: 248 583 1114; web: www.lucksmusic.net; e-mail: sales@lucksmusic.net. Instrumental printed music of all publishers (specialists in orchestral literature), as well as its own orchestral reprint editions; extensive catalog of works for rent; searchable online catalogs; PDF catalogs of solo and ensemble music of publishers worldwide.

OMI—Old Manuscripts and Incunabula, PO Box 6019, FDR Station, New York, NY 10150. Tel: 212 758 1946; fax: 212 593 6186; e-mail: immels@panix.com. Music facsimiles of all publishers; no online database; publishes annual catalogs of in-print facsimiles by medium of performance (keyboard, plucked strings, etc.).

Theodore Front Musical Literature, 16122 Cohasset Street, Van Nuys, CA 91406. Tel: 818 994 1902; fax: 818 994 0419; web: www.tfront.com; e-mail: music@tfront.com. Printed music of all types by all publishers, books on music, CDs, videos; searchable database of books and scores published worldwide since 1994, with full bibliographic descriptions and annotations (online ordering is enabled; pre-1994 publications can be ordered offline); separate listings of new publications updated bimonthly; monthly notification of new publications sent to customers by post or e-mail; separate online listing of out-of-print and antiquarian titles available for sale; publishes occasional specialty catalogs; approval plans for U.S. and European scores and recordings available; out-of-print searching.

Libraries that want to keep their music purchasing close to home may identify local retailers that can provide at least some of the services available from the established vendors, and at competitive costs. Names and contact information, by state and by country, of additional retailers of printed music can be found at the websites of several major music publishers, such as Carl Fischer Publications (www.carlfischer.com) and Hal Leonard Corporation (www.halleonard.com). The Retail Print Music Dealers Association also has a directory of its members at www. printmusic.org.

European Vendors of Printed Music

Several European library book vendors have taken a broader cultural view than their U.S. counterparts and *do* distribute music scores from the geographical areas that they represent. These are Blackwell's Book Services (United Kingdom, standing orders only), Casalini Libri (Italian-language areas), Otto Harrassowitz (Europe and selected publishers in other parts of the world), Librairie Erasmus (France), Puvill Libros (Spain, Portugal, Andorra, and Mexico), and Iberbook International (Spain). Of these, both Casalini and Harrassowitz have extensive coverage of music scores in their online databases, where libraries can search and verify publication details, and where registered library customers can order online. Puvill Libros includes some scores and compact discs in its online database, though the coverage is far less thorough than that found with Casalini and Harrassowitz. Blackwell's and Erasmus's databases are of books only, but each can supply music scores as well as music books from the areas they represent.[11]

Blackwell's Book Services: 50 Broad Street; Oxford OX1 3BQ, UK. Tel: 44 01865 792792; fax: 44 01865 791438; web: www.blackwell. co.uk. Continuation orders for music sets and series (books and scores) of the United Kingdom; online database of books only (searches stock in the United States and United Kingdom, all prices quoted in pounds sterling); for monograph orders see Blackwell's Music Shop.

Blackwell's Music Shop, 23–25 Broad Street, Oxford OX1 3AX, UK. Tel: 44 01865 333580; fax: 44 01865 728020; web: www.music. blackwell.co.uk/printedmusic; e-mail: music.ox@blackwell.co.uk; web: www.music.blackwell.co.uk/printedmusic. Monographic orders for printed music, books, and CDs published in the United Kingdom; searchable online database includes printed music only; for book database and continuation orders (books and printed music) see Blackwell's Book Services.

Casalini Libri, via Benedetto da Maiano, 50014 Fiesole (FL), Italy. Tel: 39 055 5018 1; fax: 39 055 5018 201; web: www.casalini.it; e-mail: info@casalini.it. Printed music, books, periodicals published in Italy, Vatican City, the Republic of San Marino, Italian cantons of Switzerland, and Malta; searchable databases (online ordering enabled) with English-language interface; music scores included in the books ("I libri") database, where searches can be limited to the subject "Music" and to a thematic group, including "Musicology" (books) or "Musical Scores"; bibliographic records (full bibliographic descriptions) available in downloadable MARC format; contributes vendor bibliographic records to OCLC WorldCat and the RLG Union Catalog; new-issue notifications available by post or electronically; approval plans available.

Iberbook International, Arquitecto Gaudi, 1, 28016 Madrid, Spain. Tel: 34 91 352 8262; fax: 34 91 352 8260; web: www.iberbook.com; e-mail: customerserv@iberbook.com. Printed music of Spain; music books of Spain, Portugal, portions of Latin America; searchable database (online ordering enabled) with English-language interface, where searches can be limited by Dewey classification (780 for music books and scores); bibliographic records (full bibliographic descriptions) available in downloadable MARC format; contributes vendor bibliographic records to OCLC WorldCat and the RLG Union Catalog; database coverage of printed music is extensive but not comprehensive; approval plans available; OP searching for books from Spain. Iberbook was acquired by Puvill Libros in early 2004.

Librairie Erasmus, 28, rue Basfroi, 75011 Paris, France. Tel: 33 1 43480320; fax: 33 1 43481424; web: www.erasmus.fr; e-mail: erasmus@erasmus.fr. Printed music, books, periodicals published in France and francophone Switzerland; online database of books only.

Otto Harrassowitz, 65183 Wiesbaden, Germany. Tel: 49 611 50300; fax: 49 611 530560; web: www.harrassowitz.de; e-mail: service@harrassowitz.de. Printed music from all of Europe, Australia, New Zealand, Japan, Israel; books and periodicals from Europe; searchable database (online ordering enabled) with English-language interface; searches can be limited to various music categories and by LC classification; bibliographic records (full bibliographic descriptions) available in downloadable MARC format; contributes vendor bibliographic records to OCLC WorldCat and the RLG Union Catalog; supplementary music reference lists accessible by password (instructions for obtaining passwords on the website); volumes in the most important monuments of music from Europe (including those of Eastern European countries and Israel), composers' collected editions from Europe (with a few titles from Israel and Japan, including those currently in progress), composers' thematic indices, music facsimiles published as monographs or in series, early-music series and sets featuring music composed 1350–1600, and new classical music; new-issue announcements available by post or electronically; approval plans available; selective OP searching (books only).

Puvill Libros, Estany, 13 Nave D-1, 08038 Barcelona, Spain. Tel: 34 93 2988960; fax: 34 93 2988961; web: www.puvill.com; e-mail: info@puvill.com. Printed music, books, CDs, periodicals of Spain, Mexico, Andorra, Portugal; searchable database with English-language interface; searches can be limited to broad or narrow spans in the LC classes M, ML, and MT; bibliographic records (full bibliographic descriptions) available in downloadable MARC format; contributes vendor bibliographic records to OCLC WorldCat and the RLG Union Catalog; new-issue announcements available by post or electronically; approval plans available.

Vendor Records in OCLC and RLG

Among the European vendors of music and books, Casalini Libri, Otto Harrassowitz, Iberbook International, and Puvill Libros contribute MARC bibliographic records to OCLC WorldCat and the RLG Union Catalog. (From France, Touzot Librairie Internationale also contributes records for books published in that country, but Touzot does not sell music.) These vendor records, originally created for distribution to customers to notify them about new publications, include the data needed by bibliographers who are deciding whether to purchase a new title and by acquisitions staff who place the orders: full bibliographic descriptions, publishers' numbers, prices, and sometimes descriptive notes. In the mid-1990s, Puvill Libros became the first to contribute its records for Spanish publications to OCLC WorldCat as a way to assist libraries in moving orders and new books through the acquisition process. Casalini, Harrassowitz, Iberbook, and Touzot soon followed suit, and today one can find records in OCLC and RLG created by these vendors for new books—and for a few scores—sometimes months before full-fledged cataloging records are available. These preliminary records can be downloaded by OCLC and RLG member–users into local library systems, where they can be used for acquisitions and cataloging purposes.

Although as of this writing only a small selection of records for printed music are contributed by Puvill and Casalini in this fashion, libraries that register with any of the three vendors who include music in their databases—Harrassowitz, Puvill, and Casalini—can select music records online, and FTP them into local systems with almost as much ease as capturing records from OCLC and RLG.[12] In other words, vendors' MARC records for printed music can be harvested from Harrassowitz, Puvill, and Casalini, while their records for books about music can be found in OCLC and RLG, as well as in the vendors' own databases.

Vendor records in OCLC and RLG omit some fields that are required for full cataloging: Library of Congress subject headings (some records contain uncontrolled subject-index terms, encoded in MARC field 653), LC classification, bibliographic and contents notes, and added entries. These vendors also follow their own paths in choice of forms and spellings of names. Often, therefore, they use "incorrect" personal and corporate names and series titles, and their records may also contain typographical errors and inaccurate MARC tags, and may duplicate "real" records.[13] Despite these problems, the very convenience afforded by these records means that libraries do use them for acquisitions. While policies will vary among libraries about how to deal with conflicting headings and other errors caused in local online catalogs by vendor records, acquisitions staff will save themselves grief by doing some record cleanup up front, such as overlaying unapproved name and series title headings with ones found in local authority files. The time taken to use correct headings will reduce the likelihood that a record will be overlooked in the online catalog or the on-order file if a second request for the same edition is received.

The music editions sold by European library vendors can also be acquired from U.S. sources, but sometimes there are economic advantages to ordering from the countries of publication. Even within continental Europe, cross-border price differentials can be significant, as was noted earlier. Small daily currency fluctuations are of little consequence when ordering a score priced in euros or British pounds sterling that may not be invoiced and shipped until weeks or even months later, when the rates might be different. Still, acquisitions staff may find it prudent to follow trends in the currency exchange rates. The daily exchange rate used is stated on each invoice issued by most European vendors, and current rates can be found at any of the currency-conversion utilities available on the web, such as the Universal Currency Converter at www.xe.com/ucc.

U.S. Vendors of Recorded Music

Unlike printed music, recorded music has penetrated numerous commercial spheres, and music compact discs and cassettes can be purchased today in retail establishments in almost any town in the United States. The Universal Product Codes used on the bar codes of recordings mean that they can be managed as wholesale and retail inventory as easily as Campbell's soup.

When working with a new recordings vendor, it is prudent to determine what its backorder policies are. Some will declare a disc "not available" and return the library's order if it is out of stock at the distributor's warehouse; other vendors will backorder, persisting until the disc is again available, or until it is determined with some certainty to be out of print ("deleted").

The vendors listed here are among those that accept library purchase orders for in-print audio and video recordings (dealers in out-of-print recordings are discussed in chapter 9). Additional retailers who deal only in *video* formats are listed in chapter 7. As noted above, Theodore Front Musical Literature deals in music audio and video recordings in addition to printed music; at its website is information about classical, jazz, and world music releases since and including 2001; recordings in series; and Grammy nominees and winners (contact information for Front is on p. 71).

AAA Music Hunter, 205 Pearl Street, Suite 5C, New York, NY 10038. Tel: 212 269 2388; fax: 212 269 7478; e-mail: musichunter@ computer.net. Audio and video; not online.

Compact Disc Source/A-V Source, 1125 Florence Avenue, Evanston, IL 60202. Tel: 847 869 9999; fax: 847 869 9997; web: www.cdsourceinc.com; e-mail: cdlibrary@aol.com. Audio and video; no searchable database; approval plans available.

Compact Disc World, 635 Montrose Avenue, South Plainfield, NJ 07080. E-mail: compactdiscworld@hotmail.com. Audio and video; no website.

Gary Thal Music, Inc., PO Box 164, Lenox Hill Station, New York, NY 10021. Tel: 212 473 1514; fax: 212 288 4126. Audio and video; no website; monthly lists of new releases, mostly classical, mailed to clients.

H & B Recordings Direct, PO Box 309, Waterbury Center, VT 05677. Tel: 800 222 6872; fax: 802 244 4199; web: www.hbdirect. com; e-mail: staff@hbdirect.com. Searchable database (online ordering enabled); audio and video recordings; additional discount with annual "membership."

JRH Media Services, Inc., 741 Bethlehem Pike, Flourtown, PA 19031. Tel: 888 557 8900; fax: 888 558 3500; e-mail: jrhmedia@ bellatlantic.net. Audio and video recordings; no online database; search service available.

Multicultural Media, 56 Browns Mill Rd., Berlin, VT 05602. Tel: 802 223 1294; fax: 802 229 2834; web: www.worldmusicstore.com; e-mail: info@multiculturalmedia.com. World music audio and video recordings; searchable database (online ordering enabled).

Musical Heritage Society, 1710 Highway 35, Oakhurst, NJ 07755. Tel: 732 531 7003; fax: 732 517 0438; web: www.musicalheritage. com; e-mail: CSManager@musicalheritage.com. Distributes CDs on the MHS label only (recordings on this label are not generally available from other vendors or at retail outlets); searchable database and online ordering enabled for members; library purchase orders accepted offline without a membership requirement.

Music Library Service Company, 313 Campbell Street, Wilmington, NC 28401. Tel: 800 849 2323; fax: 910 762 8701; web:

www.mlscmusic.com; e-mail: info@mlscmusic.com. Audio and video; approval plans; searchable database (online ordering enabled); collection development tools offered online.

Professional Media Services Corp., 1160 Trademark Drive, Suite 109, Reno, NV 89511. Tel: 800 223 7672, 775 850 3825; fax: 800 2538853; web: www.promedia.com. Audio and video; online database for registered clients; cataloging shelf-ready service available.

Rhinebeck Records, PO Box 262, Salt Point, NY 12578. Tel: 914 266 3500, 800 446 2084; fax: 914 266 4432; e-mail: rhinebeckrecords@compuserve.com. Audio recordings; no online database; search service available.

In addition to these vendors, many libraries also acquire recordings from online retailers like CDNow.com, CDConnection.com, TowerRecords.com, Amazon.com, and others. These stores have searchable databases, large inventories, competitive pricing, and speedy delivery. Amazon and Barnes & Noble offer corporate accounts with deferred monthly billing for libraries that do not use credit cards (see their respective web sites for details). These corporate accounts can be a problem, however, for libraries that have payment procedures or cycles that would prevent full settlement within thirty days. Borders Books and Music offers among its business and professional services a deferred payment card for 20 percent discounts on music and books purchased in Borders stores (see www.bordersstores.com/bbps/welcome.jsp for details and to apply). Borders purchasing cards cannot be used, however, for online purchases; Borders is "teamed" with Amazon.com, and its online sales are merged with that marketing giant.

Notes

1. The terms used to refer to a commercial firm that supplies materials from publishers to libraries have varied over the years: "retailer," "dealer," "jobber," "vendor," "agent," "wholesaler," and "supplier" have been at times in and out of favor. "Vendor" seems to be in current fashion.

2. A 40 percent discount is typical for scores from mainstream publishers, part of which may be passed on to the library.

3. Michael Ochs, "What Music Scholars Should Know about Publishers," *Notes* 59 (2002): 291.

4. The same strategy also sometimes produces results for rental scores. See the discussion of rental music in chapter 2.

5. See A-R's website at www.areditions.com/rr/share/csharing.html for more information about how this policy works and for contact information.

Notes (continued)

6. United States Code, Title 17, sec. 107, www.copyright.gov/title17.

7. Ambassador Book Service, 42 Chasmer Street, Hempstead, NY 11550; tel: 516 489 4011, 800 431 8913; web: www.absbook.com; e-mail: ambassa-dor@absbook.com. Baker & Taylor, 2550 West Tyvola Rd., Charlotte, NC 28217; tel: 704 998 3100, 800 775 1800; web: www.btol.com; e-mail: btinfo@btol.com.

8. Amy Kaneko, director of mass-market specialty sales at San Francisco–based Chronicle Books commented on the divide between books and music in bookstore operations: "The books and the music departments: Never the twain shall meet, and they operate very separately," as quoted by Chris Morris, "Music Books: A Tough Sell," *Billboard* 115 (19 July 2003): 59.

9. See, for example, Audrey Eaglen, *Buying Books: A How-to-Do-It Manual for Librarians*, 2nd ed., How-to-Do-It Manuals for Librarians 99 (New York: Neal-Schuman, 2000); *Understanding the Business of Library Acquisitions*, 2nd ed., ed. by Karen A. Schmidt (Chicago: ALA, 1999); *Vendors and Library Acquisitions*, ed. by Bill Katz (New York: Haworth Press, 1991); and *Guide to Performance Evaluation of Library Materials Vendors*, compiled by the Collection Management and Development Committee of ALA (Chicago: ALA, 1988).

10. An example will be instructive: In mid-2003, the study score for a string quartet by the Polish composer Grażyna Bacewicz was listed at the website of its publisher in Poland, Polskie Wydawnictwo Muzyczne (PWM), at a retail price of U.S. $34.95 (libraries and individuals can purchase at PWM's site, either by credit card or by payment of a pro forma invoice in advance of shipment to the library). Simultaneously, the same edition was offered for sale by library vendor Otto Harrassowitz in Wiesbaden, Germany, for €45.50 ($51.50 at the exchange rate of the day). Theodore Presser, PWM's sales representative for the United States, Canada, and Mexico, listed the same score for $60. It sometimes pays to shop around.

11. In 2002, Blackwell's split its music distribution into two components: music monographs—scores, books about music, CDs—came under the aegis of Blackwell's Music Library Services, distributed from Blackwell's Music Shop, while standing orders for music sets and series—the *Works* of Henry Purcell and the series Musica Britannica, for example—continue to be serviced by Blackwell's Book Services.

12. In OCLC WorldCat and the RLG Union Catalog, these contributed vendor records can be identified by their "library" codes, as follows: Harrassowitz: OHX (OCLC) and XHAR (RLG); Casalini: C3L (OCLC) and XCAS (RLG); Puvill: PL# (OCLC) and XPUV (RLG); Touzot: TZT (OCLC) and XTOU (RLG); Iberbook: IBI (OCLC) and XIBE (RLG).

13. See chapter 6 on preorder searching for more about spelling conflicts in vendor catalogs. A study by Laura D. Shedenhelm and Bartley A. Burk of Spanish-language vendor records revealed the types and levels of these errors: "Book Vendor Records in the OCLC Database: Boon or Bane?" *Library Re-*

Notes (continued)

sources & Technical Services 45 (January 2001): 10–19. See also Charlene Kellsey, "Cooperative Cataloging, Vendor Records, and European Language Monographs," *Library Resources & Technical Services* 46 (2002): 105–10.

PREORDER SEARCHING

Bibliographic preorder searching and verification are activities that can accomplish several purposes. First, a search of the library's catalog and order file determines if the item is already held by the library, was ordered previously and has not yet been received, or is expected on a standing order or approval plan. Next comes verification of the accuracy and thoroughness of the information in hand and the quest for additional information that may be needed to place the order (see chapter 7).

In the past, these procedures involved tedious consultation of multiple print bibliographies, catalogs, and local card files, and the laborious transcription by hand of data onto paper workforms. Automation has simplified the procedure, and in libraries where there is an emphasis on organizational streamlining, it now may be integrated into a homogenous order process, or even into the selection process. Who does this searching and verification can vary depending upon the size, type, and organization of the library. Whether done in a separate searching unit of a large research library or by the music selector, it is important that music items be searched by staff who know musical terminology in multiple western European languages and are familiar with the varieties of publication formats in which a musical work can be published.[1] They must be able to recognize that the *Studienpartitur* found in the local catalog differs markedly in both form and function from the *Spielpartitur* described in the publisher's catalog in hand, although in other respects they may appear to be the same edition.

Purchase requests can be received in the acquisitions unit in many forms. Some possibilities include a marked publisher's or dealer's catalog; a copy of an advertisement or a review; a printout from an online vendor's or bibliographic database; a personal e-mail or handwritten note; a published or specially prepared bibliography; and printed or web forms designed by the library for the requestor to populate with data and to submit. web forms are advantageous for requests from individuals, since they leapfrog any possibility of illegible handwriting, and essential fields can be programmed to be mandatory: an e-mail address or telephone number of the requestor and the source of the requestor's information are handy to have in case some follow-up is needed. Yet, all of these request formats are subject to omission and error; even publishers' catalogs sometimes truncate or misstate crucial bibliographic elements, requiring the searcher to fill in the blanks.

Caveat Inquisitor

Pitfalls for the searcher abound. The need to acquire printed editions from foreign lands and the multinational nature of the recording industry render preorder searching for music arguably more complicated than for many other kinds of publications. A single musical work may be available in printed form from multiple publishers, with title pages in a variety of languages. Some genres of works may also be printed in several formats to suit different rehearsal and performance needs. A unique recorded performance can be reborn on a new label, and with different accompanying tracks. Consequently, searches cannot be undertaken casually, or with the idea that initial failure to find the exact item being searched in the local catalog means that the library has no other viable edition or version of the same work—it may be camouflaged from view. The following paragraphs describe some of the snags that can trip the unwary music preorder searcher and verifier of musical editions.

Names

Searching by the correct composer, author, and performer names would seem to be a no-brainer, but when working through a roster of composers or performers that potentially represents a global array of languages and alphabets, what may seem obvious on first examination can turn out to be less so. If the person's or organization's name is unfamiliar or contains more diacritical marks than one normally is accustomed to seeing, verifying the spelling ought to be an early step in the search process. Even if local library procedures do not require or encourage use of authorized name and series headings on purchase orders, acquisitions staff still must *search* by correct names and titles if they are to be confident of the results of an online search. While libraries entering records into their own catalogs and into shared bibliographic databases are expected to be consistent in applying national standards for names and other headings, publishers and vendors are bound by no such obligation. Their catalogs and advertisements often are anagrammatic puzzles that must be solved before unwitting searchers formulate queries based on a publisher's or vendor's "incorrect" names and titles.

Consider that even a relatively common name can have variant spellings (see fig. 6.1).

Hofman, Srdjan, 1944– (Serbian composer)
Hofmann, Leopold, 1738–1793 (Austrian composer)
Hoffman, Richard, 1831–1909 (English American composer)
Hoffmann, E. T. A., 1776–1822 (German author and composer)

Figure 6.1. Variant Spellings of "Hofman," "Hofmann," etc.

César Franck may be rendered as "Caesar," Georg Philipp Telemann as Georg "Philippe," Dutch violinist and composer Willem de Fesch as "William," Welsh American composer Hilary Tann as "Hillary," Israeli American composer Shulamit Ran as "Shulamat," and so forth.[2] While these counterfeit spellings may seem benign, each has the potential to torpedo a name or keyword search.

Diacritics

The diacritics used in some languages can also be problematic; they are not mere decoration, as they often affect not just pronunciation, but alphabetization. The umlaut that is encountered frequently in German and other languages is a ubiquitous, and sometimes treacherous, wild card. ALA filing rules for card catalogs state that "all diacritical marks associated with, and modifications to, recognizable English letters are ignored," and automated catalogs routinely disregard them as well.[3] Publishers and vendors, though, seem to have a hard time letting them go. Arnold Schoenberg—who anglicized his name by converting the original "ö" to "oe" after emigrating to the United States—is still resolutely "Schönberg" on German and Austrian publications. German-born Georg Friedrich Händel similarly Englished his name to "George Frideric Handel" after becoming a British subject in 1727, but the original spelling with umlaut is frequently seen in modern editions, as is the orthographic conversion of that spelling to "Haendel." Corporate names and titles are affected as well: the German music publishers Bärenreiter and Hänssler become "Baerenreiter" and "Haenssler" in vendor announcements, and the monographic series Tübinger Beiträge

zur Musikwissenschaft is regularly seen converted to "Tuebinger Bei-
traege."

Transliterations

In the United States, the National Authority File (NAF)—created
by the Library of Congress and participants in NACO, the name authority component of the Program for Cooperative Cataloging (PCC)—is
used almost without exception in music collections as the standard for
names, uniform titles, and series.[4] Elsewhere in the world, however, libraries may follow other systems. The differences are most obvious in
the conversion of non-Roman alphabets, such as the Cyrillic characters
of the Russian language. Figure 6.2 illustrates how the names of Russian composers Aleksandr Scriabin, Dmitriĭ Shostakovich, and Peter
Ilich Tchaikovsky (shown first in Cyrillic)—composers whose works
are found in libraries of all sizes, and in publishers' and vendors' announcements from many countries—appear in the catalog of the Library of Congress (line 1) and in the national bibliographies and libraries of Britain (line 2), France (line 3), and Germany (line 4).[5]

	Александр Скрябин	Дмитрий Шостакович	Пётр Ильич Чайковский
1.	Aleksandr Scriabin	Dmitriĭ Shostakovich	Peter Ilich Tchaikovsky
2.	Aleksandr Skriabin	Dmitriĭ Shostakovich	Petr Il'ich Chaĭkovskiĭ
3.	Alexandre Scriabine	Dmitri Chostakovitch	Piotr Ilitch Tchaïkovski
4.	Aleksandr Skrjabin	Dmitrij Šostakovič	Pëtr Il'ič Čajkovskij

Figure 6.2. Russian Name Variants in Libraries of Four Countries

A searcher working in a library catalog in the United States with, say, a
marked issue of the *British Catalogue of Music*—published in the
mother tongue—must become aware that a name or keyword search for
"Skriabin," as it is used in that catalog, is unlikely to produce the
needed result.

While searchers will quickly assimilate the LC-authorized U.S.
spellings of these and other well-known composers, more troubling will
be announcements of new editions of works by the likes of Ukrainian
composer "Valentin Silvestrov" ("Valentyn Vasyl'ovych Syl'vestrov"
is the authorized form), the prominent Danish composer "Per Noer-
gaard" (correctly, "Per Nørgård"), or even the Russian "Alexander Gla-
zounov" (authorized form is "Aleksandr Dmitrievich Glazunov"). This
is not a job for literalists.[6]

Titles of Works

Many musical works do not have distinctive titles—how many composers have written a Second Symphony?—or are printed and recorded with titles rendered in various languages—the ballet *Swan Lake* as *Le lac des cygnes*, *Schwanensee*, *The Enchanted Lake*, *El lago de los cisnes*, and probably many other variations on the original Russian *Lebedinoe ozero*. Music librarians have devised a system of uniform titles, created according to fixed rules as outlined in AACR2R, that enables libraries to uniquely identify and bring together under one heading in the catalog all printed and recorded editions and versions of each work by a composer, regardless of how it is presented in the edition itself. Mozart's symphony known popularly as the "Jupiter" has been published under a variety of titles: *Jupiter Symphony*, *Sinfonia in do maggiore (Jupiter) K. 551*, and *Symphonie mit Fuge Nr. 41 (Jupiter)* are a small sample. Application of the uniform title "Symphonies, K. 551, C major" brings all of these together. Likewise, "Lebedinoe ozero" for all versions of *Swan Lake* works the same magic. Searchers faced with works such as these should understand the principles of constructing uniform titles for music and how to identify the correct ones so as to retrieve the relevant records for a work in the home library, and in OCLC's WorldCat and RLG's Union Catalog.[7] A handy vade mecum that brings together the uniform titles of several major composers is the Music OCLC Users Group's publication *The Best of MOUG*, which lists authorized titles for many of the works by thirteen major composers and title cross-references for works of seventeen Slavic composers.[8]

Translations and Omissions

Some publishers and vendors think they do their customers a favor by rendering foreign-language titles into English in their advertising. This is not a tactic that will endear them to librarians, who may find themselves in bibliographic purgatory if they cannot determine what is the title proper of a given publication. Some compact disc recordings of serious music, moreover, have no proper titles at all: composers and performers are named on the disc and container, but no collective album title graces the recording. Reviewing media, consequently, tend to treat *actual* compact disc titles as unessential, and may omit them, leaving the searcher working from one of these reviews to rely upon keyword combinations of composer, performer, and label names to retrieve them online.

Multiple Editions and Formats

Printed Music

Public-domain music may be published in multiple printed editions, often in multiple formats or versions. Joseph Haydn's Symphony no. 94 in G major (the "Surprise" Symphony, H. I, 94), for example, is available for purchase at this writing in competing editions from Universal (conductor and study scores, orchestral parts), Kalmus (conductor score and parts), Warner (study score), Breitkopf & Härtel (conductor score and parts), Boosey & Hawkes (study score), Dover (study score) and Henle (conductor score); as well as in arrangements for string or school orchestra from Carl Fischer, Ludwig, and Highland; and in arrangements for chamber ensemble from Bärenreiter and Doblinger. In large-scale vocal works, the extravagance of formats can be dizzying: conductor score, study score, vocal score, orchestral parts, chorus score or chorus parts, libretto, excerpts (overture or individual arias, for example), and transcriptions are all publication formats commonly associated with opera. The selector must make clear to the searcher precisely which edition and format is wanted, whether a substitute is acceptable, or if a different edition already held by the library absolves the searcher from further action. The searcher must also be alert for the often subtle variations that may distinguish the various bibliographic descriptions of an edition when multiple formats of scores are encountered.

Recorded Music

While it is unusual for a copyrighted musical work to be printed by more than one publisher, the compulsory license provisions of the current United States Copyright Act mean that multiple *recorded* versions of nondramatic copyrighted music may be available at any one time, by different performers on various labels. The reasons for this go back to the early twentieth century, when the player-piano roll was the reigning recording medium. The Aeolian Company, a leading manufacturer of these rolls, had exclusive contracts with most of the music publishers of the day to record and distribute rolls of all of the compositions that they controlled. In writing the 1909 Copyright Act, Congress sought to prevent the creation of a monopoly in this area. Thus, the act provided that if the copyright owner permitted the use of a composition for "mechanical" reproduction (that is, the mass production for sale of piano rolls or other recording media), then anyone else could also mechanically reproduce the work, after making written notice to the copyright owner and payment of a statutory royalty fee for each copy produced. The written notice, together with the fee, constituted a "compulsory license." The copyright owner controlled the right of *first* reproduction, after which anybody else could record the copyrighted work.

The compulsory license provisions were retained when the present revision of the United States Copyright Act was enacted in 1976.[9] While composers and music publishers have argued against the continuation of compulsory licensing, representatives of the recording industry have advocated successfully for its retention. One result of decades of compulsory licensing has been hundreds of recordings of Hoagy Carmichael's "Stardust" since its composition in 1927.[10] On a different level, it means that no fewer than fourteen versions of John Cage's *Sonatas and Interludes for Prepared Piano* were released in the 1990s and additionally that, at this writing, two competing projects to record the composer's complete piano music are under way.

"New" Editions

Printed Music

A printed music edition sometimes reappears several years after initial publication with some variation in the production process, such as a modified title, a new publication date, an additional or revised publisher's number, being newly typeset rather than a reproduction of the composer's manuscript score, and so forth. These "new" editions frequently do not feature revised music, but are merely dressed-up versions of the original. If the cosmetic changes are significant enough, or if they affect a critical part of the bibliographic description, the searcher who sticks too closely to the newly scripted version could overlook its prior incarnation, perhaps already in the library's collection, or could mistakenly assume that the new version contains revised music. The following two citations illustrate this:

> Riccio, Giovanni Battista, 17th cent. *3 canzonas : for violin [trumpet], trombone, and basso continuo.* Ed by Glen Smith ; continuo realization by Leslie Bassett. London: Musica Rara, c1978. Pub. no. MR 1939. Score (14 p.) and 4 parts.

> Riccio, Giovanni Battista, 17th cent. *Tre canzone : for violin (trumpet), trombone and basso continuo.* Ed. by Glenn Smith ; continuo realization by Leslie Bassett. Wiesbaden: Breitkopf & Härtel, 2000, c1978. Pub. no. MR 1939. Score (14 p.) and 4 parts.

The latter is a reprint of the former, though the language of the title has changed, the editor's name is spelled differently, and the imprint is changed (Breitkopf & Härtel acquired Musica Rara after the original edition's publication). Without some direct statement from the publisher that the music itself is revised, one can reasonably assume that it is not. Here lies danger.

A more insidious example is the *Ten Works for Guitar and Flute or Violin* by Mauro Giuliani, published in ten volumes (collectively comprising also volume thirty-five of Giuliani's *The Complete Works in Facsimiles of the Original Editions*).[11] Each of the ten works also can be purchased separately. In 1999, the same facsimiles appeared again from the same publisher, this time in two volumes titled *Works for Violin, Flute, Violoncello, and Guitar*. Only after examination of the 1999 version did the bibliographic relationships of these publications become clear from the editor's new introduction:

> These two volumes, in their present form, are unchanged except for their binding from the old Volume 35 which I published in 1986, which consisted of the ten works in the form of sheet music in a slipcase. Now the ten works of Volume 35 are available in this volume form for those who prefer them in that form [i.e., pieces bound together in two volumes], while still also being available as separate sheet music if desired. No other changes have been made.

In other words, identical music, but different titles, and in different bindings. For added confusion, the same music has been produced by the same publisher in newly engraved (nonfacsimile) format. The librarian whose guard is down might unwittingly end up with more versions of this music than wanted: ten facsimiles collectively identified as volume 35 (as *Ten Works for Guitar and Flute or Violin*) of the collected edition, sold together in a slipcase; one or more of the ten separately available parts of volume 35, each with its own title; the same ten parts bound together as two volumes (as *Works for Violin, Flute, Violoncello, and Guitar*); and all of the same music newly engraved as part of the *New Complete Works*.

Recorded Music

The situation with recorded performances can be even more confounding: there may be multiple recorded versions of almost *any* music. The warhorses may be available concurrently in dozens of versions, and different record labels may even have released the identical performance of a work, particularly if it is a historic one; Maria Callas's "Lisbon" *Traviata*, recorded live in performance in 1958, has been released on the Angel, EMI, Historical Recordings Enterprises, Melodram, and Movimento Musica labels, and perhaps others as well.[12] Reviewers, perhaps citing information from the review copy in hand, often point out that a "new" recording is in fact a reissue, but selectors will not necessarily have come across this important piece of information. That at least one of the principal artists on the recording is long departed from the concert stage, whether dead or retired, may signal that the new issue is in fact a reissue, but even that kind of evidence is inconclusive: not every item in a record company's archive will necessarily have been released when it was originally captured. A practical, but not infallible, way to match a prior release of a particular performance with a later one is to perform a keyword search in OCLC World-Cat, the RLG Union Catalog, or even the library's own catalog, using the composer's and multiple performers' names, and checking any potential matches for information about dates of the original performance or recording sessions.

Works in Collections

An edition chosen by the music selector may also occur in anthologies whose contents are not analyzed in the library's catalog. Joseph Haydn's *Klaviersonate D-Dur = D major* (H. XVI, 37), edited by Georg Feder and separately published by Henle (1991, publisher's no. 177), is the same edition that the library might have acquired earlier when it was included in the second of the three-volume *Sämtliche Klaviersonaten* of Haydn, edited by Feder (Henle, 1972, publisher's no. 240), which is itself a reprint for practical use of the equivalent volume in the Haydn collected *Werke* (Ser. 18, vol. 2, 1970, publisher's no. 5452), which also, by the way, is published in study score format (1995, publisher's no. 9240). The identical edition of this sonata also appears in a two-volume selection from the earlier three-volume set: *Klaviersonaten: Auswahl = Piano Sonatas: Selections* (vol. 1, 1991, publisher's no. 152). Thus, Henle offers no fewer than five opportunities to acquire Feder's edition of this sonata. Of course, the music selector may *want* to acquire the same edition in multiple formats, and, in such a case, should communicate that information to acquisitions staff.

Nonstandard Publishers' Numbers

Nonstandard music publishers' numbers (see chapter 4) are not generally reliable for use in keyword searches because of their susceptibility to variation in presentation. This is particularly true of publishers' numbers for recordings. They are often truncated in reviewing sources—the removal of alphabetic or numeric prefixes is common—rendering them incompatible with the complete numbers that usually are found, and indexed, in online cataloging records. Some examples: The EMI label's publisher number for violinist Itzhak Perlman's Grammy-winning *American Album* is shown in various contexts as "55360," "5 55360," "CDC5 55360-2," and "7243 5 55360 2 0." Soprano Renée Fleming's recording *Bel Canto* (Decca) displays the publisher's number as "289 467 101-2" in the OCLC WorldCat cataloging record; when reviewed in the British journal *Gramophone*, the initial three-digit prefix was dropped. Publisher's numbers on recordings on the Naxos label begin with an "8," separated by a period from the remaining six numbers; *American Record Guide* routinely omits the "8"s. These are but a few examples of the variations that are seen in music publishers' numbers, and that can produce misleading results when used in searches.

Standard Publishers' Numbers

Standard ISBN and ISMN numbers, because they are unique, can be useful search keys in local catalogs, as well as in OCLC WorldCat and the RLG Union Catalog (omit the dashes when keying in the numbers). Searching by ISMN, however, is not foolproof: because of its relatively recent origin, its absence from an online record can mislead. A publisher may newly assign an ISMN when reprinting an edition that originally was published without one. In a case like this, searching by the ISMN would not retrieve earlier printings. Furthermore, catalogers sometimes fail to encode the ISMN in the MARC record, even when it appears on the published item. The ISBN, on the other hand, is so ubiquitous in the book world that catalogers are unlikely to overlook it, even when it is used on printed music.

"First Publication" or "First Recording"

It is prudent to be distrustful of any claim of "first." Time and again, earlier recordings and printed music editions are found on the library's shelves that refute the claims of publishers and reviewers who have not done their homework. Do not neglect to search the local catalog for works claimed not to have been published before; the library may already own the work in an acceptable edition.

Conclusion

The types of inconsistencies and variations described in the preceding paragraphs are encountered daily in the acquisition of music, and they reinforce the impression that not everything in the course of this activity is what it initially seems. Employers in library acquisitions units would be well cautioned that an important trait to look for in a searcher, in addition to sound musical knowledge, is a healthy dose of skepticism. It ultimately may be most efficient for the music selector to personally do much of the preorder searching, so that the often subtle chain of decisions that occur during the music selection process is not broken by the time an order actually is issued.

Notes

1. The glossary in this manual defines many of the English-language and foreign-language terms that are encountered in the course of searching, verifying, and acquiring musical publications. Most readers of this manual will likely agree that music collection development, reference service, and cataloging require musical knowledge acquired through years of formal study *before* entering music library work. Unfortunately, a few library administrators cling to the fiction that all librarians fall from the same library school cookie cutter, and therefore are interchangeable, as are the other staff who serve throughout the library system. But the staff member who has been successful in searching, verifying, and ordering titles for the history collection may not be qualified to perform the same tasks for the music collection. Musically literate staff are essential at all phases of the acquisitions process if it is to be efficient and cost effective.

2. All of the spelling examples in this sentence are from a single U.S. vendor catalog that came across my desk in 2002.

3. American Library Association, Filing Committee, *ALA Filing Rules* (Chicago: ALA, 1980), 10.

4. Publicly available online as Library of Congress Authorities, http://authorities.loc.gov. For a thorough examination of authorities in library catalogs, see Robert L. Maxwell, *Maxwell's Guide to Authority Work* (Chicago: ALA, 2002).

Notes (continued)

5. For Library of Congress transliteration practices, see *ALA–LC Romanization Tables: Transliteration Schemes for Non-Roman Alphabets: Approved by the Library of Congress and the American Library Association*, 1997 edition, compiled by Randall K. Barry (Washington, DC: Library of Congress Cataloging Distribution Service, 1997); available on the web at http://lcweb. loc.gov/catdir/cpso/roman.html. Library of Congress's authorization of "Tchaikovsky" actually deviates from its published transliteration practice (which would result in "Chaĭkovskiĭ"), so as to use the spelling common in the United States in accordance with AACR2R general rule 22.1A: "In general, choose, as the basis of the heading for a person, the name by which he or she is commonly known" (*Anglo-American Cataloguing Rules*, 2nd ed., 1998 revision [Ottawa: Canadian Library Association; Chicago: ALA, 1998], 381). Peter Ilich's brother and librettist, however, is authozed by LC as "Modest Ilich Chaĭkovskiĭ." There's more: another Russian musical family includes the composer "Boris Aleksandrovich Chaĭkovskiĭ" (b. 1925) and his nephew, composer "Alexandre Tchaikovski" (b. 1946).

6. The transliteration complication is not, of course, restricted to music publications. In the 1990s, a researcher asked 145 Russian-speaking undergraduate and graduate students at three universities to transliterate a series of Russian names and titles, testing their skills in retrieving materials in a romanized Online Public Access Catalog (OPAC). The test list of nineteen Russian words contained a total of 93 letters. Not one student got all correct. The average number of transliteration errors by each student was 21.6, meaning that none of these students, who supposedly knew the language, could effectively retrieve Russian-language publications in library catalogs. See Alena Aissing, "Cyrillic Transliteration and Its Users," *College & Research Libraries* 56 (1995): 207–19.

7. Several libraries have put music uniform-title primers on their websites for the benefit of library users and staff, and these can be usefully employed to instruct searchers in the basics. Two examples: Indiana University's Cook Music Library, www.music.indiana.edu/collections/uniform/uniform.html; and the University of Washington Music Library, www.lib.washington.edu/music/uniftitl.html. For a more thorough discussion of music uniform titles, see Richard P. Smiraglia, with the assistance of Taras Pavlovsky, *Describing Music Materials: A Manual for Descriptive Cataloging of Printed and Recorded Music, Music Videos, and Archival Music Collections*, 3rd ed., Soldier Creek Music Series 5 (Lake Crystal, MN: Soldier Creek Press, 1997), 171–212.

8. *The Music OCLC Users Group Presents the Best of MOUG: A List of Library of Congress Name Authority Records for Music Titles of Major Composers*, 7th ed., compiled by Judy Weidow (Austin, TX: Music OCLC Users Group, 2000).

9. Copyright Act of the United States, Title 17 of the United States Code, sect. 115, www.copyright.gov/title17/92chap1.html#115.

Notes (continued)

10. It has been claimed that this song is the most recorded in history. Some 630 versions are documented at its website: www.4stardust.com.

11. Mauro Giuliani, *Ten Works for Guitar and Flute or Violin,* ed. by Brian Jeffery (London: Tecla Editions, 1986).

12. It is worth noting that federal U.S. copyright protection was not extended to sound recordings until 1972, although pre-1972 recordings are often protected by common law and state statutes. For more information on this topic, see Robert W. Clarida, "Pre-1972 Sound Recordings" (December 2000), Legal Language Services, www.legallanguage.com/lawarticles/Clarida007. html.

7

PREORDER VERIFICATION

Bibliographic elements normally verified before placing an order include the correct names of authors, composers, and performers; the title proper; series title and volume or issue number; publisher name and date of publication; edition number if other than the first; and publisher number(s). Verification that the item is indeed in print and available for purchase, and its price, may also be a part of the procedure. Not infrequently, revelation along the way of some new piece of information—such as that the composer's name is spelled incorrectly on the request or that the item is part of a hitherto unidentified series to which the library may be subscribing—requires a da capo, sending the searcher back to the beginning.

If the on-order record is to be displayed to library users online, verification and use of authorized names and titles ensures that they will collocate correctly in the catalog. Authority control—the procedures that ensure catalog headings are consistent—is central to the maintenance of accurate and useful library catalogs. Catalog users rightfully expect that personal and corporate names, series titles, uniform titles, and subject headings, with an accompanying system of "see" and "see also" references, are used consistently within a catalog, and catalogers spend a large percentage of their time to assure that it is so.[1] With the introduction of library networks such as OCLC and RLIN (Research Libraries Information Network), it became essential for libraries to conform with national standards in order to take advantage of the savings afforded by shared cataloging.

General Resources

OCLC WorldCat and the RLG Union Catalog

The verification search itself takes place in whatever relevant databases the library can access, whether they be web, CD-ROM, print, or other formats. OCLC WorldCat and the RLG Union Catalog, each of which contains millions of bibliographic records contributed by member libraries, are the most comprehensive resources for all music formats, as they include bibliographic information for scores, audio and video recordings, books about music, manuscripts, microforms, multimedia, and so forth.[2] Thus, one or both of these bibliographic utilities will usually be the first, and in many cases the only, stop in the bibliographic verification procedure, whether for music materials or for other kinds of publications. Yet, newly printed and recorded music is generally slower to appear in OCLC and RLG than are new books. In the United States, the Cataloging-in-Publication (CIP) program at the Library of Congress means that most trade and scholarly books in this country are cataloged from publishers' proofs, usually months before any books are actually produced, and the preliminary cataloging records are added to OCLC WorldCat and the RLG Union Catalog (Library of Congress as the cataloging agency is identified by "DLC" in the OCLC MARC record, and by "DCLC" in RLG records; all name and title headings in these records will have been authorized by the Library of Congress). Music scores and audio and video recordings, however, are ineligible for CIP cataloging, and so a new publication in any of these formats will not appear in OCLC or RLG until some member–library actually acquires the item and catalogs it online.[3]

New books from Europe also have preliminary cataloging records created by several Continental library vendors, and these are also loaded into the OCLC and RLG databases, usually far in advance of any of the books actually reaching libraries in America (see chapter 5). As of this writing, vendor records for printed music and sound recordings are embargoed, though an occasional renegade infiltrates.

For a great many publications, identification of a publication's record in OCLC WorldCat or the RLG Union Catalog will complete the verification; a printout of the record, attached to the purchase request, can be forwarded for purchase-order creation. Even if a matching record is not found at this stage, it can be useful in many cases, while still online, to check the local authority file for the names and titles on the item being searched, to be printed out and forwarded with the purchase request, in case an order record must be created from scratch.[4] For verifications that need to continue further, it is useful to establish a checklist of the main sources to be queried (different publication formats often require different sources) and an agreed-upon set of symbols that the searcher can pencil onto the purchase request to show which sources have been examined, and the results.

If the cost of an item is unknown, it sometimes will be found following the encoded ISBN number (MARC field 020, subfield c). Take note, however, that any price entered there will be the retail cost of the item when *new*, which may no longer be valid if searching retrospectively.

National Library Catalogs

National libraries are responsible for collecting all of the publications issued in their respective countries. Their online catalogs, consequently, are good resources for verifying publications issued there. Although the Library of Congress is not a true national library, it is the United States' best analogue. Many national libraries have not converted their early holdings to machine-readable form, so their online catalogs are best used for verification of recent publications. Introductory web pages usually describe the chronological coverage and formats that are online. Some of these libraries maintain discrete printed music areas of the catalog or allow the searcher to filter by format. Catalogs that are in non-English-speaking lands often have user interfaces in English.

There are several websites that host links to the online catalogs of national libraries. Among ones that may be handy to bookmark are

Gabriel: The Gateway to Europe's National Libraries, Conference of European National Libraries (CENL), www.bl.uk/gabriel.

National Library Catalogues Worldwide, University of Queensland, www.library.uq.edu.au/natlibs.

Web Accessible National and Major Libraries, International Federation of Library Associations and Institutions (IFLA), www.ifla.org/II/natlibs.htm.

These sites are listed by institution name in this manual's bibliography under "Music Acquisitions Resources," along with a selection of library directories in printed format.

Union Catalogs

Several major online union catalogs that merge the holdings information of libraries in particular countries or regions can supplement the data in OCLC WorldCat and the RLG Union Catalog and may be particularly useful for verification of music editions originating in the areas served by the catalogs. Among these are

AMICUS Web, twenty-five million bibliographic records held by more than 1,300 Canadian libraries, including the National Library of Canada; advanced searches can limit to document types "sound recordings" and "video recordings," but not to scores (though printed music is included in the catalog); interface in English or French; available at www.nlc-bnc.ca/7/2/index-e.html.

CCFR, Catalogue collectif de France, union catalog of fifteen million holdings of fifty-six French municipal libraries, university libraries and research institutes (including full contents of SUDOC, below), and the Bibliothèque national de France; can filter for musical sound recordings ("documents sonores musicaux") and videos ("documents projetés ou vidéos"), but not printed music, though search results display by format, including "partitions imprimées" (printed scores); interface in French only; available at www.ccfr.bnf.fr.

COPAC, catalog of the Consortium of University Research Libraries (CURL; COPAC is the acronym for CURL Online Public Access Catalog), twenty-five university and legal deposit libraries in the United Kingdom, plus the British Library and National Library of Scotland; cannot limit search by document type; available at www.copac.ac.uk/copac; also available as CURL Union Catalog to members of RLIN.

ICCU, Istituto centrale per il catalogo unico delle biblioteche Italiane e per le informationi bibliografiche, union catalog of forty-three Italian libraries, including the two national libraries in Rome and Florence; separate database of printed and manuscript music includes documents from more than 500 public and private libraries; opening web pages in English or Italian; search templates in Italian only; available at http://opac.sbn.it.

SUDOC, Système universitaire de documentation, catalog of more than five million holdings in about 3,000 libraries at French universities and research institutes; interface in English or French; available at www.sudoc.abes.fr.

National Bibliographies

National bibliographies are periodic listings of publications issued within the boundaries of a single nation. Some also list publications *about* the nation, or material written by citizens of that nation wherever published, and publications issued anywhere in the national language. National libraries, which acquire publications through obligatory legal copyright deposit, are the sources for the data in national bibliographies. These bibliographies, in their printed or online versions, are more useful for *selecting* new music publications (even though the entries in them are not always the most current) than for preorder verification, because they typically lack cumulative indexing. Nevertheless, they are described here because of their relationships to their national libraries and for the sake of inclusiveness.

In this manual's bibliography are listed national bibliographies from countries that produce discrete bibliographic music components, either as separately published music supplements or music sections within a general classification scheme, such as the 780s in the Dewey Decimal System. Some countries have recently discontinued the paper versions of their bibliographies in favor of CD-ROM or web publication, notably Belgium and France, which now put this information on the web. The United States produces no national bibliography at all.

Verifying Scores

Publishers' Catalogs

Current publishers' catalogs of printed music vary widely in the quantity and quality of information that they contain. They generally are reliable for indications of availability, the publisher's numbers, and sometimes prices, but they typically omit many of the details that librarians rely upon for ordering: exact bibliographic titles, editors' names, the dates of publication (though dates of composition often are stated), or even composers' given names.

Catalogs on the Web

Astute music publishers mount their catalogs on the web, and more of them are doing so as time passes. Some of these can be searched by a variety of entry points, such as composer name, publisher's number, or instrumentation. Others are mere PDF or HTML reproductions of printed catalogs. Because of the *potential* for frequent updating, they are usually to be preferred over printed catalogs, if, in fact, the publisher in question still even produces one. Not all publishers, however, seem to be conscientious about regularly updating their online catalogs.

Several professional, academic, and commercial websites provide links to music publishers. It may be convenient for acquisitions units to bookmark some of these gateway sites, including the ones listed here.

AcqWeb, "Music Publishers and Vendors," http://acqweb.library. vanderbilt.edu/acqweb/pubr/music.html.

Cook Music Library, Indiana University, "Music Publishers," www.music.indiana.edu/music_resources/publ.html.

Deutscher Musikverleger-Verband = German Music Publishers Association, "Music Publishers," www.dmv-online.com/projects/ DMV-ONLINE/html/ENGLISH/publishers/index.html.

Music Publishers' Association [of the United Kingdom], "MPA Members" and "Printed Music Distributors List," www.mpaonline. org.uk.

Music Publishers' Association of the United States, "Directory of Music Publishers," www.mpa.org.

Musica Virtual Choral Library, "Search in Musica Database: Search for Publishers," www.musicanet.org.

MusicalAmerica.com, "Industry Links," available to paid subscribers at www.musicalamerica.com.

Northern Lights Internet Solutions, "Publishers' Catalogs: Sheet Music," www.lights.com/publisher/db/formats-Sheet-Music.html.

If looking for a particular publisher's site, simply entering its name into an Internet search engine often produces the desired result. Similarly, if searching for an edition by a contemporary composer whose publisher is unknown, entering the composer's name into a search engine often will have one, or both, of two results: a hit on the composer's home page, where information about where and how to acquire editions may be found; or a hit on the composer's *publisher's* site, where biographies and works lists of its stable of composers are featured.

Printed Catalogs

Libraries that want to maintain a file of current printed catalogs of music publishers' editions should get into the habit of consulting each new "Music Publishers' Catalogs" column that appears in the quarterly issues of MLA's *Notes*. Listed there are new catalogs received by the column editor since the journal's previous issue, with postal addresses of the publishers who have submitted them and web addresses for those whose Internet sites include their catalogs. The scope note that accompanies the column in each September issue of the journal states that "also included are stock order blanks, agents' catalogs, catalogs of books on music, catalogs of single series, substantial publishers' catalogs of single composers, and rental catalogs. Excluded are catalogs that are exclusively retail. The list also includes catalogs published by national music centers and by licensing agencies."[5] These printed catalogs can range from a one-page listing of new issues to an extract of the publications for a particular instrument, to a new *Gesamtkatalog* that purports to list every available edition from a publisher. Catalogs may be sent to the library unsolicited. Otherwise, new catalogs wanted for the library's file can be requested by mail, or, in many cases, electronically at publishers' websites, which often feature a "request our catalog" or "contact us" e-mail link. Some publishers issue complete printed catalogs annually; others issue revised catalogs infrequently or not at all.

Printed publishers' catalogs are an endangered species, due to the oft-superior convenience of web catalogs, which are easily revised and are, therefore, ephemeral. This is unfortunate, as printed and manuscript publishers' catalogs have played important roles in reconstructing the histories of individual music publishers and of music publishing in general. This type of documentation of music publishers' activities and products is at risk of disappearing.

Each music selector or acquisitions unit must decide what resources it wants to expend acquiring and maintaining printed publishers' catalogs. Good management of them, however, requires that they be *dated*; if a date is not printed on a new catalog, the date it is received by the library should be stamped or written prominently on it. Unlike the contents of a medicine cabinet, publishers' catalogs do not carry expiration dates, so the user needs some clue as to the currency of its content. Years can elapse before a catalog is revised, and one that has been in the library's files for a decade or longer is unlikely to contain much data of use for acquisitions purposes.

Vendor Databases

If a work's publisher is unknown or if the publisher's catalog is inadequate for the task at hand, music retailer and vendor databases are useful verification sources. The best ones include full bibliographic citations, sometimes supplemented by descriptive notes about levels of difficulty, commissions, prizes won, and so forth. The American vendors named here handle music of all publishers; the European vendors handle music only from particular geographical areas (see chapter 5 for more information about these vendors).

U.S. Vendor Databases

> **Byron Hoyt Music**, www.byronhoyt.com, searchable database listing printed music of all publishers; full bibliographic descriptions, many annotated, with prices and images of covers.

> **Educational Music Services**, Music-in-Print CD-ROM database listing printed music of all publishers; revised continually by EMS, which developed it for internal purposes; annual versions can be licensed for use by EMS's customers; abbreviated entries, with prices.

> **J. W. Pepper & Son**, www.jwpepper.com, searchable database listing printed music of all publishers; abbreviated bibliographic descriptions, with prices; some annotations.

> **Theodore Front Musical Literature**, www.tfront.com, searchable database of printed music and books on music published worldwide since 1994; full bibliographic descriptions with prices; some annotations.

Non-U.S. Vendor Databases

All of the European vendors listed below offer full service for firm and standing orders, journal subscriptions, approval plans, and personalized announcement services for new publications. Online interfaces are in English. Their databases contain complete bibliographic descriptions of books and printed score editions, with prices given in euros (U.S. customers are billed in dollars). Full database access to each vendor requires registration, which is free. All four of these vendors contribute bibliographic records for new book publications to OCLC WorldCat and the RLG Union Catalog (as of this writing, OCLC and RLG continue to prohibit vendor records for printed music).[6] Libraries registered with these vendors can establish FTP (file transfer protocol) accounts with them in order to download MARC records for books and scores into local systems for use as acquisitions records. This is particularly convenient for new European score editions, which typically are added to vendor databases long before they find their way into American libraries, and make their appearance in OCLC WorldCat and the RLG Union Catalog.

Casalini Libri, www.casalini.it, searchable database listing printed music and books on music published in Italy, Vatican City, the Republic of San Marino, the Italian-speaking cantons of Switzerland, and Malta; full bibliographic descriptions.

Harrassowitz Music Services, www.harrassowitz.de/mus_services. html, searchable database listing printed music and books on music from all European countries, Japan, Australia, New Zealand, Israel, and selected publishers in other countries (generally excluding North America); full bibliographic descriptions.

Iberbook International, www.iberbook.com, searchable database listing printed music and media published since 1995 in Spain and books on music from Spain, Portugal, and selected Latin American countries; full bibliographic descriptions. Iberbook was acquired by Puvill Libros in early 2004.

Puvill Libros, www.puvill.com, searchable database of printed music and books on music published in Spain, Portugal, and Mexico; full bibliographic descriptions.

Other Databases

Andante.com, "Music In Print," www.andante.com, the vocal, guitar, woodwind, and orchestral databases licensed from Musicdata prior to their sale to emusicquest (see that entry, which is unrelated to this one); by paid subscription.

emusicquest: The Music-in-Print Series, www.emusicquest.com, individual searchable databases of, in 2003, sacred choral, classical vocal, orchestral, classical guitar, woodwind, piano, string, and "miscellaneous" music in print;[7] several individual databases are also available on CD-ROM; data compiled from catalogs solicited from publishers worldwide (671,829 entries as of May 2003); several of the original Musicdata printed volumes, which are the basis of the online versions, are available in paperback reprints from emusicquest (see the bibliography of this manual for a listing of original volumes, and the emusicquest website for availability of reprints).

Specialty Online Resources

Some online retailers specialize in music for a particular instrument or musical genre. The depth of coverage and the quality of the information provided at these sites varies markedly from one to another, and some of them undoubtedly have their champions both inside and outside the library world. It is not possible to include a comprehensive directory of specialty retailers in this manual; readers who want to investigate other retailers can find links to dozens of them worldwide at the website of the Hal Leonard Corporation (www.halleonard.com; select the "how to order" link).

Despite this disclaimer, the following specialty retailers are ones that I have found to be occasionally useful for verification purposes, though they do not fit neatly into categories already discussed:

ejazzlines.com, www.ejazzlines.com, full line of jazz printed music, CDs, videos, books; credit cards and institutional purchase orders accepted.

Guitar Gallery, www.guitargallerymusic.com, searchable database of guitar music and instructional videos of all publishers; abbreviated entries; credit cards and institutional purchase orders accepted.

Musica Bona, www.musicabona.com, Czech classical music of all publishers (scores, CDs, books); full bibliographic descriptions with prices in U.S. dollars and euros; credit card or prepay by check with mailed order form; several discount plans available.

Musica Virtual Choral Library, www.musicanet.org, reference database of the International Federation for Choral Music; free on the web or by purchase on CD-ROM; interfaces in English, French, German, and Spanish; as of November 2003, contained 135,000 references for musical works and editions, with directories of composers, authors of texts, and publishers (also listed earlier in this chapter with the directories of publishers).

Robert King Music Sales, www.rkingmusic.com, brass music of all publishers; abbreviated entries; credit cards and institutional purchase orders accepted; Robert King is a subsidiary of the French music publisher Alphonse Leduc.

Shar Music, www.sharmusic.com, string music of all publishers; abbreviated entries; credit cards and institutional purchase orders accepted.

Prices of Printed Music

If the price of a printed music edition is unknown, it is often a good idea to spend time confirming it in one of the resources described herein, rather than to submit an order with an estimated price. A few music publishers seem to follow no rational formula when setting prices for new editions, particularly of contemporary composers published in Europe. When purchasing trade and scholarly books, one usually can make some general assumptions about their likely price ranges based on the number of pages or volumes, bindings, number of color plates, and their places of publication.[8] Suppositions about printed scores, however, can be astonishingly off the mark. Consider the 2003 publication of a sixty-four-page score of a work by Italian composer Luigi Nono (1924–1990) for voices, orchestra, and electronics, which was listed that year for sale at the Harrassowitz website for a hair-raising €1,560 (about $1,765 in mid-2003).[9]

A fail-safe step that the library can take to reduce the likelihood of receiving a budget-busting edition is to notify regularly used vendors of acceptable pricing guidelines, stating dollar ceilings or percentages above estimated costs that should trigger a price quotation to the library and a request for confirmation. Vendors may be able to code the instructions into the library's customer record in their automated accounting and invoicing systems. Or, in some automated library systems, it may be possible to have pricing guidelines be printed directly on the purchase orders.

Verifying Audio and Video

For half a century, the librarian's primary guide to available audio recordings was the *Long Playing Record Guide*, published monthly beginning in 1949 by William Schwann, a Boston record shop owner. Schwann's aim was to list all recordings generally available in the United States. The form of entries remained essentially unchanged throughout the journal's history, with works listed alphabetically by composer, subarranged by title, then by principal artist—a separate entry for each work on each recording—with anthologies listed in a separate section by instrument or musical genre. Although the publication changed title, frequency, and format numerous times over the ensuing decades, and despite fluctuations in the thoroughness and quality of its content, *Schwann* was rarely far from the reach of any librarian responsible for acquiring recordings.[10]

Today, the print version of *Schwann* is gone, done in, in part, by the web.[11] British and German equivalents thrive, however, as *R.E.D. Classical Catalogue, Bielefelder Katalog Klassik*, and *Bielefelder Katalog Jazz*.[12] These catalogs provide excellent indexing and analytics of recordings issued in the United Kingdom and Germany, for those who wish to work with printed verification tools.

Another printed guide to current sound recordings is *Phonolog*, which in 1948 began providing indexing of available recordings—primarily *popular* music recordings—by way of a loose-leaf updating service.[13] In 2000, *Phonolog* was taken over by Muze, Inc., which continues the publication as a multivolume annual, now covering all genres of music from pop to jazz to classical. A companion annual, *Videolog*, provides similar information for video products. The loose-leaf updates to *Phonolog* are now history, though there are midyear supplements for both of the annual publications. That *Phonolog* and *Videolog* now appear only in annual print editions is indicative of their publisher's primary focus on Internet-linked in-store music information centers.[14] From its beginnings, *Phonolog* was marketed as a tool for record retailers, not librarians, and it rarely was seen in any but the largest urban libraries, undoubtedly in part because of its high subscription cost.

Web Retailers

Since 1994, when CD Now was the only well-established web retailer of sound recordings, the recorded music business has exploded in cyberspace. A number of web vendors now specialize in compact discs and video recordings or include these media alongside books and other merchandise in their inventories, and their online databases are substantial. The following selective list of retailers of new and used recorded music includes but a few of those selling audio and video recordings, in all musical genres and available recording formats.[15] Some of them—Amazon, Borders, Music Library Service Company—are notable for offering institutional accounts and discounts to libraries that do not have access to, or prefer not to use, credit cards. All of the following include a broad selection of video as well as audio recordings.

Amazon, www.amazon.com; select the "international" link to visit Amazon's sites in Europe, Japan, Canada, and Australia, where many CDs not listed on the U.S. site will be found (note: most DVDs and videocassettes sold at the European and Australian sites will be incompatible with North American playback equipment, as described in the "International Video Standards" section in chapter 3).

Barnes & Noble, www.barnesandnoble.com; data taken from All Music Guide (www.allmusic.com) and All Movie Guide (www.allmovie.com); verification searches and purchases can be made at all three of these web locations.

Borders Books and Music, www.borders.com; "teamed" with Amazon (shared shipping, billing, and customer service); institutional accounts can be used in Borders stores (with 20 percent discount off list prices for libraries), but not for online shopping.

CD Now, www.cdnow.com; "teamed" with Amazon (shared shipping, billing, and customer service).

Music Library Service Company, www.mlscmusic.com; searchable database access requires registration; institutional purchase orders accepted (see "U.S. In-Print Recorded Music Vendors" in chapter 5 for fuller entry for this vendor).

Tower Records, www.towerrecords.com; select the "TowerRecords.co.uk" link to visit the United Kingdom site, where many CDs not listed on the U.S. site will be found (note: most DVDs and videocassettes sold at the U.K. site will be incompatible with North American playback equipment, as described in the "International Video Standards" section in chapter 3).

Whether a library chooses to purchase from Internet retailers or not, their large databases are useful for determining the status of a particular recording, or whether a particular musical work is available on any recording at all (some merchants retain deleted recordings in their listings, identifying them as "out of print"). An "advanced" or "classical" search function often is available for those whose requirements are more specific than, say, what recordings by Bob Dylan are available. The details given about each recording vary from site to site, but usually one can find full track listings (complete table of contents), sample audio files, date of the original release, label name and publisher's number, performers' names, and an image of the cover (sometimes useful in enlarged view for verifying an album's exact title or other information that may be abbreviated in, or absent from, a review or other source). Even if not ordering from the retailer whose site lists a wanted recording, acquisitions staff can take the retailer's information and send it to a mail-order dealer. Though none of these vendors can be expected to list all available releases of all labels, a quick search of three or four of their databases can produce a plausible supposition about whether a particular work or recording is available for purchase through normal U.S. outlets. It also can provide easy price comparisons if online ordering is an option.[16]

Record Label Websites

If the label name of a recording is known, the company's website can be the most direct way to verify its availability and the retail list price. Many labels maintain online catalogs of their issues, and direct online sales sometimes are offered, most commonly by the independent labels.[17] There are several comprehensive online directories of label sites, with links to the individual sites (for print directories of record labels, see chapter 3).

Allrecordlabels.com, http://allrecordlabels.com; more than 5,000 links; online form permits labels to submit new entries; includes links also to online music stores and other music sites; browse by musical genre, geographical location, format, and recent additions.

MusicalAmerica.com, www.musicalamerica.com; corresponds to the annual print *Musical America International Directory*; search by label name or location in the categories "Record Companies" (United States and its territories and Canada) or "International Record Companies" (rest of the world); available by paid subscription.

Record Labels on the Web, www.rlabels.com; more than 5,000 links; search by label name or musical genre; online form permits labels to submit new entries.

Some online label directories focus on a particular type of music: classical, jazz, folk, etc.

ClassicalNet, "Recording Labels and Distributors," www.classical.net/music/links/commercial/musiclabel.html, 200 links to classical music CD labels.

Dirty Linen Folk & World Music, "Record Company Addresses," www.dirtylinen.com/linen/109, more than 1,000 addresses and links to international folk and world music recording labels.

International Record Review, "Directory of Record Company Website Addresses," www.recordreview.co.uk, 450 links to classical record labels.

Jazzitude, "Jazz Record Labels," www.jazzitude.com/labels.htm, 60 links to jazz labels.

World Music Central, "Record Labels," www.worldmusiccentral. org, 165 addresses and links to international world and traditional folk music recording companies, by country.

Other Web Resources

Andante.com, "Recordings in Print," www.andante.com; by paid subscription; simultaneous searches of Amazon.com, Barnes & Noble, Tower Records.

Gramofile, at the website of the British monthly *Gramophone*, www.gramophone.co.uk, where is found access to full texts of "over 30,000 reviews in the world's largest single classical archive. More than 100 new critiques are added to Gramofile each month"; access is free with online registration.

Pricing of Compact Discs

Journals that review compact discs rarely quote prices for the recordings described in their pages.[18] The labels' recommended "list" prices can usually be found at their websites, but many retailers and library vendors sell recordings at discounted prices. Unlike retail prices for printed music, those for recorded music historically have had remarkably uniform pricing structures. No label would remain long in business if it priced recordings tens of dollars more than another label offering similar artists and repertoire.[19] The library, therefore, may choose to omit the step of verifying actual prices when ordering recordings, and simply estimate them. One tactic is to average the costs on the invoices of the library's principal audio vendor over a period of time, and to use that figure to encumber each new title ordered.

A few compact disc reviewing sources indicate an *approximate* price for each recording by using a coding system. What these categories actually mean in cash money can vary from one reviewing source to another, and from one country to another (retail prices of compact discs in the United Kingdom, for example, are generally higher than in the United States). These cost estimates, therefore, should be used only as general guidelines. In the United States, the following price ranges were approximations as of 2003 of what the list prices of these categories represented:

super budget	less than $4.99
budget	$4.99–$8.99
midprice	$9–$12.99
full	more than $12.99

With experience, one soon learns that releases on, for example, the Naxos Classical Label, to name a well-known budget label, typically list (as of 2003) for around $6.98, whereas Hyperion releases list for around $19.98.

DVD and VHS

Vendors of compact discs can, as a rule, also supply video recordings. Several online retailers, however, have video-only databases that are useful for verifying availability. As a rule, only principal performers and directors are identified; distributors' names and their catalog numbers usually are omitted. Opera and concert productions are listed together with theatrical releases. These vendors accept online orders with credit cards and institutional purchase orders by mail and fax.

DVD Planet, 16672 Beach Blvd., Suite L, Huntington Beach, CA 92647. Tel: 800 624 3078; fax: 714 892 8369; web: www.dvdplanet. com; e-mail: orders@dvdplanet.com. Videos on all topics.

Facets Multi-Media, 1517 West Fullerton Ave., Chicago, IL 60614. Tel: 800 331 6197; fax: 773 929 5437; web: www.facets.org; e-mail: sales@facets.org. Videos on all topics; database retains listings for out-of-print titles.

Note should be made of three production and distribution companies that specialize in, or feature, classical music in their videos:

Films for the Humanities & Sciences, PO Box 2053, Princeton, NJ 08543. Tel: 800 257 5126; fax: 609 275 3767; web: www.films.com; e-mail: custserv@films.com. Documentaries and educational videos, biographies, concerts; purchase price includes public performance rights.

Kultur International Films, 195 Highway 95, West Long Branch, NJ 07764. Tel: 800 573 3782; web: www.kulturvideo.com; e-mail: info@kultur.com. Opera, ballet, concert performances, and profiles.

Video Artists International & VAI Audio, 109 Wheeler Ave., Pleasantville, NY 10570. Tel: 800 477 7146; fax: 914 769 5407; web: www.vai-music.com; e-mail: inquiries@vaimusic.com. Classical and jazz DVD, VHS, and CDs.

Musical video recordings intended for home viewing typically range in price between $19.95 and $29.95, similar to videos of feature films. Notable exceptions are documentaries and instructional videos that bundle public-performance rights into the purchase price (see the section on "Video Performanc Rights" in chapter 3 for more about this topic), and these can cost several times the typical home-use video.

Notes

1. It has been estimated that authority work comprises about half of all cataloging costs. See Barbara B. Tillett, "Authority Control: An Overview," in *Authority Control in Music Libraries*, ed. by Ruth Tucker, MLA Technical Reports 16 (Canton, MA: MLA, 1989), 4.

2. A 2003 snapshot of music titles in the RLG Union Catalog is available on CD-ROM, as *International Bibliography of Printed Music, Music Manuscripts, and Recordings*, 2nd ed., 2 discs (Munich: K. G. Saur, 2003); it includes bibliographic records for about 870,000 printed music editions, 37,000 music manuscripts, and 782,000 sound recordings.

3. For more about the purpose and scope of CIP, see http://cip.loc.gov/cip.

4. Library of Congress Authorities also can be searched on the web at http://authorities.loc.gov.

5. *Notes* 58 (2001): 155.

6. The Paris-based firm of Jean Touzot Librairie Internationale (http://search.touzot.fr) contributes records for French books to OCLC and RLG, and its online database is freely available for verification of in-print titles (no registration required for search-only access). Touzot does not, however, catalog or sell printed or recorded music.

7. Reviewed by Alec McLane in *Notes* 60 (2003): 506–8. The content of the original string volume publication edited by Margaret K. Farrish is omitted due to copyright restrictions: *String Music in Print*, 2nd ed. (New York: R. R. Bowker, 1973).

8. See the annual price indexes of music publications found in each December issue of *Notes*, where average costs of literature submitted to the journal for review, and listed in the quarterly "Books Recently Published" column, are divided according to their languages of publication: arithmetic-mean prices for 2002 (published in the December 2003 issue) ranged between $35.32 (for books in English) and $23.67 (for Spanish-language texts). Also listed, by various musical-subject categories, are price indexes of printed music from the "Music Received" column. While it might be tempting to use the mean prices from the *Notes* price indexes when estimating prices on purchase orders, the compiler, Brad Short, warns in the 2003 issue that "it is suggested that these figures be used with some care. Some categories have so few items that the arithmetic mean prices should be considered tenuous at best. They represent the best guess of what prices were for a given year. These calculations are intended to be used for library collection-planning purposes only."

9. *1° Caminantes . . . Ayacucho: 1987*, text by Giordano Bruno (Milan: Ricordi, 2003, c1987), listed at www.harrassowitz.de. That's $27.58 per page!

Notes (continued)

10. See, for example, complaints by Gary A. Galo, "The State of *Schwann*," *ARSC Journal* 27 (1996): 259–62.

11. The terminal version of *Schwann* in printed form was as a multipart publication from Stereophile of Santa Fe, New Mexico: *Schwann Opus* (1991–2001, quarterly), listing classical recordings by composer; *Schwann Spectrum* (1991–2001, quarterly), listing jazz and popular recordings by performing group; and *Schwann Artist* (1996–1999, annual), listing classical recordings by performers' names. After the demise of the print catalogs, a web version continued as *Schwann Online*, which conflated in a single subscription database more than 3.5 million recordings of every musical genre, including "current" as well as archived records. In mid-2003, the database continued to be available to subscribers, but my sampling of its content revealed that no new records appeared to have been added since 2001; I found no 2002–2003 releases *at all* by several independent U.S. labels.

12. *R.E.D. Classical Catalogue* (London: Retail Entertainment Data, 1996– , annual); updated by monthly cumulative supplements; also available online by subscription: see www.redpublishing.co.uk for information; *R.E.D.* is better known to many readers by an earlier title, *Gramophone Classical Catalogue* (founded 1953), and variants thereof. *Bielefelder Katalog Klassik* and *Bielefelder Katalog Jazz* (Bielefeld: Bielefelder Verlagsanstalt, 1953– ; semi-annual, updated by CD-ROM three months after each issue); titles and imprints vary. A French equivalent, the annual *Diapason: Catalogue général* (Paris: Diapason-microsillon, 1956–1997), ceased publication in 1997, to be reborn a few years later as *Diapason: Catalogue classique* (Suresnes: Emap France, 2003–).

13. *Phonolog Reporter* (Los Angeles: Trade Service Publications, 1948–2000); frequency of the loose-leaf updates fluctuated between biweekly and three per week.

14. More about *Videolog* and the current incarnation of *Phonolog* is found at the publisher's website: www.muze.com.

15. I have used these online merchants for library purchases with satisfaction; readers may have had equally satisfactory experiences with other online recorded music retailers. Links to these and some seventy additional classical Internet sites that have databases of recordings for sale on the web or by mail order are found at the ClassicalNet website: http://classical.net/music/links/commercial/musicretail.html, with the advice that "buyers should exercise caution and make sure that services, products, prices, and return policies are clearly understood before purchases are made."

16. A shopper's primer for a few sites is Steven Ritter's "Buying Discs on the Internet," *American Record Guide* 64 (January–February 2000): 58–62.

17. As noted elsewhere in this manual, due to selective distribution strategies, not all recordings listed in the complete catalogs of multinational recording companies will be available in all territories.

Notes (continued)

18. An exception is *BBC Music Magazine* (London: BBC Magazines, 1992– ; www.bbcmagazines.com/music), the monthly music news and reviewing journal from Britain whose covers bill it as "the world's best-selling classical music magazine." This journal offers an ordering service for any item reviewed in its pages (a mail-order form is included in each issue), and the BBC Music Magazine Direct price is quoted, in pounds sterling, for each title reviewed.

19. A notable exception is Stockhausen-Verlag in Kürten, Germany, which produces printed scores and compact discs of the works of German composer Karlheinz Stockhausen (b. 1928). In mid-2003, CDs of Stockhausen's music from this publisher were retailing for around $35–$50 per disc.

THE ORDERING PROCESS

Regardless of the type of materials that are being acquired, the goals of the ordering process are essentially the same: to obtain materials as quickly and as inexpensively as possible; to use efficient procedures to keep operational costs low; to work with a high level of precision; to monitor and accurately control and report fund encumbrances and expenditures; to pay vendors in a timely fashion and to maintain cordial and professional relations with them; to monitor and evaluate vendor performance on an ongoing basis; and to report promptly the availability or nonavailability of materials that have been requested by selectors and library users.

The basic ordering procedures are common to all types of library materials and are discussed in detail in the general acquisitions guides cited in the bibliography herein.[1] The present manual will not rehearse in detail the general procedures that are covered thoroughly in those books, but will focus on techniques pertinent and useful for music orders.

Collating Order Requests

Publication Format

A common first step in the ordering process is to sort purchase requests into groups according to predicted order-preparation procedures. Major categories into which requests naturally fall for a music collection are the different formats of publication. Printed music and recordings, for example, are usually acquired from different vendors than are used for books. Books, printed music, and recordings, therefore, might logically proceed through the order pipeline in discrete groups. Subdivision within a format may also be required by the library's materials-budget funding hierarchy: some libraries use separate funds for acquisition of composers' collected editions and monumental sets, for large-ensemble performance materials (orchestral, band, and choral parts), for reference books, and so forth. Further subdivision by country of publication may also be appropriate if the library makes significant use of music vendors abroad. The fewer variables that a library requires vendors to use—a single account number and a single shipping and billing address, for example, would be ideal—the fewer delivery and invoice errors are likely to occur.

Order Types

There are three basic types of orders—firm orders, standing orders, and subscriptions (approval plans will be considered separately)—and each is handled differently in the library at every step, from preorder searching, through cataloging and shelf preparation. Terms used to categorize these orders can vary from one library to another, but they fall into these groups essentially because of the way the bills are paid.

> **Firm orders**, sometimes known as "monographic" orders, are used for publications for which the library expects to pay only once, though they may be multivolume, multipart, or multiformat editions. Firm orders would be used for a three-volume printed edition of Beethoven's Piano Trios that includes a score and separate string parts in each volume; for a DVD recording of Mozart's opera *Don Giovanni*; and for *The New Grove Dictionary of Music and Musicians*, 2nd edition, of which all twenty-nine volumes were published simultaneously. The majority of orders for a music collection will be firm orders. The serials monster that has ravaged science and social sciences acquisitions budgets in recent years has not had quite as grim an effect on the humanities; there are few costly electronic resources devoted to music, and musical journals are comparatively inexpensive.

> **Standing orders**, sometimes known as "continuation" or "recurring" orders, are used for publications that appear in successive volumes or parts and for which the library expects to pay for each volume as it is received, until the standing order is cancelled or the publication ceases. Standing orders would be used to acquire all the volumes in a publisher's series, such as Recent Researches in the Music of the Baroque Era from A-R Editions, and for the volumes appearing in a composer's complete edition, such as the *Sämtliche Werke* of Richard Wagner, published by Schott Musik International. Vendors and publishers often solicit "subscriptions" to such editions, though libraries usually reserve the term for another type of order (see below). Standing orders are characterized by their unpredictability: new volumes

arrive unexpectedly (years can elapse between volumes, so that disabling automated claiming procedures can be a good idea), and prices can vary considerably from one volume to the next. For these reasons, some libraries do not encumber funds for at least some standing orders, choosing instead to absorb an unanticipated financial hit when each new and expensive volume arrives. Standing orders are essential for acquiring long-term, prestige publishing projects, like composers' complete editions, as there are often significant price breaks for libraries that have standing orders for them (as well as penalties for those that cancel prematurely). Volumes in these series are often published out of numerical order, and the numbering schemes can be baroque. Consider the publication hierarchy in figure 8.1 of Wolfgang Amadeus Mozart's *Neue Ausgabe sämtlicher Werke* (New Edition of the Complete Works):

> **Serie** VIII: Kammermusik = Series VIII: Chamber Music.
> > **Werkgruppe** 20: Streichquartette und Quartette mit einem Blasinstrument = Works Category 20: String Quartets and Quartets with a Wind Instrument.
> > > **Abteilung** 1: Streichquartette = Section 1: String Quartets.
> > > > **Band** 2: Streichquartette, Bd. 2 = Volume 2 of String Quartets.

(This arrangement is not strictly hierarchical: *Werkgruppen* are numbered continuously through all of the primary category, the *Serien*.)[2]

Figure 8.1. Hierarchy in the Mozart *Neue Ausgabe sämtlicher Werke*

Standing orders can also be established for some ongoing recording projects, such as the Romantic Piano Concerto series on the Hyperion label. Some recording projects can be difficult to track, however, as they are prone to title changes as new discs come out: the title proper on one disc can become a series title on the next, and a reviewer may describe a new release as part of an ongoing recording project, though there is no discographic evidence on the item itself to identify it as such. New releases suspected to be part of ongoing recording projects may need the attention of the most experienced searchers to determine whether a standing order is already established.

Subscriptions are placed for editions that are paid regularly and on a predictable schedule, typically once per year. These include periodicals, annuals, and online databases. Periodical publications consisting solely of printed music first appeared in England and France as early as the 1690s, and flourished through the nineteenth century.[3] In the twentieth century, this tradition continued in modified style with such journals as *Sing Out* (1950–), featuring melodies and lyrics of folk songs along with articles about them, and the California-based *Source* (1967–1973), containing printed scores and recordings by avant-garde composers of the midcentury.[4] Today, the practice survives principally in the musical supplements that accompany some music journals, either bound in, or as separates: examples include *Saxophone Journal*, of which most bimonthly issues are accompanied by a compact disc with accompaniments for play-along, or a masterclass, to be used with printed music and instructional text in the journal; and the British monthly *Gramophone*, which comes with a compact disc recording of a work featured in the issue.

Vendor Assignment

Once the requests have been searched, verified, and sorted, library staff must next decide who will get the order. This discussion has already taken place at some length in chapter 5, but a brief review is appropriate here concerning some of the factors that should influence the decision, along with more detailed explication of some issues specific to music orders. If choosing from among the library's regular vendors, the most important criterion, of course, is which one has given the library the best service at the best price in the past.

What is the format? Logically, orders for compact discs should not be sent to vendors who deal only in print material, and vice versa; the vendor of choice should be one who specializes in the type of material being ordered.

What is the urgency of the need? If a compact disc is required immediately for course reserves, a visit to a local record retailer might produce same-day results. If local stores do not have the exact disc wanted or an acceptable substitute, many web retailers have extensive inventories and indicate online the number of copies of a disc currently in stock and the estimated shipping date.

Where is the item published? A printed music edition is often most economically acquired from a vendor in its country of publication, though there are no hard and fast rules here. Vendors and retailers in the United States *do* routinely handle printed editions from other countries, and costs and delivery times can be competitive; they can also be dramatically higher. Comparing prices in publishers' and vendors' online databases can be informative at this stage.[5]

In the case of sound and video recordings, international distribution practices result in not every recording being readily available in every country, so that an opera or song recital released on compact disc in, say, Germany may not be distributed by the publisher in the United States.[6] Ordering from a vendor or online retailer in Germany may be the surest way to acquire the desired recording if it cannot be obtained readily from U.S. vendors and retailers. DVDs and VHS cassettes also have asynchronous distribution patterns, but there are risks, if ordering these formats from abroad, that they will be incompatible with U.S. video standards and playback equipment. For libraries in North America, VHS cassettes should be in NTSC format. Most players in this area of the world will not play PAL or SECAM formats; DVDs should be coded for region 1 or 0.[7]

Purchase-Order Preparation

The form and type of purchase order that is produced will depend upon the size and sophistication of the library's acquisitions operation: it may be a single printed card, slip, or sheet of paper for each item; it may be a multititle order form; it may be an e-mail message or attachment sent to the vendor; or it may be part of an automated process that is submitted electronically through the vendor's website. Whatever form it takes, the purchase order should include (1) a unique library-assigned purchase-order number that allows the vendor to track what has been shipped and the amount owed for each shipment, and enables the library to match the shipment with in-house order records when it is received; (2) the library's full address, with separate "ship to" and "bill to" addresses if appropriate, including e-mail and telephone numbers (both voice and fax) if questions about the order arise; (3) the library's customer number if the vendor has assigned one; (4) complete bibliographic information about each title ordered, including full title and subtitle, editor's name if applicable, publisher's name and catalog number(s), full series title and volume number if applicable, principal performer(s) on recordings, the advertised or estimated price, and format and number of copies wanted; and (5) any specific terms related to the order, such as "send score only," or "rush for delivery by October 31st if possible."

When orders are for works not advertised by or listed in the catalog of the vendor to whom the order is sent, it is useful to cite the library's source of information. This is particularly true if the order is prompted by a new publisher's direct mail solicitation, or by a review in a journal that names the composer as the source of the edition. The vendor may not have received that mailing or seen the review, so passing along the publisher's web or postal address or e-mail, or all of these, will enable the vendor to contact the publisher if it is previously unknown to the vendor.

Editions

Often, multiple printed editions of public-domain works in the standard repertoire are available from several publishers. The publishers Henle, Peters, and Wiener Urtext, for example, have competing editions of much of the oft-performed piano repertoire. Multiple performances and recordings of copyrighted as well as public-domain music may be available from several different labels. When a specific musical edition is required, and only that edition is acceptable, the information given to the vendor should be the most complete and accurate possible, as described in the following paragraphs. Sometimes, though, the library will accept *any* edition, if, for example, an older edition has gone out of print or the need for speed makes the library less discriminating than usual. A note to the vendor that a "substitution is acceptable," or "any CD of this work acceptable for earliest delivery" will give the vendor leeway to fill the order without undue back-and-forth.

Formats

Excepting the hardback–paperback dichotomy, the concept of format may be unique to music. A work may be published in miniature score, full (conductor's) score, condensed score, vocal score, libretto, and set of parts, to name a few possible variants. A sonata for clarinet and piano is usually assumed to be available only as score-plus-part, but concertos are routinely published as both full and miniature scores, as well as in arrangements with the orchestra reduced for a piano. Works for larger ensembles may be published as a set of parts, as a score (miniature or full size), as a set including both, or as single or multiple copies of a performance score.[8] A work that incorporates electronic sounds may require a compact disc or prerecorded tape for rehearsal and performance that is included with the set or sold separately. The purchase order must state *exactly* what format is required.

For some library acquisitions units, "score" merely means printed music, whatever the specific format. The term may sometimes, in fact, be used on a purchase order merely to alert library staff that the item needs special treatment when it arrives ("Give this to the music cataloger"), rather than to inform the vendor of the format. Music vendors have learned to ignore "score" on purchase orders when used alone, unless it is clear from the bibliographic description of the work or some other evidence that it is being used precisely. In most cases the term can and should be qualified to make its usage clear: "study score," "vocal score," "conductor's score," "score and parts," and so forth. If the order is printed from a MARC bibliographic record in the library's online system, tweaking the acquisitions module so that the physical description in field 300 automatically prints on the purchase order will assist the vendor in identifying the format that is wanted. Even with this enhancement, it is rarely excessive to enter manually as a note the format that is wanted, even if it duplicates information printed from the bibliographic record.

Performance parts for an orchestra should specify the number of parts required for each of the string sections, as described in "Music for Large Ensembles" in chapter 2. The number of scores or parts needed for a chorus should also be specified.

Medium of Performance

Many musical works have titles that are not indicative of their medium of performance. There is nothing in the title of Schumann's *Thème sur le nom Abegg varié* to indicate it is for piano, of Donald Erb's *Suddenly It's Evening* to tell you it is for cello, or of Marlos Nobre's *Rememorias* to recommend it to guitarists. Or consider a title like *Fratres* by Estonian composer Arvo Pärt, who used it on several distinct versions of the same work: for violin and piano, for string quartet, for cello ensemble, for wind octet with percussion, and the list goes on. Composers also sometimes arrange their own works, or works by others, for different performance media. Pachelbel's famous canon for three violins and continuo has been adapted for just about every ensemble imaginable.

Many other works have generic titles based on musical forms, such as "Sonata" and "Concerto." "Symphony" will usually be assumed to be for orchestra, unless it is a "symphony" for solo organ, of which there are many. Any title of the sort "Sonata, op. 4, no. 6," therefore, may be meaningless to the vendor without identification of the instruments that are to perform it. Vendors and publishers usually organize their stock by medium of performance, or by format, not in one grand alphabetical order by composers' names. They must know the medium of performance in order to know where to check their stock for the item you are ordering without having to do additional research.

Some songs and vocal collections may also need further details on the medium of performance, since vocal works often are printed in multiple editions to suit voices of high, medium, and low ranges. Franz

Schubert's songs for voice and piano, for example, are published by C. F. Peters in seven volumes: volumes 1–3 are each available in three vocal ranges (high, medium, low), though volumes 4–7 are printed only with the songs in the original keys as Schubert composed them. If multiple ranges of a vocal edition are published and a specific one is wanted, the order should indicate it. In applicable cases, it may be sufficient to specify "original key."

For all of the above reasons, the medium of performance should be stated explicitly on the purchase order, either as part of the bibliographic title, or as an added note to the vendor.

Uniform Titles

The uniform title for each work should appear, if possible, on the purchase order.[9] Uniform titles contain all of the title, enumeration, key, and other information needed to identify precisely what musical work by the composer is being ordered, though not the particular edition itself. While adequate information to identify the work may also be found in other components of the order, this fail-safe feature provides added insurance that sufficient information to identify the musical work will be communicated to the vendor. If ordering using MARC records downloaded from one of the bibliographic utilities, local acquisitions systems usually can be adjusted to print uniform titles from field 240 on the purchase orders.[10]

Publisher's Number

Include on the purchase order *all* of the publisher's catalog numbers that are associated with an edition. (See chapter 4 for more information about music publishers' numbers.) Automated acquisitions systems commonly print an ISBN number on the purchase order as a matter of course, if the edition has such a number; the printing of other kinds of publishers' numbers (from fields 024 and 028) may require some tinkering with the system. If such a fix cannot be accomplished locally, publishers' numbers should be entered manually on the purchase orders. They are important information for identifying particular editions and versions. Publishers that release a musical work in multiple formats will usually assign a variant number to each one, presenting the library and the vendor with another way to distinguish among them.

Publisher's Imprint vs. Publisher's Agent

The editions of many foreign and some small domestic music publishers are distributed in the United States by an agent.[11] These business relationships frequently are stated on the title pages of the editions that are sold in the country of the agency and consequently are repeated in library cataloging records: the Durand edition of Lili Boulanger's *Quatre mélodies pour chant et piano*, for example, has its imprint recorded in the OCLC WorldCat cataloging record as "Paris: Éditions Durand; Bryn Mawr (USA): T. Presser Co., 2000." While this may accurately reflect the publisher–agent relationship as of the year 2000, distributorship of Durand editions subsequently was transferred to the Hal Leonard Corporation. The move of Durand from Presser to Hal Leonard was widely known at the time it happened, but many other publishers change agencies over the course of a year with little ado. While it is acceptable to include the name of the former distributor (Presser) on a new order for the Boulanger songs (the vendor can sort out the correct publisher–vendor relationship), the name of the original publisher (Durand) should appear in *all* cases. Naming only the agent, even if it is the correct one, gives a false impression to the vendor of who is the actual publisher and can delay the order.

Vendor's Catalog Number

When ordering from a vendor that assigns its own internal catalog numbers to the materials it advertises, include that number on the purchase order if ordering from that vendor. Using the vendor's catalog number, however, does not absolve the library from also furnishing the other elements described in this chapter, including the publisher's number; provide the fullest possible information on all orders. When ordering material from one vendor that has been advertised by another, however, inclusion of the other vendor's catalog number is of little use and may actually create confusion.

Try to distinguish between the vendor's internal catalog numbers and numbers assigned by publishers. One way to recognize these distinctions, though occasionally fallible, is that if the numbers in a vendor's catalog have various prefixes and are of various lengths, they probably are publishers' numbers.

Approval Plans

Poor bibliographic control of printed music and the multinational nature of the print and recorded music industries conspire to steer many libraries into the use of approval plans to acquire music, both printed and recorded.[12] Generally, approval plans call for the library to create a profile of the subjects, publishers, formats, and so forth, that it needs; the approval-plan vendor then monitors the output of new publications and selects and ships to the library those that conform to its profile and its approval-plan budget.[13] The library can return unsatisfactory materials to the vendor for credit.[14] Depending upon the needs of the library, notification slips containing bibliographic descriptions, and sometimes annotations, may be sent in place of the scores or recordings in agreed-upon categories in the profile. Libraries also can opt to receive *only* notification slips, in which cases the plans usually are known as "form selection" plans rather than approval plans.

Approval plans historically have been justified as a way to bring new publications into the library in a timely fashion and to build a core collection, while saving staff time that otherwise would be spent processing firm orders. In music collections, a more practical consideration is often in play: the available musical expertise is spread too thin to devote the many hours per week necessary to develop a collection *and* to provide music reference service, catalog new scores and recordings, train and oversee staff and part-time employees, maintain the playback equipment, and so forth. Few institutions can afford to hire a music collection-development specialist who has the expertise and the time to manage the existing collection, analyzing it for retrospective needs, while also selecting and adding current publications. The music vendor with approval plans is deus ex machina for many libraries in this environment.

Printed Music

There are three principal music vendors who offer approval-plan service for printed music, and each one has more than a quarter century of experience servicing them. Each supplies editions published in different, though overlapping, geographical areas: Theodore Front Musical Literature (the Americas, including the United States, Canada, and Mexico, plus Australia and New Zealand, with selective coverage of South America; and Europe), Otto Harrassowitz (Europe, with selective coverage available for Japan, Israel, Australia, and New Zealand), and

J. W. Pepper & Son (North America).[15] Front and Harrassowitz describe their services in detail at their websites (www.tfront.com and www.harrassowitz.de/mus_approval_plan.html), where printable planning worksheets are also found; details about Pepper's plan, including a worksheet, can be requested from the vendor. The worksheets cover basic decisions to be made about types of music and formats to be included, geographical and chronological coverage, per-volume price limits, the library's requirements for invoicing and statistical reports, and so forth. As a rule, libraries are not restricted by these basic worksheet forms; in consultation with the vendor, additions and modifications can be made to suit the library's needs.

Writing an approval-plan profile for printed music is arguably a more onerous task than writing one for books. In addition to selecting what "subjects" (performance media and types of music) the library will acquire, choices must be made about publication formats, since multiple ones may be available for a single edition: full score, study score, and solo with piano for a concerto, for example; full score, study score, and vocal score for dramatic music; score alone, parts alone, and score *with* parts for chamber music; and so on. (Not every relevant format will be offered for sale for every edition; for some chamber-music works, for example, only study scores are available for purchase.) Libraries at music conservatories, where performance is emphasized, are likely to profile to receive chamber-music parts in addition to scores, whereas academic institutions at which limited or no instrumental instruction is offered may opt to forgo the parts and acquire only scores.

Furthermore, many new score publications do not contain new music; rather, they are editions of previously published music that now is in the public domain: works, for example, by the so-called Viennese classicists (Haydn, Mozart, and Beethoven). Some publishers disseminate only this type of music: Wiener Urtext Edition and G. Henle Verlag are two examples. Others specialize in the reprinting, without editorial changes, of out-of-print editions by unrelated publishers (see chapter 9 for a directory of some of these publishers). If the library's approval plan aims to bring in pre-twentieth-century repertoire, the profile should indicate which categories of these editions will be acceptable. The profile might contain, for example, an exclusion list of publishers for which the vendor should send only *forms* for the music selector's decisions. Conversely, some libraries may choose to receive *all* new issues from publishers like Wiener Urtext and Henle, whose editions are generally well respected; the library thus may want to acquire them, regardless of whether they duplicate music already owned in other editions. Front and Pepper both provide convenient lists of publishers that are normally covered by their plans; these lists can assist the librarian in identifying publishers to be specifically excluded or to be collected comprehensively.

Front, Harrassowitz, and Pepper all provide helpful supplementary resources to assist the library in writing its profile, including, from each, an extensive list of twentieth- and twenty-first-century composers to aid the library in identifying modern composers whose works it wants to receive automatically and those it does not. Front's list of about 3,200 composers that are represented in its American and European plans is by far the most extensive of the three, due to the more comprehensive geographic coverage of its plan; Harrassowitz's list of about 1,585 composers represents those published principally in Europe; Pepper's 1,480 names includes composers published in North America.[16] On first examination, these lists can be intimidating. Keep in mind, however, that the majority of composers named do not publish new editions every year—many of them are dormant for long periods of time—and rarely do more than a few new editions by any one composer appear in a single year.

Harrassowitz and Pepper sort their contemporary composers into three rankings, based upon the composers' prominence and their performance and recording histories. The library thus can opt to receive scores only by well-known and prominent composers (the first rank) or can add the second rank of less well-known and established composers; libraries with larger budgets may choose to acquire also the third-tier composers who are just emerging and are not yet widely performed and recorded.[17] Front declines to pigeonhole the composers on its list, stating at the website:

> We have deliberately avoided categorizing composers according to some arbitrary value judgment assigned to their work or to the historical/musical significance of their total output. We consider that such categories are not only inflexible and limiting, but also predicate and dictate how music libraries should build their collections.

If the library chooses not to accept the composer strata posed by Harrassowitz and Pepper, the music selector, if in an academic institution, would be well advised to seek the input of the school's composition and performance faculty in working through these lists. In fact, it would be a good idea to consult them in *any* case, as these instructors almost certainly will be more in touch with the current composition "scene" than just about any library's music selector. What may result is a composer list with names drawn from multiple areas of the vendor's choices, perhaps even with names added of local composers who are not affiliated with mainstream publishers and who may still be below the vendor's radar. What should derive from the process is a list of contemporary composers whose publications the library will accept more or less unconditionally (within established price guidelines), with the understanding that notification slips will be sent for other composers.

Vendors' Aids

Additional aids from Front and Pepper include lists of continuing music series published in the geographic areas that they cover. It is important for the library to harmonize its current series standing orders with the new approval-plan profile in order to prevent duplications: if the library subscribes to any relevant series with other vendors, the profile should specify that new publications in those series be excluded; alternatively, the library may opt to transfer the standing orders to the approval-plan vendor, who will then ensure that duplicates are not sent. In practice, vendors normally exclude new volumes in ongoing series from approval shipments—exceptions being first volumes of *new* sets and series—but informing the vendor about the specifics of the library's standing orders is unlikely to be regarded as superfluous information. The more specific the profile, the less chance there will be miscommunication between library and vendor, and the need to return unwanted publications.

Additional sorts of music reference lists are posted by Harrassowitz at its website, describing available (and, in some cases, forthcoming) volumes in several categories: major ongoing composer collected editions and monuments of music published in Europe; music facsimiles published as monographs as well as in facsimile series; ongoing numbered series of music composed after 1900; and thematic catalogs of composers' works. Access to these lists is password protected, though passwords are available to library customers upon request.

Format and Other Considerations

Other areas that should receive attention during the writing of a profile are as follows: under what conditions the vendor should send reprint and revised editions, practical editions extracted from collected editions and historical sets, score anthologies, facsimiles, arrangements, choral octavos, music for children or beginners, method books, and parts for orchestra and band; what languages and alphabets of vocal music and librettos are acceptable; and what binding is preferred if multiple formats are available. Ideally, appropriate library personnel—including selectors and acquisitions and accounting staffs—and the vendor's approval-plans manager will work through these issues together during the development of a library's profile. It should not be a unilateral endeavor.

Following are summaries of a few specifics about each of the three vendors' basic plans as outlined in their literature.

Front, North American, Australian, New Zealand, and selected Central and South American editions; also European editions; provides lists of European and North American publishers, and of continuing music series normally included; shipments include annotated bibliographic slips for each title sent; plans also are available for books about music; customized search service available for out-of-print editions; titles "temporarily" out of print kept on continuous backorder; shipments invoiced at 10 percent off retail prices; full details at www.tfront.com.

Harrassowitz, European editions from up to forty-two countries; selective coverage beyond Europe available for Japan, Israel, Australia, and New Zealand; can select "approval plan" (scores are sent; returns are accepted) or "form selection" (bibliographic information is sent, from which firm orders can be initiated) in all categories and at every level of the profile; estimated annual cost projections are given for various levels of coverage of both new and older music; approval plan also available for German, Austrian, and Swiss books about music; shipments invoiced at current retail prices; full details at www.harrassowitz.de/mus_approval_ plan.html.

Pepper, North American editions; divides new publications into categories of (1) contemporary composers, to which Pepper's composer list applies, (2) earlier composers active before about 1900, and (3) popular music including rock and folk music, country and western, urban blues, and other similar categories (library can omit or modify any of the three categories in its profile); in each category, Pepper can provide annual dollar value for scores issued in recent years; shipments invoiced at current retail prices; no details on the plan are given at www.jwpepper.com.

All three vendors provide management reports tailored to suit the library's needs: these might include total expenditures to date and by month, number of scores sent and average price, a list by composer of all scores sent during the year, and so forth.

Recorded Music

Approval plans for recorded music are a relatively recent addition to the acquisitions librarian's arsenal. Among vendors who actively promote their audio and video approval plans to libraries are Compact Disc Source/A-V Source and Music Library Service Company (contact information for both is at "U.S. Vendors of Recorded Music" in chapter 5), and Theodore Front Musical Literature (contact information at "U.S. Vendors of Printed Music" in chapter 5).[18]

Label Selection

As a rule, profiles built around specific labels work best. As with score approval plans, coverage can be limited by geography (European labels, North American labels, Pacific Rim labels), musical genres (classical, jazz, world, etc.), and special interests (historical releases, composers' or performers' series, historical periods, etc.). Areas of special interests will typically be defined by the library's present collection and future goals. The vendor can help the library choose the labels that specialize in the type of music of interest and can estimate the cost to the library of acquiring their releases in a typical year. Consider also visiting the online directories of specialty labels listed in chapter 7, where the music profiler can review the particular repertoire recorded by labels that specialize in classical, folk, and world music.

Standard Repertoire

Compact disc plans often exclude a standard-repertoire approach, due to the numerous competing labels and recordings in this category. A plan may, however, choose to acquire this repertoire on some labels, but not on others: yes, for example, to Deutsche Grammophon, which has contracts with leading artists and ensembles, but no to Naxos, which records lesser-known artists, albeit at super-budget prices. Recordings of recognized merit may also be included, such as Grammy Award nominees or winners, "Editors' Choices" in the reviewing journal *Gramophone*, and, for popular music, *Billboard* chart toppers in selected categories.

Contemporary Composers

The library may wish to coordinate its music score and compact disc acquisitions by using the same contemporary composers list for both formats. Caveat emptor: unlike *printed* editions of copyrighted music, which usually are available from only one publisher, the compulsory-license provisions of the copyright law of the United States mean that any performer and any label can issue a second—or tenth—recording of a copyrighted musical work once the copyright owner has exercised the right of first recorded publication.[19] Therefore, the possibility of multiple printed editions of pre-1924 and other public-domain music extends, in the recorded realm, to music of *all* eras.

Reissues

Another area of danger is reissues: a recording of a particular performance may be licensed to any number of labels, which can reissue it, often paired with different complementary repertoire than was on the original release. To avoid acquiring duplicate recordings of a unique performance, the library should consider whether to exclude reissues entirely from an approval plan.

Conclusion

Approval plans must be monitored ceaselessly if they are to be successful: bibliographers and acquisitions staff need to be attentive to current publishing activity in the subjects, publishers, and formats covered by the library's profile in order to know when an expected title is overdue or missing. The intellectual "selection" process continues at some level, even if it results in few firm orders being placed, and each shipment must be evaluated carefully for titles that stray outside the profile's parameters.

Notes

1. See, for example, the procedures summarized in Audrey Eaglen, *Buying Books: A How-to-Do-It Manual for Librarians*, 2nd ed., How-to-Do-It Manuals for Librarians 99 (New York: Neal-Schuman, 2000), 100–108.

2. Useful resources for monitoring European score series currently published are "Monuments of Music from Europe" and "Composers Collected Editions from Europe" at the *Music Scores Acquisitions Services* area of vendor Otto Harrassowitz's website, www.harrassowitz.de/mus_services.html. Volume numberings are shown there, including forthcoming volumes, as are prices of

Notes (continued)

in-print volumes. These resources are password protected; instructions for obtaining a password are found at the above web address.

3. Imogen Fellinger, "Periodicals," *Grove Music Online* (2001), www.grovemusic.com, at part I/2.

4. Michael D. Williams, *Source: Music of the Avant Garde: Annotated List of Contents and Cumulative Indices*, MLA Index and Bibliography Series 19 (Ann Arbor, MI: MLA, 1978).

5. An example is given in chapter 5, note 10, of the significant price differences that can occur depending upon the source of supply. Here is another: G. Henle Verlag of Munich, Germany, publisher of the ongoing collected edition of *Beethoven Werke*, states the list price at its website (www.henle.de) of the clothbound series 1, volume 1, of this edition, containing the First and Second symphonies of Beethoven, as €94 ($106.50 at the mid-2003 exchange rate). By clicking on the site's U.S. flag, one is taken to G. Henle USA, where the price of the volume for American customers is quoted as $165—a premium of more than 50 percent for the "privilege" of purchasing it domestically.

6. See "International Distribution" in chapter 3 for an explanation of why this is so.

7. See "International Video Standards" in chapter 3 for more information about these standards and regions.

8. See the glossary for definitions of particular formats.

9. More about uniform titles for music is found in chapter 6.

10. The uniform title is one of several fields included in the "Automation Requirements for Music Materials" for acquisitions, submitted 29 February 2000 by the Automation Subcommittee of MLA: "In addition to other basic bibliographic elements (1xx, 245, 260), the system will allow entry and printing of the following fields on purchase orders: 02x (standard numbers; it will be possible to print multiple 02x fields); 240 (uniform title); 300 (physical description)," www.musiclibraryassoc.org/committee/co_adm_autoreq.htm, sec. IV. To this list I would add fields 4xx (series statement) and 511 (participant or performer note for recordings).

11. See chapter 2 for fuller discussion of these kinds of arrangements.

12. A 1996 survey of academic libraries (seventy-five respondents) revealed that 93 percent of them were using approval plans of some kind, with most libraries reporting multiple plans (847 plans reported in all): *Evolution and Status of Approval Plans*, compiled by Susan Flood, SPEC Kit 221 (Washington, DC: Association of Research Libraries, Office of Management Studies, 1997). The data summary of the survey stated that music compact discs and foreign music cassettes were covered in several plans (no details were reported); printed music was not identified in the survey. The literature on approval plans is substantial; the bibliographies included in the bibliography of the present manual cite many of the recent publications on the subject. Among general guides, see particularly the *Guide to Managing Approval Plans*, ed. by Susan Flood, Acquisitions Guidelines 11 (Chicago: ALA, 1998). I have not

Notes (continued)

identified any articles or books that specifically address approval plans for music.

13. Approval plans are widely perceived to be workable only for medium-to-large academic libraries, although printed-music approval-plan budgets as small as $1,500 per year have been accommodated, according to plan descriptions at Theodore Front Musical Literature (www.tfront.com). Compact Disc Source/A-V Source recommends budgeting at least $100 per month for an audio plan (www.cdsourceinc.com/standing_orders.htm).

14. A return rate of 10 percent or more means the library and the vendor need to review the profile, according to Flood, *Guide*, 22.

15. Contact information is given in chapter 5. Pepper's plan was established by European American Retail Music in 1973; European American has since been absorbed by Pepper. A fourth firm, Blackwell's Library Services, dropped its approval-plan service for scores published in the United Kingdom during a 2001 reorganization that transferred music firm-order operations to Blackwell's Music Shop in Oxford, England; Blackwell's Library Services continues to service standing orders for printed-music sets and series.

16. Front's and Harrassowitz's lists can be useful to reference librarians, as well as to acquisitions staff, as sources for birth and death dates of composers who have not achieved sufficient stature to be included in standard music dictionaries and encyclopedias. Pepper's list does not include dates.

17. Libraries that are members of a consortium, or otherwise have liberal interlibrary lending agreements with sister institutions, have been known to divvy up the lists of lesser-known composers, with each library in the group responsible for acquiring scores by composers whose names begin with a section of the alphabet.

18. I am indebted to Christine Clark, president of Theodore Front Musical Literature, for providing information about Front's CD approval plans. Much of the discussion in this section of the manual derives from Front's plan.

19. Section 115, www.copyright.gov/title17/92chap1.html#115. Compulsory licensing is discussed in this manual in the "Multiple Editions and Formats" section of chapter 6.

SECONDHAND AND
OUT-OF-PRINT MUSIC

Assorted circumstances can motivate the acquisition of secondhand and out-of-print materials. Replacement of lost, missing, and mutilated titles is a continuous pursuit in most libraries. The acidic paper that afflicts much printed music of a certain age also plays a role in the initiation of replacement purchases.[1] Vinyl recordings of performances and repertoire not reissued in digital format become scratched and worn from everyday use, particularly as new generations of listeners lack the experience to handle them carefully. Added copies of a heavily used score might be wanted for course reserve, and retrospective purchasing may be required to support a new area of study or to fill identified gaps in the collection. Sometimes the very nature of music publication formats and the way those formats are used by musicians drive the need to acquire out-of-print music: a set of string quartet parts is returned with such an accretion of penciled rehearsal markings that future borrowers are likely to shun it, or the cellist in the group has left the country, inadvertently taking her part along. In either scenario, the set becomes unusable and all or part of it will need to be replaced. To meet these diverse needs, music acquisitions staff frequently must turn to the secondhand marketplace.[2]

Also contributing to the need to acquire out-of-print editions is the trend that began in the 1980s of publishers allowing their publications to go out of print more quickly than previously. In 1979 the U.S. Supreme Court ruled in *Thor Power Tool Company v. Commissioner of Internal Revenue* that merchandise in a company's warehouse is subject to taxation, even though it represents income that has yet to be realized. This decision had an unanticipated effect on the publishing and recording industries: they began producing smaller print runs, reducing their inventories, and allowing even standard repertoire to go out of print more quickly. *Thor* taught librarians to order new publications promptly, lest they miss the opportunity to acquire them new, or at all.

Printed Music and Books

A differentiation sometimes is made between secondhand and antiquarian music and books and their respective dealers (though the terminology, and the shadings of distinction may vary from dealer to dealer).[3] "Secondhand" is used here for preowned trade and scholarly books and published scores of the sort that populate the shelves of a typical music library's collection. "Antiquarian" is used loosely to refer to collectible items: rare printed music and music literature, manuscripts and autographs, iconographic items, and memorabilia. The catalogs of antiquarian dealers often feature detailed bibliographic descriptions with provenance and full-color illustrations of some of the more interesting and important offerings to tempt the selector. Readers who consider such goods to be extravagances suitable only for special collections should consider their pedagogical value for the study of music manuscript and printing practices of the past. Even the best facsimile reproductions cannot substitute for the visual and tactile sensations that are conveyed by holding, and beholding, an original, early published or manuscript score.

Ordering from Dealers' Catalogs

Procedures for ordering from catalogs distributed by secondhand and antiquarian dealers differ little from those for other types of orders. Speed, though, is paramount: orders should be placed as soon as possible after a new catalog is received. The dealer likely has only one copy of each out-of-print title listed (though some dealers advertise a mix of out-of-print and in-print titles in the same catalog), and if the library covets a particular title, chances are that others who received the same catalog will want it as well. It is a good idea to e-mail or telephone the dealer to verify the current availability of desired titles (some titles may already have been sold, even before the catalog came off the press) and to request that titles be reserved for your library until purchase orders can be sent. If telephoning, have the dealer's catalog at hand to identify the catalog itself (usually by a number or title on its cover) and the particular numbered items within the catalog to facilitate the dealer's verification of their status. These catalog and item numbers also should appear on any e-mail or other correspondence to the dealer, including on the purchase orders. The exhortation about speed should extend also to the issuing of confirming orders after the dealer has agreed to reserve items. A dealer may specify a maximum period during which the titles will he held; even if no limit is stated, dealers cannot be expected to reserve items for much more than a few weeks, particularly if other buyers are clamoring for the same title. Dispatch purchase orders promptly.

When choosing printed music from secondhand dealers' catalogs, selectors should pay careful attention to the condition of the items as described by the dealers.[4] Editions intended for use in performance have an inherent problem: music that is actually *used* by performers tends to get used *up*; after repeated read-throughs in rehearsals and performances, scores and parts may not survive in such a condition even to be described by a dealer as "fair." While much printed music is listed among the offerings of dealers who sell used books about music, in my experience, it is rare to locate a "good" exact replacement for a worn or deteriorating performance edition; its published siblings have not likely endured in any better condition than the copy to be replaced.

Secondhand Sources

Several dealers in the United States and abroad specialize in used and out-of-print scholarly music books and printed music. The dealers listed below are some of those who distribute printed catalogs of their stock, or portions thereof, or who list their offerings on the Internet.[5]

Bel Canto Books, Box 55, Metuchen, NJ 08840. Tel: 732 548 7371; web: www.abebooks.com/home/belcantobooks, with link to searchable inventory at Abebooks (formerly the Advanced Book Exchange). Music and dance; print catalogs; book search service.

Elliott M. Katt Books on the Performing Arts, 35570 Bella Vista Dr., Yucaipa, CA 92399. Tel: 909 797 8689; e-mail: filmbook@ earthlink.com; web: www.abebooks.com/home/filmbook, with link to searchable inventory at Abebooks (formerly the Advanced Book Exchange). Music, dance, etc.; book search service.

J. B. Muns Fine Arts Books and Musical Autographs, 1162 Shattuck Ave., Berkeley, CA 94704. Tel: 510 525 2420; fax: 510 525 1126; e-mail: jbmuns@aol.com. Print catalogs; no website; book search service.

Marsha Berman Musical Literature, 2417 Fourth St., Santa Monica, CA 90405-3616. Tel: 310 399 3674; fax: 310 399 2054; e-mail: music@mberman.com; web: www.abebooks.com/home/marshaberman, with link to searchable inventory at Abebooks (formerly the Advanced Book Exchange). Berman is a former music librarian.

Martin Silver Musical Literature, 7221 Del Norte Dr., Goleta, CA 93117-1326. Tel: 805 961 8190; fax: 805 961 8290; e-mail: silver@silcom.com; web: www.silcom.com/~silver, with links to searchable inventory at Abebooks (formerly the Advanced Book Exchange) and Bookavenue. Silver is a former music librarian.

Montagnana Books, 2734 Garrison Ave., Evanston, IL 60201. Tel: 847 864 5991; fax: 847 864 6064; e-mail: montagnana@earthlink.net; web: http://montagnanabooks.com. Specialist in the violin family; print catalogs; latest catalog and special items available on the website.

The Opera Box, Box 994, Teaneck, NJ 07666. Tel: 201 833 4176; fax: 201 862 0474; e-mail: ajpischl@cs.com; web: www.abebooks.com/home/operabox, with link to searchable inventory at Abebooks (formerly the Advanced Book Exchange). Opera and voice.

R. Mahlon Jones Books & Scores, 2157 Ridge Ave., Evanston, IL 60201. Tel: 847 864 7035; e-mail: rmjbks@yahoo.com. Printed catalogs issued; no website.

Rosemary Dooley Secondhand Books on Music, Crag House, Witherslack, Grange-over-Sands, Cumbria LA11 6RW, UK. Tel: 44 0 15395 52286; fax: 44 0 15395 52013; e-mail: musicbks@rdooley.demon.co.uk; web: www.booksonmusic.co.uk. Printed catalogs issued; no website.

Theodore Front Musical Literature, 16122 Cohasset St., Van Nuys, CA 91406. Tel: 818 994 1902; fax: 818 994 0419; e-mail: music@tfront.com; web: www.tfront.com, includes a listing of out-of-print offerings. Printed music, books, recordings; book search service.

Travis & Emery, 17 Cecil Court, London WC2N 4EZ, UK. Tel: 011 44 20 7240 2129; fax: 011 44 20 7497 0790; e-mail: enquiries@travis-and-emery.com; web: www.travis-and-emery.com. Printed catalogs issued; no online catalog or database.

Antiquarian Sources

Antiquarian dealers can be of service to librarians in ways other than offering desirable titles for library collections: they can act as agents for the library when auctions of music collections are held; they may be in a position to refer potential donors to the library; and they can appraise collections for donors (in which cases the library needs to be aware of relevant provisions of the tax laws). The library that is lucky enough to have at its disposal special funding for antiquarian purchases, or that is simply well fixed through conventional funding sources, would be well advised to build a good relationship with a dealer whose material is of serious interest to the library, making its particular collection interests known. A dealer with choice new items is likely to offer them first to a valued customer with known interests in the field.

Many secondhand and antiquarian dealers do not have shops as such, but operate from home by post, e-mail, and fax. Most are amenable to showing their current stock by appointment if the music selector has plans to be in the vicinity, and to reserving preliminary selections made during such a visit until they can be checked against the library's holdings. Depending upon circumstances, it may be possible to search the selected titles in the library's online catalog while on site, using the dealer's Internet connection.

There is only one major full-time antiquarian music dealer presently active in the United States who maintains a high profile in the music library community: J. & J. Lubrano of Lloyd Harbor, New York. A denser concentration of antiquarian music dealers is found in Europe than in the United States, and this should not be unexpected, since much of antiquarians' stock-in-trade is of European origin. Fifteen members of the Antiquarian Booksellers' Association of America and sixty-six members of the International League of Antiquarian Booksellers describe music as one among several of their specialties, and sometimes they publish catalogs featuring their musical items. Most of these dealers have databases that can be searched through links at the two associations' websites, where they also can be searched collectively.[6] The following are some of the music antiquarians who distribute printed catalogs, or describe their offerings on their websites:

Dan Fog Musikantikvariat, Graabrodretorv 7, DK-1154 Copenhagen, Denmark. Tel and fax: 45 33 11 40 60; e-mail: dan-fog@inet. uni2.dk; web: www.antikvar.dk/dan-fog. Searchable online database.

Erasmushaus Musik, Mozartstrasse 17, D-70180 Stuttgart, Germany. Tel: 49 0 7 11 60 02 46; fax: 49 0 7 11 6 20 77 46; e-mail: kohl@erasmushaus-musik.de;   web: www.erasmushaus-musik.de. Print catalogs published; searchable online database.

J. & J. Lubrano Music Antiquarians, 351 West Neck Rd., Lloyd Harbor, NY 11743. Tel: 631 549 0672; fax: 631 421 1677; e-mail: lubrano2@optonline.net; web: www.lubranomusic.com, where iventory can be browsed and searched. Print catalogs published.

Libreria musicale Gallini, via Gorani 8, 20123 Milano, Italy. Tel and fax: 0272 000 398; e-mail: gallinimusica@tiscalinet.it. Print catalogs published; no website.

Lisa Cox Music, The Coach House, Colleton Crescent, Exeter, Devon EX2 4DG, UK. Tel: 44 0 1392 490290; fax: 44 0 1392 277336; e-mail: music@lisacoxmusic.co.uk; web: www.lisacoxmusic.co.uk. Print catalogs published; recent catalogs online; no searchable database.

Musikantiquariat Dr. Michael Raab, Radspielerstrasse 17, D-81927 Munich, Germany. Tel and fax: 089 91 57 80; e-mail: dreiraaben.muenchen@t-online.de; web: www.dreiraaben.de. Recent catalogs online; no searchable database.

Musikantiquariat Dr. Ulrich Drüner, Ameisenbergstrasse 65, D-70188 Stuttgart, Germany. Tel: 49 0 711 486165; fax: 49 0 711 4800408; e-mail: antiquariat@musik-druener.de; web: www.musik-druener.de. Recent catalogs online; no searchable database.

Musikantiquariat Hans Schneider, Mozartstrasse 6, D-82323 Tutzing, Germany. Tel: 0 81 58 3050; fax: 0 81 58 7636. Print catalogs published; no website.

Musik-Antiquariat Heiner Rekeszus, Herrngartenstrasse 7, D-65185 Wiesbaden, Germany. Tel: 06 11 308 2270; fax: 06 11 308 1262; e-mail: Mus-Antik-Rekeszus@t-online.de; web: www.musantik.de. Recent catalogs online; no searchable database.

Paul van Kuik Antiquarian Music & Music Literature, Bram Limburgstraat 70, 2251 RR Voorschoten, Netherlands. Tel: 31 071 561 9833; fax: 31 071 561 7397, e-mail: P.Kuik@paulvankuik.nl; web: www.paulvankuik.nl. Recent catalogs online; no searchable database.

Wurlitzer-Bruck, 60 Riverside Dr., New York, NY 10024. Tel: 212 787 6431; fax: 212 496 6525; e-mail: music@WurlitzerBruck.com; web: www.wurlitzerbruck.com. No catalogs issued; selected stock viewable online.

Searching for Specific Titles

Browsing through antiquarian and secondhand dealers' catalogs with the anticipation of selecting some appealing offerings can be an enjoyable activity. Searching for particular titles, however, is more problematic. Finding one sought-after title among the billions of used books offered daily for sale by tens of thousands of dealers could reasonably supplant the needle-in-a-haystack cliché for librarians. Before there was Internet commerce, acquiring out-of-print books was labor intensive, time consuming, and, more often than not, futile. Success rates varied, sometimes depending upon the type of material being sought. In the mid-1990s, several academic libraries estimated finding between 10 and 40 percent of out-of-print books that they sought, though in some cases searches could last for years; other libraries reported doing few or no out-of-print searches at all due to the amount of labor involved.[7] While the 10 to 40 percent range perhaps applies to scholarly books about music, scholarly editions of printed music appear in dealers' catalogs with less frequency.

The Internet has improved access to secondhand dealers and their stocks, but the traditional searching methodologies continue to be used. A library may perform its own out-of-print searches or farm the work out to someone else. Some of the traditional library book vendors, both in the United States and Europe, will search the out-of-print market for books ordered from them that are discovered to be no longer in print. Among the vendors that offer this service are Midwest Library Service (www.midwestls.com), Coutts Library Services (www.couttsinfo.com), and Blackwell's Book Services (www.blackwell.com) for North American publications; and Otto Harrassowitz (www.harrassowitz.de) for books published in German-language areas. The length of time vendors will search varies: Midwest searches for ten weeks, Blackwell's for one year before canceling an order; Harrassowitz will search indefinitely. (Although Harrassowitz is a vendor of scores as well as books, printed music is excluded from its out-of-print search service.)

Searches for out-of-print titles can also be initiated through one of the professional book-search services.[8] Several specialty music out-of-print dealers will also perform searches for scores as well as books, as noted in the annotations of the directory information in this chapter. These dealers will scour the out-of-print market, usually at no cost or obligation to the library, and reply with a price quotation when the desired book or score is found. Ads placed by libraries and by dealers in journals catering to the secondhand trade, listing books wanted and books available, have long been a feature of these searches. One such marketplace was the *AB Bookman's Weekly*, which for more than half a century was the most influential magazine in the out-of-print book world.[9] This journal ceased publication in 1999, however, done in by the Internet, and the growing popularity and ease of online book buying. The monthly *Library Bookseller* continues to be used by several libraries for this purpose.[10]

Many libraries establish and maintain lists of out-of-print books, scores, and recordings that the library wants to acquire—commonly referred to as want lists or desiderata lists. These lists can be built from a variety of sources: lost, damaged, and deteriorated titles in the collection that need to be replaced; orders returned from vendors marked

"OP"; retrospective needs identified by library selectors; and so forth. The venerable 3" x 5" index card was long the format of choice for managing want lists and for submission to search services. Today's database management software packages, such as Microsoft Access, and bibliographic management programs like ProCite or EndNote are ideal for managing such lists. The data can be indexed and searched in ways appropriate to the particular library, updated efficiently, and the file periodically sorted and filtered to send to a search service or out-of-print dealer in a variety of formats to suit each dealer's preference: as an electronic file for matching against the dealer's own database; as printed lists, labels, or cards; or other format as agreed with the dealer.

It is not a good idea to send the same desiderata list to multiple dealers simultaneously; if several dealers are competing for the same title for a library, it likely will be perceived in the trade as more "desirable," driving up the price. If the library wants to work with more than one dealer, each should be given the exclusive right to search the list for a designated period of time, before the unfilled parts of the list are submitted to another dealer.

Secondhand Sources on the Internet

The Internet has revolutionized access to out-of-print and secondhand materials. Many dealers of rare and used books and music have their own websites that librarians can browse, and from which they can order directly. Some of these web catalogs are merely HTML or PDF versions of the printed catalogs mailed to customers, but increasingly dealers are taking advantage of the way a searchable online database can substitute for an inventory of current offerings. In addition to, or as substitute for, maintaining a discrete online database, dealers large and small can also become members of services that aggregate the inventories of thousands of booksellers into a virtual marketplace, providing access to millions of new and used books at the click of a mouse. Often a dealer will join several of these services. Each of these multidealer services operates in a similar manner: searches can be executed by author or title (some offer advanced search capabilities for qualifying a search by LC class, price and publication-date ranges, preferred condition, and so forth). Some sites search *each other*, so that a query at BookFinder, for example, can produce hits from rival Alibris. Some services accept want lists electronically, which they will search continually against the entire online database. Generally, payment is to the aggregator rather than to individual dealers, so that only one payment is required if titles from several dealers are purchased from a single "shopping cart."

At most of these sites, a credit card is required for purchasing online (exceptions are noted below). Libraries unable to use credit cards can use the online dealer contact information to get in touch with dealers directly and purchase offline when a search produces favorable hits. Though the focus in all of these Internet services is on books, much printed music also is to be found.

The following are among the largest of the secondhand book marketplaces:

> **Abebooks**, www.abebooks.com, self-styled "world's largest online marketplace for used, rare, and out-of-print books"; formerly known as Advanced Book Exchange; advanced search features; online glossary; want-list service; invoicing available to libraries; in December 2003, more than 760,600 entries were retrieved using the keyword "music."

> **AddAll Used and Out-of-Print**, www.addall.com/Used, "40 bookstores, 20,000 dealers, and millions of books"; advanced search features; no want-list service.

> **Alibris**, www.alibris.com, listing "over 30 million used, new and hard-to-find titles"; advanced search features; invoicing available to libraries; online glossary; want-list service.

> **Bibliofind**, www.bibliofind.com, "millions of rare, used, and out-of-print books through the world's No.1 online bookstore"; partnered with Amazon.com (shared billing and shipping services); no advanced search features or want-list service.

> **Bookfinder**, www.bookfinder.com, "the forty million titles available constitute the largest book catalog available"; can limit to English, French, German, or Italian books; online glossary; no want-list service.

Photocopy and Digital Imaging

Increasingly, libraries are turning to the digital scanner to replace lost, missing, and deteriorated editions, and to add new out-of-print titles to their collections. It has long been fairly common practice for libraries to use traditional microfilm and photocopy techniques to acquire copies of out-of-print titles. With digital capture technologies and improved printing capabilities, libraries are now capable of generating high-quality facsimiles from out-of-print originals borrowed from other libraries, or requesting copy service from the owning library, thus eliminating titles from their desiderata lists that may have languished there for years. And the advantages over traditional photocopying are notable: the digital files that are created by scanning can be accessed repeatedly to reproduce copies with 100 percent accuracy and without degradation of quality; text can be aligned accurately and registered front-to-back when printed; and sophisticated editing capabilities permit image quality that can be superior to the scanned originals. This type of acquisitions work can involve multiple departments and units in the organization: acquisitions departments that initiate the procedures, interlibrary loan to borrow copies for scanning, copyright clearance offices when protected intellectual property is involved, and preservation departments that may do the actual imaging.[11]

Many printed music editions, unfortunately, are poor candidates for digital scanning. Scores and parts, particularly of instrumental music, are typically of greater height and width than the average book and may not fit the scanning windows of common letter-size devices. Tabloid-size flatbed scanners are available that will accept pages up to 11 x 17 inches, and such a scanner is required for capturing these larger editions.[12] Furthermore, if a multipart chamber-music edition is the scanned object, professional binding may be required for the final product to be presented in the correct configuration and to open flat on a music stand. The department doing the scanning will probably be geared up for books, and some adjustments in addition to the difference of sizes may be required. The fine lines of music staffs and phrasing marks, for example, may have different scanning requirements for optimum legibility than does plain text. In all cases the condition of the original will affect the scanner settings and may require some experimentation and adjustment on a case-by-case basis, particularly if the original paper is yellowed or spotted.[13]

Copyright Issues

Whenever reproduction of an original text is involved, staff must evaluate whether there is need to obtain permission to copy. Works published before 1923 are in the public domain in the United States and do not require copyright permission in any case.[14] If scanning to *replace* publications already in the collection that are "damaged, deteriorating, lost, or stolen, or if the existing format in which the work is stored has become obsolete," no permission is normally required if a "reasonable effort" has been made to acquire an *unused* copy at a "fair price."[15] It is up to the library to interpret "reasonable" and "fair" in these cases and to keep thorough, written documentation of its efforts to obtain the item from standard trade sources or the copyright holder. The U.S. copyright law thus shields a library from liability if it duplicates a work borrowed from another library to replace a copy in its own collection, or if it duplicates one of its own editions to provide a replacement copy for another library. Few libraries, however, seem to be willing to duplicate copyrighted material under *any* circumstances without the copyright owner's permission, even if the copy would be covered by the limitations on exclusive rights granted to libraries in section 108 of the Copyright Act.

If the library never owned the title—that is, it is *not* being replaced—and it is protected by copyright, permission to copy should be sought from the copyright owner. At the MPA website is found contact information for music publishers in the United States, and information about distribution and copyright agents in the United States for foreign publishers. At this site there also is a printable form that libraries can fill in and submit to publishers or other copyright owners to request permission to copy out-of-print music.[16] The MPA site also has a "Copyright Search Center" that includes a step-by-step summary to acquiring permission to copy out-of-print music.

Commercially Published Reprints

Orphaned public domain score editions sometimes are adopted by reprint publishers for reintroduction to the buying public. This is a convenient, and often inexpensive, way to replace editions whose original publishers are no longer in business or no longer have them available for sale.

Following are listed some publishers that specialize in music score reprints or include a substantial number of music reprints in their catalogs. Not included here are publishers of early-music facsimiles that are intended primarily to illumine performance and publication practices of earlier eras: publishers such as Éditions Fuzeau, Georg Olms, Minkoff Éditeur, Performers' Facsimiles, and so forth.

CD Sheet Music, distributed by Theodore Presser Company, 588 N. Gulph Rd., King of Prussia, PA 19406. Tel: 610 525 3636; fax: 610 527 7841; e-mail: questions@cdsheetmusic.com; web: www. cdsheetmusic.com. CD-ROMs containing PDF reproductions of thousands of pages of public-domain editions of standard repertoire, and some licensed copyrighted music; full contents listed at the website; reprint sources not identified; institutional subscriptions for web access available through Byron Hoyt Sheet Music as a discrete special collection from ebrary (www.ebrary.com): www.byronhoyt.com/ebrary/ebrary_interest.html.

Classical Vocal Reprints, 3252 Cambridge Ave., The Bronx, NY 10463. Tel: 718 601 1959; fax: 718 601 1969; e-mail: ClasVocRep@aol.com; web: www.classicalvocalrep.com. Catalog of more than 3,000 vocal reprint editions; reprint sources not identified.

Dover Publications, 31 East 2d St., Mineola, NY 11501. Fax: 516 294 9758; web: www.doverpublications.com. Over 600 scores and 100 books about music; online and print catalogs; reprint sources identified.

Edwin F. Kalmus, Box 5011, Boca Raton, FL 33481. Tel: 561 241 6340; fax: 561 241 6347; e-mail: efkalmus@aol.com; web: www.kalmus-music.com. More than 7,200 works, principally orchestral and operatic; online and print catalogs; reprint sources not identified.

Elibron Classics, Adamant Media Corp., 50 Cutler Lane, Chestnut Hill, MA 02467. Web: www.elibron.com (online sales only: credit card or check). More than 40,000 music scores on paper and as PDF files; reprint sources not identified.

Masters Music Publications, Box 810157, Boca Raton, FL 33481. Tel: 561 241 6169; fax: 561 241 6347; e-mail: webmaster@masters-music.com; web: www.masters-music.com. Music for keyboard, woodwinds, brass, strings, chamber ensembles, voice; online and print catalogs; reprint sources identified.

Musikproduktion Jürgen Höflich, Enhuberstraße 6–8, D-80333 Munich, Germany. Tel: 49 0 89 522081; fax: 49 89 525411; e-mail: hoeflich@musikmph.de; web: www.musikmph.de. Miniature score reprints of "wrongfully neglected" works; online catalog; reprint sources identified in the editions.

Recital Publications, 738 Robinson Rd., Pembroke, NH 03275. Tel: 603 228 4259; fax: 603 228 4618; e-mail: info@recitalpublications.com; web: http://recitalpublications.com;. Vocal music; print catalog.

Unfortunately, some of these reprint publishers do not inform potential buyers exactly what it is they are reprinting, though it sometimes is possible to deduce this information. Many scores published by Edwin F. Kalmus, for example, are obviously extracts from the nineteenth-century collected editions published by the Bach Gesellschaft, the Handel Gesellschaft, and so forth, though they are not so identified in the publisher's catalogs or in the editions themselves. Masters Music Publications, on the other hand, does identify in its online catalog the reprint sources (publishers' names and dates of the originals), as does Dover Publications. If the library's goal is to acquire music exactly as manifest in an earlier original edition, this reprint-source information is important. If, on the other hand, the concern is to replace or acquire new *repertoire*, as opposed to a particular editorial expression of the music, then the reprint source may not matter very much to the library.

In the context of reprints, it is worth mentioning ProQuest UMI Books On Demand (http://wwwlib.umi.com/bod), which makes available nearly 150,000 out-of-print books from the fifteenth century up to the present on a broad range of subjects, including nearly 2,000 titles on music. It addition to books about music, a number of scores are also available from Books On Demand, including many volumes reprinted from several of the nineteenth-century publications of composers' complete works, volumes important to scholarly research in music whose original editions are crumbling to dust on library shelves all over the world.

Recordings

Secondhand and out-of-print sound recordings of both the analog and digital varieties are widely bought and sold on the Internet. This online marketplace includes specialty dealers, search services, auction sites, aggregators that comb through the stock listings of thousands of used-recordings dealers worldwide, and marketing giants like Amazon.com that list new merchandise side by side with used versions being offered by third-party merchants. These sites are analogous to the secondhand book sites described earlier and operate in much the same fashion.

Among the websites with searchable databases of used and out-of-print recordings are the following:

Alibris, www.alibris.com, new and used; can filter by LP or CD; musical videos included in the "movies" category, with filters for DVD or VHS; institutional billing available.

Berkshire Record Outlet, www.berkshirerecordoutlet.com, deletions and cutouts (all items are unused); can filter by LP, CD, DVD, VHS, Laser Disc, label name, and price; institutional purchase orders accepted.

BuyUsed.co.uk, www.2ndhand.org.uk, searches multiple used-CD vendors and aggregators (Alibris, Amazon, Djangos, GEMM, Half.

com, NetSounds, SecondSounds, Second Spin), and links searcher directly to hits at each vendor's site.

GEMM: Global Electronic Music Marketplace, www.gemm.com, aggregator of thousands of sound-recording vendors rated by a five-star system based on buyer feedback, turnaround time, fill rate; advanced search features and want-list management available; some vendors accept purchase orders; see following entry for videos.

GEMMvideos, www.gemmvideos.com, video equivalent of the preceding entry.

Mikrokosmos, www.mikrokosmos.com, classical LP and 78-rpm recordings; credit cards and prepayment accepted; specialist in East-European recordings.

The chances of locating a particular LP recording on the out-of-print market are generally better than of finding a particular out-of-print compact disc. Several factors work together to make this so: manufacturers are producing fewer copies of each release than in the LP era, and this trend is likely to accelerate as growing numbers of consumers purchase music as downloaded files; there is a growing tendency of labels to destroy stocks of deleted titles rather than releasing them to the secondhand market; and few recorded music enthusiasts are selling off their CDs, as happened with LP collectors beginning in the 1980s. The following are some of the firms that will perform searches for particular titles of recorded music:

CDtrackdown, www.cdtrackdown.com, out-of-print classical domestic CDs and in- or out-of-print foreign releases.

Parnassus Records, www.parnassusrecords.com, LPs and out-of-print CDs.

The Record Collector, www.therecordcollector.net, searches for LPs only.

Yankee Music Search, www.yankeemusic.com, audio recordings in all formats.

The following is an online guide to these sites and to others that deal in used and out-of-print recordings:

Music Selection Sources on the WWW, "Web Resources for Out-of-Print Sound Recordings," www.halcyon.com/aseaberg/opmusic. html, compiled by Anna Seaberg for King County Library System, Washington State.

Notes

1. A 1990 survey of the miniature-score collection of the Indiana University Music Library revealed that 78 percent of those scores tested for high acidity with a pH testing pen (only 2 percent tested for *no* acidity): Marlena Frakowski, "The Survey of Miniature Scores Deterioration in the Indiana University School of Music Library" (Indiana University Music Library, 1990, unpublished printout), 8. This survey was undertaken as a project for the seminar in music librarianship that is a component of the music-specialization course of study of the Indiana University School of Library and Information Science.

2. For another discussion of this topic, with a somewhat different focus, see Linda Fidler, "The Acquisition of Out-of-Print Music," in *Out-of-Print and Special Collection Materials: Acquisition and Purchasing Options*, ed. by Judith Overmier (New York: Haworth, 2002), 5–15; published simultaneously as vol. 27 of *Acquisitions Librarian*.

3. My categorization of a dealer as antiquarian or secondhand in this manual is based on perusal of their catalogs over a period of years, or on their characterizations of themselves, and should not be considered prescriptive. Many dealers handle both kinds of materials.

4. Several of the used-book dealers and aggregators identified in this chapter have glossaries at their websites that define terms used in the trade, including those commonly used to describe the condition of items for sale. See also the link to glossaries at Books & Book Collecting, www.trussel.com/f_books.htm. Unfortunately, dealers are inconsistent in their use of the commonly used terms of condition; some are conservative in describing condition and prefer to err on the side of downgrading, while others may think every book they sell is in "fine" condition.

5. Additional book dealers who include music as one among several specialties are listed and indexed by subjects in *Sheppard's Book Dealers in North America: A Directory of Antiquarian and Secondhand Book Dealers in the USA and Canada*, 13th ed. (Farnham, Eng.: Richard Joseph, 1996). Directories of dealers operating in other geographical locations are also published by Richard Joseph.

6. Figures are from mid-2003. Antiquarian Booksellers' Association of America, http://abaa.org; International League of Antiquarian Booksellers, www.ilab-lila.com.

7. Douglas Duchin and Celia Scher Wagner, "Trials and Tribulations: Out-of-Print 101," *Library Acquisitions: Practice and Theory* 20 (1996): 341–50. This article, which is based on interviews with librarians and used-book dealers, is a good overview of the issues and methods used by libraries doing out-of-print work prior to the use of the Internet for purchasing.

8. For links to the websites of a number of general book-search services, go to the Books and Book Collecting site at www.trussel.com/f_books.htm; there also is an index of dealers who perform book searches in *Sheppard's Book Dealers in North America*.

Notes (continued)

9. *AB Bookman's Weekly: For the Specialist Book World* (Newark, NJ: Sol M. Malkin, 1967–1999); successor to: *Antiquarian Bookman* (1948–1967).

10. *The Library Bookseller: Books Wanted by College and University Libraries* (Berkeley, CA: Scott Saifer, 1949–).

11. For descriptions of two university-library OP scanning operations, see L. Suzanne Kellerman, "Out-of-Print Digital Scanning: An Acquisitions and Preservation Alternative," *Library Resources & Technical Services* 46 (2002): 3–10; and Lee A. Krieger, "OP Scanning: An Acquisitions and Preservation Solution," *Library Collections, Acquisitions, and Technical Services* 24 (2000): 424–26.

12. A digital camera may not be an adequate substitute: "At the time of this writing [January 2003] most consumer and professional digital cameras do not have sufficient resolution for archival capture of cultural heritage materials. Lens[es] used in these types of cameras are designed for capturing three-dimensional scenes and may introduce distortions to flat materials," according to *Western States Digital Imaging Best Practices*, version 1.0 (January 2003), by the Digital Image Working Group of the Western States Digital Standards Group, www.cdpheritage.org/westerntrails/wt_bpscanning.html. This is a useful guide for decision making when planning a digital imaging project.

13. Note that gray-scale images do a better job of reproducing older scores than do black-and-white scans, which sometimes drop out parts of the originals. MLA's journal *Notes* requires scans of 1200 dpi (dots per inch) for line art (including scores) that is to be reproduced in the journal: "Information Guidelines for Authors of Articles and Reviews" (September 2003), at the association's website, www.musiclibraryassoc.org.

14. Works published after 1923 may also be in the public domain in particular circumstances: if published between 1923 and 1978 without a copyright notice; if published between 1978 and 1 March 1989 with a notice, but without subsequent registration; if published between 1923 and 1963 with a notice, but not subsequently renewed. For these and additional criteria for identifying public domain works, see Lolly Gasaway, University of North Carolina: "When U.S. Works Pass into the Public Domain," www.unc.edu/~unclng/public-d.htm.

15. Copyright Act of the United States, sect. 108 (c), www.copyright.gov/title17/chapter01.pdf. Some restrictions apply.

16. "Library Requisition for Out-of-Print Copyrighted Music," www.mpa.org/copyright/forms.html. A separate form is available for use by individuals to make requests. This form is approved by the Music Publishers' Association, the National Music Publishers' Association, and the Music Library Association. Additional information on obtaining permission to copy copyrighted music is found in Richard Stim, *Getting Permission: How to License and Clear Copyrighted Materials Online and Off* (Berkeley, CA: Nolo Press, 2000), including a chapter on "Copyright Research."

MISCELLANEA

Microfilms

Sometimes the library is asked to acquire microfilms of original source materials that have not been commercially published as facsimiles.[1] Such requests are common particularly at institutions supporting research in Western "classical" music, for which the composers' original manuscripts and early printed editions are held, for the most part, in European libraries and archives. An essential task for the scholar who is writing a musicological study of a work, or preparing a new edition of it, is examination of the manuscripts and first editions that document its creation and early publication history. Many instrumentalists, vocalists, and conductors also want their performances to be informed by original sources. If the scholar or performer is unable to visit the libraries owning the original sources to examine them firsthand, and if published facsimiles are not available, next best are microfilms of the sources acquired directly from the libraries that own the originals. A microfilm can never be a perfect stand-in for the original, particularly in the case of detailed manuscript studies, but film reproduction is a useful tool of which the advantages are appreciated by scholars.

Libraries of the world that possess original source materials are accustomed to receiving inquiries about the availability of microfilm reproductions of them, and many are prepared either to photograph them in-house or to send the work out to a local photographer. In the past, many European libraries were reluctant to furnish reproductions of their treasures to other institutions. Walter Rubsamen, writing of Italian librarians during the period of rebuilding after World War II, complained of the prevailing mindset that "a library's importance is measured by its manuscript holdings, which lose their intrinsic value if they are photographed. . . . The precious manuscripts in their charge are viewed viewed almost as personal property that should be kept under lock and key, safe from the prying eyes of intruders."[2] A decade later, obstacles that continued to restrict the availability of microfilms from Europe prompted Richard Hill to write, as the editor of *Notes*, that "perhaps some day the librarians of the world may grow up and put away their jealous custodial perquisites in favor of aiding scholarship."[3] A few years still further on Hans Lenneberg observed that "one finds no sign of concerted efforts to simplify the international exchange of microfilms although such exchange is essential in carrying out research in old music."[4]

Although attitudes and conditions have improved steadily since these music librarians expressed their frustrations, American institutions wishing to purchase microfilms from abroad still face impediments. While most European libraries and archives now will provide microfilms as a matter of course, a few continue to embargo all sales of copies of their resources to other libraries. Individual scholars, as a rule, get better treatment than libraries, and often are able to purchase for private research copies that are strictly no-sale to libraries.

The owners of the original resources commonly impose restrictions on the copies, typically forbidding publication, duplication, or lending of the films outside the local institution. In 1977 Siegrun Folter published the results of an international survey of libraries regarding the restrictions then being imposed upon the use of microfilms supplied to others.[5] Of 223 libraries replying to Folter's questionnaire, only 3 explicitly absolved users from obtaining written permission to make additional copies of their resources. Folter included several examples of the agreements that purchasers were required to sign, providing examples of the restrictive terms. Today, a few libraries state no explicit restrictions on the copies they supply (Universitätsbibliothek Basel and Statens Musikbibliothek Stockholm, for example); most have some restrictions (British Library, Biblioteca nazionale di Torino, Rijksuniversiteit te Utrecht, Bibliothèque royale Albert Ier); some will not copy an entire source (Bischöfichle Zentralbibliothek Regensburg); and a few still refuse outright, or simply do not reply.

Verifying the Request

When a microfilm request is received by the library, acquisitions staff or the bibliographer assisting the scholar should verify the citations, if at all possible, in relevant secondary sources such as thematic catalogs of the composers' works; in union catalogs such as the *Répertoire international des sources musicales* (RISM)[6] and the *Census-Catalogue of Manuscript Sources of Polyphonic Music, 1400–1550;*[7] or in the catalogs of the libraries concerned. To aid in finding appropriate verification tools, there are extensive annotated lists of "Reference Works on Individual Composers and Their Music," and of "Catalogs of Music Libraries and Collections" in Duckles and Reed's bibliography, *Music Reference and Research Materials.*[8] The monographic works described therein are normally found in libraries' music reference collections, shelved, respectively, by the Library of Congress class numbers ML134 for composer catalogs (A–Z by composer) and ML136 for library catalogs (A–Z by location).

Many of the libraries that own original sources have websites that enable searching of their online catalogs for verification of bibliographic citations and call numbers, or at very least of current addresses to which inquiries can be directed. A few—such as the British Library, Library of Congress, and the Bibliothèque nationale de France—provide specific instructions for ordering reproductions of their resources, including quotations of applicable fees. In some cases there are online order forms that can be filled in with the particulars of the manuscript or printed source wanted and printed from the web and faxed or mailed to the owning library, or, in a few instances, submitted electronically. Most of these library websites can be found expeditiously with Internet search engines, or through several gateways that manage links to the websites of major libraries of the world. Several of these are listed in this manual's bibliography, along with printed directories of libraries worldwide.

If multiple libraries own a given resource, as will often be the case with early printed editions, a step in the verification process should be to establish whether and which of the extant copies are complete. Sets of seventeenth-century vocal partbooks, for example, may lack one or more parts in this library or that one, and the verification sources may identify which sets are intact. For example, the collection *Primus liber cum quatuor vocibus, fior de mottetti tratti dalli mottetti del fiore,* published in four partbooks in 1539 by the Venetian printer Antonio Gardane (or Gardano), is listed as RISM Ser. B1 entry 1539/12, with copies identified in three libraries as follows:

D Mbs (AT) – **GB** Lbm – **I** Vib (S)

These sigla indicate that the Bayerische Staatsbibliothek in Munich (**D** Mbs) possesses only the altus and tenor parts (AT); the British Library set (**GB** Lbm) has no parenthetical qualification, and therefore seems to be complete; and the Biblioteca bertoliana in Vicenza, Italy (**I** Vib), has only the superius part (S).[9] Additional kinds of holdings qualifiers seen in RISM include "SATB inc., 5" for a set of five partbooks of which the bassus part is incomplete; "mq. A," or altus *manque* (missing), and so forth. In this case the British Library, obviously, would be the preferred source for a microfilm copy, because it owns the only identified complete set. If no library is known to have a complete set of an edition, it is sometimes possible to construct one from the holdings of two or more libraries. If multiple libraries own the complete work, a large library such as a national one would be more likely to have well-established filming procedures in place, and good quality control in the reproduction process.

Making the Request

After the bibliographic information has been verified and the owning library identified, the next step, if established ordering procedures and fees for the library are unknown, is to write the institution on library letterhead to ask if a copy of the source can be provided in the desired format, and if so, at what estimated cost. It is important to determine the approximate costs before sending a firm purchase order. If the source has not already been photographed by the library that owns it, the requesting library likely will be expected to pay the photography and processing costs of a master microfilm—a photographic negative to be retained by the owning library—as well as the cost to produce the positive copy to be sent in fulfillment of the order, that is, about double the normal cost. In addition, some provincial libraries have been known to quote fees extravagantly higher than any legitimate production costs, perhaps because they simply do not want to be bothered. The query should include:

Full bibliographic description of the title wanted

Source of information (holding library's catalog, composer's thematic catalog number, RISM number, etc.)

Holding library's call number, if known

Format desired (positive microfilm, photocopy, etc.)

Film size, type, and polarity (e.g., 35mm positive silver halide film)

Number of copies wanted

Name and address of contact at the requesting library

Date of the inquiry

It may be prudent for this initial probe to state in addition that the resource will be used for private research and is not intended for publication. While this inquiry can be brief and to the point, Larry G. Mowers—then at the Isham Memorial Library at Harvard University, and speaking on a panel at the 1968 winter meeting of the Music Library Association—advised that when corresponding abroad about acquiring microfilms, "you should be a little more courteous than usual in making your request and a little more prompt than usual in making your payment"—sound advice when your correspondent has the upper hand, and you may need to deal with the library again in the future.[10] The return reply may be a cost estimate scribbled illegibly on the original request, may be a printed agreement form with a firm price quotation to be completed and signed, may require prepayment, may be in a language unknown to you, may be a refusal, and may be a long time coming. There may also be no response at all.

Much of the protracted back-and-forth that characterized the preplastic snail-mail era happily has been ameliorated in libraries that have embraced today's web and credit card culture. The librarian with an order form that includes firm cost information, a web-retrieved citation and call number, and MasterCard or Visa can fax his way to resolution of an aggravation that formerly could require months of correspondence. With the right tools at hand—near-instant gratification!

It is almost always an exercise in futility to try to purchase or borrow a microfilm copy from a library that already has acquired a film from the owner of the original source. Responsible libraries, which almost surely will have committed promises to paper, will redirect the requestor to the original owner, either to place the order directly, or to obtain written permission for the intermediary library to duplicate its microfilm.[11]

Film Archives

Two existing film archives—one exclusively musical, and the other containing music within a broader context—have obtained from many of the original owners prior permission to duplicate their microfilms: the Deutsches Musikgeschichtliches Archiv (DMA, or DMgA) in Kassel, Germany, and the Hill Monastic Manuscript Library (HMML) at Saint John's University, Collegeville, Minnesota.

Deutsches Musikgeschichtliches Archiv

The DMA was established in 1954, partly in response to the destruction of sources and, indeed, of entire libraries, wrought by World War II. Its mission has been to preserve on microfilm documents of German musical heritage, principally from the late fifteenth to the early nineteenth centuries. As of 2003 it had acquired from libraries and archives throughout the world more than 29,000 microfilms and fiches of musical scores and treatises. Copies of these films can be purchased by libraries and by individuals for research purposes, with the customary no-copying and no-lending restrictions. The DMA has not obtained secondary distribution rights from a few libraries, and for those the DMA will redirect the requestor to the library owning the original. Catalogs of the archive have been appearing in installments since 1955, although at its website (www.dmga.de), where a cumulative index to the printed catalogs is mounted, the DMA warns that the published catalogs document only about 40 percent of the archive's holdings.[12] The DMA also sells the index in printed form.

Hill Monastic Manuscript Library

The Hill Monastic Manuscript Library is a collection of microfilms of medieval and later manuscripts, many of which are musical sources.[13] Despite the library's name, it has sources from other types of libraries in addition to monastic ones, including city, state, cathedral, and private libraries. With the permission of the owning library, the HMML provides to scholars and libraries microfilms of the manuscripts that it has photographed. The library's online catalog (under construction) and instructions for ordering are found at its website (www.hmml.org).

Other Film Archives

The Library of Congress has filmed significant portions of its music collection, including all pre-1700 manuscript and printed music, and all of its pre-1800 books about music. Most of these are available for purchase from the library. Among other significant music microfilm collections in the United States are the Isham Memorial Library at Harvard University,[14] the Musicological Archive for Renaissance Manuscript Studies at the University of Illinois at Champaign-Urbana,[15] and the Toscanini Memorial Archives collection of autograph scores of great composers in microfilm reproduction at the Library and Museum of the Performing Arts at Lincoln Center in New York.[16] These archives do not make copies of their holdings.

Quality Control

Quality control in the photography shops to which some libraries outsource their filming can be variable. Upon receipt, therefore, films should be examined carefully to assure that (1) the correct item was photographed; (2) the item is bibliographically complete; (3) if a multipart work, that no parts are reverse images (yes, this can happen if the film is duplicated from existing masters; the remedy is to cut and splice the film into a consistent configuration); (4) images are not blurred or the film scratched; (5) if wound on a reel, that the first image is tail out, and wound to feed correctly into local microreaders so that images are not reversed; and (6) that there are leaders and trailers of blank film (at least 18 inches at each end).[17]

Published Microfilm

Several commercial publishers produce and distribute music materials in microfilm. The types of materials filmed include collections of music manuscripts and early editions from major European libraries, runs of current and early music journals, program books of major orchestras, composers' collected editions, historical anthologies, musical iconography, and out-of-print monographs and scores. Surveys of some of these projects were published in the 1970s and 1980s, describing important music micropublishing projects that were then available or in progress.[18]

Following are listed some of the principal microform publishers today whose catalogs include musical materials (among these, only the Sibley Library and University Music Editions are exclusively musical); full catalogs of what they have for sale are found at their websites.

Adam Matthew Publications, Pelham House, London Rd., Marlborough, Wiltshire SN8 2AA, UK. Tel: 44 1672 511921; fax: 44 1672 511663; e-mail: info@ampltd.co.uk; web: www.adammatthew-publications.co.uk. Music publications include periodicals from 1722–1940, and manuscripts from the National Library of Scotland, Pembroke College Cambridge, and the Musikbibliothek der Stadt Leipzig.

Brookhaven Press, La Crosse, WI 54603. Tel: 608 781 0850; fax: 608 781 3883; e-mail: brookhaven@nmt.com; web: www.brookhavenpress.com. Music publications include American sheet music to 1830, music dictionaries and encyclopedias, and journals.

Harald Fischer Verlag, PO Box 1568, D-91005 Erlangen, Germany. Tel: 49 0 9131 205620; fax: 49 0 9131 206028; e-mail: info@ haraldfischerverlag.de; web: www.haraldfischerverlag.de. Music publications include reproductions of manuscripts and early editions in Augsburg libraries.

IDC Publishers, 350 Fifth Ave., Suite 1801 Empire State Bldg., New York, NY 10118. Tel: 212 271 5945; e-mail: info@idcpublishers.com; web: www.idc.nl. Music publications include early keyboard music, opera scores, and editions from libraries in the Low Countries, technical drawings of musical instruments, nineteenth-century Wagner literature, and portraits of musicians.

Primary Source Microfilm, 12 Lunar Dr., Woodbridge, CT 06525. Tel: 800 444 0799; fax: 203 397 3893; e-mail: psmcs@gale.com; web: www.galegroup.com/psm. Music publications include manuscripts and early printed music from the British Library and other English collections, monographs and scores from Harvard libraries, manuscripts from the Staatsbibliothek zu Berlin, early instrumental tutors, American sheet music, Venetian opera librettos, and journals.

ProQuest Company, 300 N. Zeeb Rd., PO Box 1348, Ann Arbor, MI 48106. Tel: 734 761 4700; fax: 734 997 4040. web: www.proquest.com. Subsidiaries include UMI, Norman Ross Publishers, Chadwyck-Healey, and ProQuest Information & Learning; music publications include U.S. and Canadian dissertations, journals, out-of-print books and scores, and research collections of manuscript and printed music and reference works.

Sibley Library, Eastman School of Music, 27 Gibbs St., Rochester, NY 14604. Tel: 585 274 1300; fax: 585 274 1380; e-mail: sibref@ esm.rochester.edu; web: www.rochester.edu/Eastman/sibley. Publications reproduce early editions from the Sibley Library collection.

University Music Editions, PO Box 192 Fort George Station, New York, NY 10040. Tel: 212 569 5340; fax: 212 569 1269; e-mail: ume@universitymusicedition.com; web: www.universitymusicedition.com. Editions include reproductions of historical score anthologies and composers' collected editions, reference books, hymnology sources, and *The National Tune Index*.

World Microfilms, Microworld House, PO Box 35488, St. John's Wood, London NW8 6WD, UK. Tel: 44 0 20 7586 4499; fax: 44 0 20 7722 1068; e-mail: microworld@ndirect.co.uk; web: www.microworld.ndirect.co.uk/wmcats.htm. Publications include early music from Westminster Abbey, Lincoln Cathedral, and Trinity College

Dublin, archives of the Broadwood piano manufacturing firm, British music journals, and records of the Worshipful Company of Musicians.

Products of these and other microfilm publishers are also listed by author and by subject (usually without prices) in the annual *Guide to Microforms in Print.*[19] The 2003 edition includes more than 3,000 entries under the heading "Music."

Music journals generally do not announce and review music micropublications, leaving the task to such specialized journals as the quarterly *Microform & Imaging Review.*[20] Since the 1970s, *Microform Review* and its successor have reviewed more than a dozen music titles.

Ordering Published Microfilms

Information in the general library literature about acquisition of commercially produced microfilms is limited and mostly outdated, and in the music library literature, it is essentially nonexistent.[21] Micropublishers typically distribute their own publications, so ordering direct from the publisher rather than through a vendor is the norm. Several publishers have periodic sales that enable regular customers to fill gaps or add new parts to ongoing projects at substantial savings. The percentage of the discount usually depends upon the total dollar amount of the order, so that a music librarian who is incrementally acquiring parts of, say, Primary Source Microfilm's series Music Manuscripts from the Great English Collections may be able to increase the discount by bundling the music order with an order for any nonmusical set being acquired from the same publisher by another of the library's selectors. A library's collection development officer often will be aware of these opportunities and can coordinate multisubject orders to achieve the greatest savings for all concerned.

Purchase orders should include full bibliographic description, and clear identification of the part wanted, if from a multipart series or set; format desired if multiples are available; type of film if there is a choice; reduction ratio (generally only one is available for any one title); number of units expected (reels or fiches); polarity (positive or negative if both are available); and the usual housekeeping matters (purchase order number, number of copies required, billing and shipping instructions, date of the order). Films generally are reproduced on demand, so cancellations are seldom possible if the copy already has been made.

Often buried in the publisher's fine print are the handling charges, which usually are a percentage of the total dollar amount of the order—typically between 3 percent and 6 percent. Add-on sticker shock for a $5,000 microfilm order, therefore, can be considerable.

Film Types

Microfilms are distributed by commercial publishers in a variety of film types, the most common ones being silver (also known as silver-gelatin, silver-halide), diazo, and vesicular. Silver is the type of film used for general photography; diazo and vesicular film are reproduction media, copied from silver original negatives. Silver film is the only type of film available from many micropublishers, as it is the most enduring for archival preservation—500 years if on polyester film, and properly stored—and is, in fact, the only type for which archival standards exist.[22] Silver film also enables the highest resolution images, and therefore is preferred where graphics with fine detail may be a concern, as would be the case with music manuscripts and early printed editions. Unfortunately the emulsion that carries the image is on the surface of silver film, making the images susceptible to scratching. Diazo film is resistant to scratching, but the dyes used in fixing the images begin to fade almost immediately, and fading accelerates when exposed to light, including the light in a reading device! Vesicular film is generally unaffected by light, but it scratches readily and can be damaged by excessive heat, including the heat generated by the bulb in a reader. Clearly, silver is the film of choice for anything that the library hopes to keep around for a long time.[23]

Conclusion

A half-century ago it was commonly prophesied that microfilm would replace print in libraries. Today, soothsayers predict that electronic formats will render both print and microfilm obsolete. Librarians who view digitization as preservation's panacea would do well to hearken to the Cassandras warning that the very speed of the digital revolution makes digital formats a risky choice for long-term information storage. Tomorrow's hardware and software will be unable to decode today's bits and bytes without a rigorous program of continual data reformatting and refreshing. Microfilm, when properly produced and stored, will be readable a century from now with no more than a lens and a light, and, furthermore, will be readily convertible to the digital medium du jour. The affordability, durability, portability, and storability of microfilms make them unlikely candidates for the bibliographic dustbin.[24]

Dissertations and Theses

The doctorate has existed in the Western world since the twelfth century, when the first doctorate of law was awarded at the University of Bologna. In the thirteenth century it was introduced to England, and the first recorded doctorate in music was awarded by Cambridge University in 1464. The antiquity of the doctorate, however, has not brought universal respect to its most tangible product, the dissertation, and there is extensive literature questioning its benefits to the individual author and as a contribution to research.[25]

For librarians, the odor of scholastic disrespect is intensified by the problems associated with acquiring, binding, classifying, assigning subject headings, shelving, and circulating these documents.[26] In one of the few monographic treatments of the dissertation, Calvin Boyer wrote that they probably are held in such low esteem by many librarians because they are a format that is perceived to require segregation, because they are little more than a training device (in other words, homework!), and they lack the network of evaluative media of the sort that vet other scholarly publications.[27] The imbalance between the amount of time required to acquire, catalog and physically process dissertations, and their perceived infrequent subsequent use have rendered them *libri non grati* in many libraries.

"Thesis" and "dissertation" have multiple dictionary definitions. In academic parlance the two terms sometimes are used as synonyms, and sometimes with distinct meanings. In the United States, a common usage has theses being written for master's degrees, and dissertations for doctorates, but this interpretation is by no means all-pervading. Library literature also embraces a bewildering array of terms in other languages that mean more or less the same thing: akademische Abhandlung, akademiska handling, concours, Dissertationsarbeit, Doktorarbeit, Fakultatsrede, Gradulationschrift, Habilitationsschrift, Hochschulschrift, Inauguralhandlung, Inauguraldissertation, proefschrift, thèse, tesi, and so forth. For this discussion, "thesis" and "dissertation" are used interchangeably to mean any written essay or treatise based on academic research that is submitted to and accepted by an institution of higher learning in order to fulfill all or part of the requirements for the awarding of an advanced degree.[28]

There is widespread belief that "good" dissertations will be published in some form or another and that their ideas will find their way into libraries through commercial routes. A number of studies have shown, however, that only a small percentage of these documents, even from highly rated programs at prestigious universities, ever achieve publication.[29] The reasons for this are varied, but include in the United States the ready availability of on-demand photocopies and microforms of them, which tends to diminish the potential for their commercial exploitation. Further, there is the reluctance of many authors, often psychologically brutalized by the doctoral process, to do the extensive rewriting required to convert them into acceptable prose. Having served the purpose of acquiring for their creators a necessary job qualification, they are never heard from again.

While few would question the responsibility of academic libraries to preserve the dissertations produced at their own institutions, attitudes toward those from other degree-granting institutions vary. Some research libraries make no distinction between dissertations and the scholarly books distributed by trade and scholarly presses, and they acquire titles containing relevant research regardless of their formats. Others purchase only theses specifically requested for faculty research. Still others purchase the requested titles, but then disown them once received, handing them unceremoniously over to the researchers to become their personal property.[30]

For libraries that do wish to acquire theses and dissertations on musical topics, the most comprehensive and best-known bibliography of them arguably is *Doctoral Dissertations in Musicology*, which is most complete in its online version. DDM-Online is a freely accessible "database of bibliographic records for completed dissertations and new dissertation topics in the fields of musicology, music theory, and ethnomusicology, as well as in related musical, scientific, and humanistic disciplines."[31] Its coverage is international—degree-granting institutions from more than thirty countries are represented—and it is updated regularly as universities and individuals submit data about dissertations recently completed or in progress. It contains all retrospective entries from its printed predecessors, *Doctoral Dissertations in Musicology*, 2nd international edition (1984), and the 2nd series, 2nd cumulative edition (1996), with additional updates and corrections.[32] Each entry includes fields to identify the title's *Dissertation Abstracts* number, *RILM Abstracts* number, and ProQuest Digital Dissertations order number.[33] DDM-Online is not a particularly reliable source for references to these other resources, however, because it depends upon the recent doctoral honorees themselves to supply the data. Once finished with their dissertations, it seems that many authors are not eager to re-visit the site where they first publicly declared their research topics and began what for many must have felt like a period of penance. The absence of any of these numbers from an entry in DDM-Online, therefore, should not be taken as evidence that the dissertation is not listed in those sources. Users of DDM-Online should take care to distinguish between accepted (completed) dissertations and those that are still in progress. An asterisk with the DDM-Online catalog number and the absence of a completion date indicate that the work is still in progress, and that a purchase or interlibrary loan request would therefore be inappropriate. Users also should not mistake DDM-Online as a source of supply; the editors of DDM-Online occasionally receive from libraries and individuals orders for dissertations which they have no capability to fulfill.

Many music theses and dissertations from many countries completed after 1968 can also be verified in *RILM Abstracts of Music Literature*, the serial print and electronic bibliography of all sorts of literature about music, with abstracts.[34] Like DDM-Online, RILM relies upon contributions by authors and a network of volunteers willing to seek out these documents and to write abstracts. The powerful searching capabilities of RILM's electronic versions can be limited to the document type "dissertation."

The United States and Canada

Libraries purchasing U.S. and recent Canadian dissertations can benefit from one-stop shopping. UMI Dissertation Services—formerly University Microfilms International, and now a subsidiary of ProQuest Information and Learning—provides the most comprehensive listing of U.S. and Canadian dissertations on all subjects through its online database ProQuest Digital Dissertations, formerly known as Dissertation Abstracts Online, which contains bibliographic citations beginning with the earliest U.S. dissertation accepted in 1861 and extending to those accepted as recently as the current year.[35] Titles from some international institutions have also been included in this database since 1988, though only a selection of these can be purchased from UMI; status of availability for each title is clearly indicated in the database.

Not every North American dissertation finds its way into the ProQuest database, and not every dissertation listed there is available for purchase. Some universities cooperate selectively and may, for example, submit only PhD theses, omitting master's or DMus theses, or both, from their submission programs. Some institutions—notably

Harvard, Stanford, the Massachusetts Institute of Technology (MIT), and the University of Chicago—long declined to contribute at all, reserving the right to reproduce and sell copies of their dissertations for themselves.[36] Harvard eventually capitulated in 1985,[37] Stanford in 1989,[38] and Chicago in 1994.[39] The University of Chicago sent its entire archive of theses to UMI for filming beginning in 1994, and Stanford documents going back to 1953 are also now available from UMI. Most pre-1985 Harvard theses and all MIT theses still must be ordered directly from the home institutions. Many of these documents are cataloged in the UMI database, but with the rubric "not available from UMI."

Theses that contain musical examples sometimes face an additional hurdle; if as little as a single measure of a copyrighted work is reproduced in the thesis, UMI requires written permission from all the copyright owners before it will distribute the document. This undoubtedly accounts for a few of the "not available from UMI" notices that appear with some titles in the database. Once a preorder search verifies that the document does in fact exist, if it fails to appear in the ProQuest database within a reasonable period of time (say, one and one-half calendar years following acceptance by the degree-granting institution), it is unlikely to do so. In such a case the only avenue for purchase usually is to request a photocopy directly from the library of the institution that granted the degree. Section 108 of the United States Copyright Act allows the reproduction of unpublished works by a library or archive for deposit in another.[40] How each library interprets this section of the law in relation to unpublished dissertations may depend upon local institutional regulations or agreements with degree recipients, or level of skittishness regarding all things copyright. Written permission of the author may be required before the institution will make a copy, in which case the school will sometimes provide the author's address.

The UMI order number given for each title in the ProQuest Digital Dissertations database and in related printed resources is critical to acquiring the correct title when ordering from UMI. Libraries with access to the database can search by title keywords and optional subject categories, degree dates, and names of institutions awarding degrees to identify the titles wanted and their order numbers. The most recent two years of citations and abstracts are available free of charge to anyone visiting UMI's ProQuest Digital Dissertations website. Music selectors at libraries that do not subscribe to the full database, therefore, can keep current with theses and dissertations by making periodic visits to the UMI site and searching for all dissertations on the subject "music" that were submitted in the preceding calendar year. Typically, 800–900

"music" titles are added annually, of which 350–400 are PhD dissertations. Libraries without access to the full database can also use UMI's
DATRIXDirect service to have UMI perform individualized searches
of the database for titles submitted in earlier chronological periods. For
a modest fee, UMI will produce a printed bibliography of up to 500 dissertation citations based on the library's choice of title keywords, with
optional subject categories, degree dates, and names of institutions
awarding degrees. The full database is available by library subscription
direct from UMI, or through the commercial online services Ovid
Online (Ovid Technologies), DataStar and DIALOG (both from the
Dialog Corporation), and EPIC and FirstSearch (both from OCLC).

UMI accepts institutional purchase orders and its own order forms
for prepaid or institutional credit card orders. Credit cards can also be
used to order online at the ProQuest Digital Dissertations database. The
cost of each dissertation depends not on the length of the document, but
on the format selected. Substantial discounts are given to "academic"
purchasers, including college and university libraries, librarians, faculty, and students.[41] All dissertations contributed since 1997 are available in downloadable digital PDF format, which is the least expensive
option; access to these is free to requestors at the originating university
of each dissertation. Other available formats, listed here in order of increasing cost per copy, are unbound paper copy, microfilm or fiche,
paper copy bound in a paper cover, and hardbound paper copy. Any
audio or other media files included as accompanying matter in the
original dissertation will not be reproduced in the UMI product.

Libraries and individuals can also establish standing orders by setting up a profile through UMI's Dissertations ASAP (Automatic Shipment As Profiled) program. Working with UMI, the library develops a
profile based on subject terms used by UMI—"music" (without any
further qualification) is the narrowest term specific to music—in combination with title keywords, names of particular degree-granting institutions, types of degree granted, and dates of degrees. This can be a
useful blanket acquisition method if the library wants to acquire, say,
all PhD dissertations accepted by Harvard, Yale, and Stanford on any
musical topic. If the library wants to apply narrower subject limitations,
however, this is not likely to be a practical method. Relying upon keywords in titles will surely overlook appropriate works, considering the
propensity of many authors of dissertations to strive for style over sub-
stance in titling their *magna opera*.[42] Furthermore, ASAP is not an "approval" plan; the books are printed on demand and are not returnable.
Librarians engaged in building comprehensive but discriminating music

subject collections, therefore, are probably better off using traditional selection methods to acquire the dissertations they want.

The United Kingdom and Ireland

Bibliographic control and availability for purchase of theses and dissertations created outside the United States and Canada is often a disordered affair.[43] The British Thesis Service of the British Library Document Supply Centre at Boston Spa sells copies of most of the doctoral theses completed at British and Irish universities since the early 1970s (more than 165,000 titles as of 2003).[44] The primary listing of British theses is the quarterly *Index to Theses*; bibliographic records contributed to this index from 1970 forward are available on the web as a searchable database, free to legitimate members—students, faculty, etc.—of organizations that subscribe to the print version.[45] Brief records can also be found in the Document Supply Centre file of the British Library Public Catalogue (http://blpc.bl.uk). An additional resource for identification and verification of British theses is the union catalog of the Consortium of University Research Libraries (CURL), which consists of twenty-five United Kingdom university and legal deposit libraries. Free access to the twenty-four million records in this database, which is known by the acronym COPAC (for CURL Online Public Access Catalog), is available at www.copac.ac.uk. The database is also available to subscribers to RLIN.

Instructions for ordering, including costs and printable forms, and online ordering for institutions with established accounts or credit cards, are found at the Document Supply Centre's British Thesis Service website. Some British universities impose restrictions or require completion of a Thesis Declaration Form, including the signature of the person who will actually use the thesis. Theses requiring a signed declaration form "may not be added to library collections," according to the service's website. A list of participating institutions, and notes about availability and copyright information for each, are also found at the Thesis Service site.

Continental Europe

On the Continent, it was long common practice to require doctoral candidates to have their theses printed and bound in book form, sometimes at their own expense, so as to provide sufficient copies to support a web of deposit and exchange agreements among university libraries, both nationally and internationally. The social and political turmoil of the 1940s brought an end to those requirements almost everywhere, though they were reinstated to some extent in the 1950s. By the mid-1970s, formal publication was an unconditional requirement only in the Netherlands, Iceland, Finland, and Norway (Nordic stoicism?), though journal publication of the research findings in abbreviated form was usually acceptable.[46]

Although formal publication requirements are now largely a thing of the past, dissertation deposit requirements in much of continental Europe remain rigorous, particularly at German universities. At the Free University of Berlin, for example, doctoral candidates in the humanities and social sciences have four deposit options, depending upon the final format chosen for the work: (1) eighty bound photocopies; or (2) three bound photocopies and eighty microfiche copies plus one master microfiche; or (3) five bound photocopies and an electronic version in PDF format; or (4) three copies produced by a trade publisher.[47] And of course, in most of Europe, copies are also required for legal deposit at the appropriate national library, with subsequent listing in the national bibliography and in the library's catalog. The availability of a growing number of national library catalogs on the web has significantly enhanced access to these documents, at least in terms of bibliographic description.

One result of all this European publishing, depositing, and exchanging is that university libraries there have accumulated dissertation collections that are enormous by American standards. The library of the Free University of Berlin, for example, houses more than 498,000 dissertations, and there are more than 669,000 at Ludwig Maximilian University in Munich, forming bibliographic plaque to clog the arteries of their cataloging units.[48] So many dissertations are acquired by European libraries through exchange that purchase may rarely be necessary. Another consequence is that a number of publishers, particularly in German-speaking Europe, have established monographic series that rely wholly or extensively upon dissertations for fodder. These publications, usually revised versions of the originals, are announced and distributed through normal trade channels. By way of illustration, the following are the music series incorporating dissertation research that are produced by just two commercial publishers:

Peter Lang (Frankfurt, Bern, New York, etc.)
    Beiträge zur europäischen Musikgeschichte (1995–)
    Beiträge zur Geschichte der Musikpädagogik (1995–)
    Europäische Hochschulschriften. Reihe 36, Musikwissenschaft
    (1981–)

Schriften zur Musikpsychologie und Musikasthetik (1987–)
Studien und Dokumente zur Tanzwissenschaft (1998–)

Hans Schneider (Tutzing)
Frankfurter Beiträge zur Musikwissenschaft (1977–)
Mainzer Studien zur Musikwissenschaft (1967–)
Münchner Veröffentlichungen zur Musikgeschichte (1959–)
Wiener Veröffentlichungen zur Musikwissenschaft (1976–)
Würzburger musikhistorische Beiträge (1975–)

Note the appearance of the name of a city in the title of each of the Schneider series, which is a clue that the dissertations produced at the local university are likely the focus of its publishing plan. University presses, too, have traditionally used dissertations as a major source for their publication programs. Several Italian university presses, for example, have dissertation series for distributing the local product on microfiche. But as a rule, the glut of documents coming out of today's doctorate factories has long since outstripped the capability to publish them comprehensively in this way.

France

Only France seems to have attempted a publication program that is in any way like those of UMI and the British Thesis Service, though it seems far less ambitious than its English-language cousins. Prior to 1943, formal publication before the defense was required in France for all dissertations, and the procedure was partially reinstated during 1957–1969. After reorganization of the national university system in 1970, official reproduction of all theses in the arts, letters, social sciences, and law submitted in France was undertaken at a "studio" established in 1971 at the university at Lille (now l'Université Charles de Gaulle): l'Atelier national de reproduction des thèses (ANRT).[49] The atelier enabled continued dissertation saturation at French university libraries, while relieving the authors of the expense of reproducing large numbers of copies privately. Between 1971 and 1983, ANRT relied upon the authors to submit their theses for reproduction. The meager number of music titles included in the published catalog of theses distributed from Lille between 1971 and 1986 suggests that many authors opted out of this service.[50] After 1983, when production was switched from photocopy to microfiche, deposit became obligatory and was the responsibility of the universities rather than the authors. Yet the relatively small number of music titles that still appear in these catalogs—only fifty-two published in the discipline "musicologie" in the year 2000, for example—suggests that universities perhaps are submitting only their best examples.[51] Libraries can order microfiches of music theses listed in the original catalog and its supplements directly from ANRT in Lille; some recent theses are available also in paper. A subseries of "Thèses à la carte"—formerly distributed in the trade in attractive paperbacks by Presses universitaires du Septentrion, and including about eighty-five music titles—are now distributed through the ANRT website.

The most comprehensive source for verification of recent French theses is SUDOC (Système universitaire de documentation), the free online union catalog of more than five million holdings of about 3,000 libraries at French universities and research institutes.[52] As of December 2003, SUDOC listed about 800 theses in musicology (accessed by searching the term "musicologie" in the "Note de thèse" field). Note, however, that theses on musical subjects are often awarded in other disciplines.

Many earlier French-language theses are described in Jean Gribenski's 1979 annotated bibliography *Thèses de doctorat en langue française relatives à la musique*.[53] All French doctoral theses in progress in the arts and humanities are registered at a central file maintained at the Université de Paris X–Nanterre. In late 2003, a search limited to the discipline "musicologie" of the file's online database returned a list of 825 dissertations in progress.[54]

Germany

A useful tool for verifying German dissertations is the Deutsche Bibliothek CD-ROM catalog *Hochschulschriften 1945–1997*, popularly known as Diss-CD.[55] This database combines information from the *Jahresverzeichnis der deutschen Hochschulschriften* published annually 1937–1970 by the Deutsche Bücherei, and dissertations added 1971–1997 to the Deutsche Bibliothek in Frankfurt. German dissertations also can be searched and verified in the web catalog of the Deutsche Bibliothek, where searches can be limited to the category "Hochschulschrift."[56] Three print bibliographies that are useful for identifying and verifying earlier German-language music dissertations are *Bibliographie Darstellende Kunst und Musik: Deutschsprachige Hochschulschriften und Veröffentlichungen ausserhalb des Buchhandels 1966–1980*, which lists "gray" literature on the arts published during the specified years, and the two volumes by Richard Schaal that index German-language musicological dissertations completed 1861–1970.[57] Dissertations in progress at German, Austrian, and Swiss universities are registered at DMS: Dissertationsmeldestelle der Gesell-

schaft der Musikforschung[58] (many entries in this database are duplicated in DDM-Online).

Spain

In Spain, a web database of more than 71,000 theses completed
since 1976 is maintained by the Ministerio de Educación, Cultura, y
Deporte: Bases de datos de tesis doctorales (TESEO).[59] In addition to
the expected searching choices (author, keyword, university, thesis
date, etc.), the search ("buscar") page includes drill-down menus of
subject categories that allow the user to search very broad topics or to
limit to narrower topics in the humanities: for example, "Ciencias de
las artes y las letras" (arts and letters), can be narrowed to the subcategory "Teoria analisis y critica de las bellas artes" (theory, analysis, and
criticism of fine arts), which can be limited further to musical topics
("Musica y musicologia").

Australia and New Zealand

There is no comprehensive distribution system for theses and dissertations produced in the Antipodes.[60] Policies for borrowing or purchasing theses varies from university to university, as do the formats in
which they are made available, but increasingly, these documents are
being sold directly by the degree-granting institutions over the Internet.
Among these are the Australian National University (http://anulib.
anu.edu.au/collections/theses.html), the University of Melbourne
(http://buffy.lib.unimelb.edu.au/services/ill/ill.html), the University of
Queensland (www.library.uq.edu.au/iad/docdeliv/uqtheses.html), and
the University of Sydney (www.library.usyd.edu.au/borrowing/docdel/
otherlibtheses.html).

Additional Resources

Additional bibliographies that list theses and dissertations, including the national bibliographies of Germany, Austria, and Italy, among
others, are too numerous to itemize here. For information about these
the reader is referred to Vincent Duckles and Ida Reed's *Music Reference and Research Materials*, which lists sixteen titles about music dissertations, and to Michael Reynolds's *Guide to Theses and Dissertations: An International Bibliography of Bibliographies*, which
describes sixty-nine titles in the chapter on music.[61]

When a thesis cannot be purchased from UMI, the British Thesis Service, or one of the French outlets, a query to the library of the de-gree-granting institution as to whether a photocopy or microform can be made is usually the only recourse for library acquisition. In addition to the aforementioned Borchardt and Thawley *Guide to the Availability of Theses* and its supplement, several directories are available to assist in making the appropriate contact: *The Directory of Music Research Libraries*, published as series C of RISM; *The Directory of University Libraries in Europe*, first published in 2000; and the annual *World of Learning*.[62]

Borrowing Foreign Dissertations

When avenues for purchase of a foreign dissertation have been ex-hausted, it may be possible to borrow a copy of a fugitive non-U.S. or non-Canadian PhD document either directly from the degree-granting university or from the Center for Research Libraries (CRL), an interna-tional not-for-profit consortium of colleges, universities, and libraries that makes available scholarly research resources to users every-where.[63] The center has a collection of more than 750,000 doctoral dis-sertations from universities outside of the United States and Canada, and it lends them freely to libraries of member institutions and to non-members upon payment of a transaction fee. This collection of disserta-tions is built by deposits from member libraries, and by exchange or deposit arrangements with almost 100 universities. The CRL includes all printed French dissertations except medical since 1952, and com-prehensive coverage of the rest of Europe. A listing of universities par-ticipating in these arrangements with CRL and the dates on which their participation began is found at the center's website. The center also will attempt to obtain on a title-by-title basis any dissertation requested by a member institution if that title is not already in the collection. Disserta-tions are not listed in the center's main catalog, but a separate database of them is being created.[64] In late 2003, the center reported more than 20,000 dissertation records in the database, with more being added weekly.

Electronic Theses and Dissertations

The 1990s witnessed the development of electronic publication and distribution of theses and dissertations (commonly abbreviated as ETDs). The leader in ETD development has been Virginia Tech Uni-versity, which in 1996 received a grant from the United States Department of Education to support a three-year project to establish a National Digital Library of Theses and Dissertations (NDLTD).[65] By early 1997 international interest broadened the scope from "National" to "Networked," and by the end of 2003 the NDLTD international federation included 196 member institutions participating at varying levels of intensity.[66] In 1997 Virginia Tech became the first university to require submission of ETDs, where they are cataloged and archived by the university library. Virginia Tech was soon followed by West Virginia University and others, some of which do not require electronic submission, but provide the option.

There are many variations among ETD programs, including the options for distribution. Choices typically include (1) unlimited availability on the web, (2) availability limited to the local university community, and (3) no access allowed for a certain period of time if, say, the author wants to reserve the potential for commercial publication. A comprehensive "Guide to Electronic Theses and Dissertations," hosted by UNESCO, is available on the web.[67]

When archived electronically on the web, usually as PDF or SGML files, dissertations can be enhanced by color images, audio and video files, and hypermedia demonstrations. Additional advantages of electronic theses and dissertations are their accessibility from anywhere at anytime, internal indexing, availability soon after submission, and potential savings in storage space and processing costs. These very capabilities of enrichment, however, can be a hindrance if examples of copyrighted music are to be included, either as image or audio files; music publishers who are willing to grant permission to reproduce excerpts in a paper document that will be the subject of limited distribution may balk at allowing free access on the web to digital reproduction of even a few measures of their works.

While ETDs broaden the potential for easy access to dissertations, as long as some electronic theses and dissertations carry restrictions on content or access, electronic publishing will not provide a solution to the problem of access by libraries to these documents.[68]

Notes

1. "Microfilm" is used throughout this section, although other formats (microfiche, photocopies, black-and-white photographs, digital image files, etc.) may also be available from some suppliers. Microfilm is usually the most economical medium for the acquisition of unpublished resources and traditionally has been preferred by libraries.

Notes (continued)

2. Walter Rubsamen, "Music Research in Italian Libraries: An Anecdotal Account of Obstacles and Discoveries," *Notes* 6 (1949): 229.

3. Richard Hill, "Notes for *Notes*," *Notes* 14 (1959): 355.

4. Hans Lenneberg, "Problems in the International Exchange of Microfilm," *Fontes Artis Musicae* 15 (1968): 75.

5. Siegrun H. Folter, "Library Restriction on the Use of Microfilm Copies," *Fontes Artis Musicae* 24 (1977): 207–43.

6. A copublication, in three series, of G. Henle Verlag (Munich, 1961–) and Bärenreiter Verlag (Kassel, 1971–): ser. A, inventory by composer of printed publications to 1800; ser. B, materials organized by topic, including polyphonic manuscripts, theory of music, Hebrew writings on music, etc.; and ser. C, library directories. Web version of ser. A/II (music manuscripts after 1600) along with ser. C (directory of libraries) is available by subscription from the National Information Services Corporation (NISC), www.nisc.com; a CD-ROM version of ser. A/II, cumulated annually, is available from K. G. Saur, www.saur.de.

7. Compiled by the Musicological Archives for Renaissance Manuscript Studies, University of Illinois at Urbana-Champaign, 5 vols. (n.p.: American Institute of Musicology, 1979–1988).

8. Vincent Duckles and Ida Reed, *Music Reference and Research Materials: An Annotated Bibliography*, 5th ed. (New York: Schirmer Books, 1997), 337–89, 391–514.

9. The sigla used in each volume of RISM are explained in the preliminaries of that volume, and also are cumulated in *RISM-Bibliothekssigel: Gesamtverzeichnis*, ed. by Zentralredaktion in den Ländergruppen des RISM (Munich: G. Henle; Kassel: Bärenreiter, 1999).

10. Quoted in Fred Blum, "Music Library Association Panel on Microforms and Photoduplication," *Current Musicology* 6 (1968): 140.

11. Much of what is written in this chapter about requesting microfilms of manuscripts and early printed editions can apply also to acquiring copies of recordings in sound archives. Recordings in these archives, it should be noted, are invariably encumbered with a bundle of rights, whose owners can include composers, artists, donors, recording companies, radio networks, licensing organizations, and others. While the archive that owns the original may be able to assist the requesting library in identifying the rights owners, it inevitably is the requestor's responsibility to clear all rights before duplication can begin. The website of the International Association of Sound and Audiovisual Archives (IASA, at www.iasa-web.org) has links to its members' sites, where reproduction policies and procedures can usually be found.

12. Deutsches Musikgeschichtliches Archiv Kassel, *Katalog der Filmsammlung* (Kassel: Bärenreiter, 1955–); index at www.dmga.de.

13. For descriptions of some of the musicalia, see Peter Jeffery, "Music Manuscripts on Microfilm in the Hill Monastic Manuscript Library at St. John's Abbey and University," *Notes* 35 (1978): 7–30; and J. Evan Kreider,

Notes (continued)

"Austrian Graduals, Antiphoners, and Noted Missals on Microfilm in the Hill Monastic Manuscript Library at St. John's Abbey and University," *Notes* 36 (1980): 849–63.

14. "Collections in the Isham Memorial Library," http://hcl.harvard.edu/loebmusic/isham-collections.html.

15. Charles Hamm and Herbert Kellman, "The Musicological Archive for Renaissance Manuscript Studies," *Fontes Artis Musicae* 16 (1969): 148–49.

16. "Toscanini Memorial Archives," *Fontes Artis Musicae* 13 (1966): 173–74; Susan Sommer, "Toscanini Memorial Archives," *Fontes Artis Musicae* 16 (1969): 149–50.

17. For a more detailed discussion of microfilm evaluation, as well as of other aspects of microfilm management in libraries, see the Association of Research Libraries' *Preservation Microfilming: A Guide for Librarians and Archivists,* 2nd ed. by Lisa L. Fox (Chicago: ALA, 1996).

18. Arne J. Arneson, "Microformats and the Music Library: A Bibliographic-Use Survey of Recent Trends," *Microform Review* 4 (1975): 25–29; reprinted in *Microform Management in Special Libraries*, ed. by Judy H. Fair (Westport, CT: Microform Review, 1978), 98–104. Stuart Milligan, "Music and Other Performing Arts Serials Available in Microform and Reprint Editions," *Notes* 37 (1980): 239–307 (this was the third, and final, listing of music serial reprints to be published in *Notes*; earlier versions appeared in vol. 24 [1968], compiled by Fred Blum, and in vol. 29 [1973], compiled by Michael Keller). William M. McClellan, "Microformatted Music Indexes," *Microform Review* 16 (Winter 1987): 21–31.

19. *Guide to Microforms in Print* (Munich: K. G. Saur, 1978–); publisher varies.

20. *Microform & Imaging Review* (Munich: K. G. Saur, 1996–), a continuation of *Microform Review*, published 1972–1995.

21. Virtually nothing useful has appeared in print since two articles by Robert C. Sullivan, "The Acquisition of Library Microforms," *Microform Review* 6 (May 1977): 136–44; 6 (July 1977): 205–11; and "Microform Developments Related to Acquisitions," *Microform Review* 14 (Spring 1985): 164–70.

22. *American National Standard Specifications for Photographic Film for Archival Records, Silver-Gelatin Type, on Polyester Base*: ANSI PH1.41-1981 (New York: ANSI, 1981); *American National Standard Specifications for Photographic Film for Archival Records, Silver-Gelatin Type, on Cellulose Ester Base*: ANSI PH1.28-1973 (New York: ANSI, 1973). Standards for optimal storage conditions are given in *American National Standard for Photography (Film): Storage of Processed Safety Film*: ANSI PH1.43-1983 (New York: ANSI, 1983).

23. Fuller descriptions of film types and their characteristics are found in numerous sources, including William Saffady's "Stability, Care, and Handling of Microforms, Magnetic Media, and Optical Disks," *Library Technology Re-*

Notes (continued)

ports 33 (1997): 613–751, as well as in the aforementioned *Preservation Microfilming*.

24. For a summary of the pros and cons of print, microfilm, and electronic formats in libraries, see Norman H. William, "Microform Publishing: Alive and Well in the Electronic Age," *Microform & Imaging Review* 25 (1996): 68–72; and Bryant Duhon, "Technology-Proof Archival," *Inform* 13 (September–October 1999): 25–26.

25. See, for example, S. H. Bush, "Undue Dominance of the Dissertation in Training for the Doctorate," *School and Society* 56 (10 October 1942): 309–18; David C. Williams, "Stop the Dissertation!" *Educational Leadership* 28 (1971): 753–56; and Roger P. Phelps, "The Doctoral Dissertation: Boon or Bane?" *College Music Symposium* 18, no. 2 (Fall 1978): 82–93.

26. Concerning the variety of cataloging practices used in 171 U.S. libraries, see Lona Hoover and Robert E. Wolverton, "Cataloging and Treatment of Theses, Dissertations, and ETDs," *Technical Services Quarterly* 20, no. 4 (2003): 3–58. For additional views, see works cited in Hoover, "Cataloging Theses and Dissertations: An Annotated Bibliography," *Technical Services Quarterly* 19, no. 3 (2001): 21–40.

27. Calvin James Boyer, *The Doctoral Dissertation as an Information Source: A Study of Scientific Information Flow* (Metuchen, NJ: Scarecrow Press, 1973), 107.

28. A broad discussion of terminology, of the history of the thesis medium, and of its nature and purpose is found in Donald Davinson, *Theses and Dissertations as Information Sources* (London: Clive Bingley; Hamden, CT: Linnet Books, 1977).

29. See, for example, the study by Manuel D. Lopez, "Dissertations: A Need for New Approaches to Acquisitions," *Journal of Academic Librarianship* 14 (1988): 297–301, and other studies cited therein.

30. I have worked in libraries where each of these attitudes prevailed at one time or another.

31. Doctoral Dissertations in Musicology—Online (1996–), www.music. indiana.edu/ddm. The site is hosted by the Center for the History of Music Theory and Literature at the Indiana University School of Music.

32. *Doctoral Dissertations in Musicology*, 2nd intl. ed., 7th North American ed., ed. by Cecil Adkins and Alis Dickinson (Philadelphia: American Musicological Society; n.p.: International Musicological Society, 1984). *Doctoral Dissertations in Musicology*, 2nd ser., 2nd cumulative ed., ed. by Cecil Adkins and Alis Dickinson (Philadelphia: American Musicological Society; n.p.: International Musicological Society, 1996).

33. See the following notes for descriptions of these resources.

34. *RILM Abstracts of Music Literature* (New York: RILM, 1967–), annual. The web version of RILM is available by subscription through OCLC FirstSearch service (OCLC Reference Services, 6565 Frantz Rd., Dublin, OH 43017, www.oclc.org), on the SilverPlatter platform from Ovid Technologies

Notes (continued)

(Ovid Technologies, 100 River Ridge Dr., Norwood, MA 02062, www.ovid.com), and through NISC BiblioLine service (National Information Services Corp., 3100 Saint Paul St., Baltimore, MD 21218, www.nisc.com). NISC also produces a CD-ROM version, *MuSe: Music Search.* Subscription to annual print volumes of *RILM Abstracts* are available from the RILM International Center, City University of New York, 365 Fifth Ave., New York, NY 10016-4309.

35. ProQuest Digital Dissertations, wwwlib.umi.com/dissertations. Canadian theses have been listed by UMI since 1990, and UMI is their designated distributor. Earlier Canadian theses can be purchased in microfiche format from the Canadian Theses Service of the National Library of Canada, 395 Wellington St., Ottawa K1A 0N4, e-mail: theses@nlc-bnc.ca. Canadian theses since 1947 have been listed in *Canadian Theses = Thèses canadiennes, 1947–1960*, 2 vols. (Ottawa: National Library of Canada, 1973), with annual or semiannual microfiche supplements. Bibliographic citations for Canadian theses are found also in AMICUS Web, the online union catalog of twenty-two million bibliographic records held by more than 500 Canadian Libraries, including the National Library of Canada: www.nlc-bnc.ca/7/2/index-e.html.

36. Every issue of *Dissertation Abstracts International, Section A: Humanities and Social Sciences* (Ann Arbor, MI: UMI, 1969–) includes a list of participating institutions.

37. Eda Kuhn Loeb Music Library of the Harvard College Library, "Collections in the Isham Memorial Library: Harvard Dissertations in Music," http://hcl.harvard.edu/loebmusic/isham-collections.html.

38. Stanford University Libraries, "Dissertations and Theses," http://library.stanford.edu/depts/ssrg/econ/dissertations.html.

39. Mary Ruth Yoe, "Bound to Change," *University of Chicago Magazine* 9, no. 4 (April 2001), http://magazine.uchicago.edu/0104/features/bound.html.

40. www.copyright.gov/title17/chapter01.pdf.

41. Consult the UMI website for current cost for each format, which includes all handling and shipping charges. Nonacademic customers pay about 45 percent more for printed dissertations than do academic customers.

42. A 1992 study comparing the titles of 371 master's theses on nonliterary subjects with their assigned Library of Congress subject headings found that 36 percent did not include the first word of the principal assigned subject headings in their titles. See Barbara Keller, "Subject Content through Title: A Master's Theses Matching Study at Indiana State University," *Cataloging & Classification Quarterly* 15, no. 3 (1992): 69–80.

43. For description of national and subject guides to dissertations, the reader is directed to Michael M. Reynolds, *Guide to Theses and Dissertations: An International Bibliography of Bibliographies*, rev. and enl. ed. (Phoenix, AZ: Oryx Press, 1985), which includes sixty-nine entries under the heading "music"; and to "Dissertations" in *Guide to Reference Books*, 11th ed., edited by Robert Balay (Chicago; London: ALA, 1996), 274–81.

Notes (continued)

44. British Thesis Service, The British Library Document Supply Centre, Boston Spa, Wetherby, LS23 7BQ, UK, www.bl.uk/britishthesis, where theses can be ordered online; e-mail: dsc-british-thesis-service@bl.uk.

45. *Index to Theses with Abstracts Accepted for Higher Degrees by the Universities of Great Britain and Ireland and the Council for National Academic Awards* (London: Aslib, 1950–). The online database at www.theses. com is available *only* by subscription to the paper format. Subscription information to the printed version is at the website, as is a demonstration subset, FAQs, and a list of contributing universities and colleges.

46. According to Friedrich-Adolf Schmidt-Künsemüller, "Ein LIBER-Seminar über Dissertationsfragen," in *Zentrale und kooperative Dienstleistung in Bibliothekswesen: Vorträge, gehalten auf dem 65. Deutschen Bibliothekartag vom 20. bis 24. Mai 1975 in Konstanz*, ed. by Fritz Junginger and Wilhelm Totok, Zeitschrift für Bibliothekswesen und Bibliographie, Sonderheft 22 (Frankfurt: V. Klostermann, 1976), 127.

47. See the requirements ("Rechtsgrundlagen für die Ablieferung der Dissertationsexemplare") posted at the Free University Library's website: www. ub.fu-berlin.de/service/benutzung_bereiche/hochschulschriften/rechtsgrund.html. General information about doctoral course programs in European countries, including dissertation publication and deposit requirements, is in Oleg Kouptsov, *The Doctorate in the Europe Region*, CEPES Studies on Higher Education (Bucharest: UNESCO, Centre européen pour l'enseignement supérieur, 1994). For a broader discussion of dissertation production, distribution, and access in Britain, Germany, and France, see John B. Rutledge, "European Dissertations: Production, Access, and Use," *Collection Management* 19 (1994): 43–67. For a snapshot of dissertation requirements, sales, and lending policies of specific degree-granting institutions worldwide, see D. H. Borchardt and J. D. Thawley, *Guide to the Availability of Theses*, IFLA Publications 17 (Munich; New York: K. G. Saur, 1981); and G. G. Allen and K. Deubert, *Guide to the Availability of Theses II: Non-University Institutions*, IFLA Publications 29 (Munich; New York: K. G. Saur, 1984), which includes information about several music conservatories.

48. Collections, including dissertation holdings, are described in *The Directory of University Libraries in Europe* (London: Europa, 2000).

49. l'Atelier national de reproduction des thèses, 9 rue Auguste Angellier, 59046 Lille Cedex, France; e-mail: anrt@univ-lille3.fr.

50. *Catalogue des thèses reproduites, 1971–1986* (Lille: LNRT, 1993).

51. See ANRT's thrice-yearly *Catalogue des thèses reproduites* for 2000. The atelier's catalog is now available online at www.anrtheses.com.fr.

52. SUDOC (2000–), http://corail.sudoc.abes.fr. Prior to implementation of SUDOC, the standard source for verification of recent French theses was the semiannual CD-ROM database *DocThèses: Le catalogue des thèses soutenues dans les universités françaises* (Paris: Chadwyck-Healey, in cooperation with Le ministère de l'enseignement supérieur et de la recherche, and with l'Agence

Notes (continued)

bibliographique de l'enseignement supérieur, 1998–2001), which indexed more than 300,000 theses in all disciplines produced 1972–2000. *DocThèses* listed the libraries holding each thesis, with practical information needed to borrow copies. The database also was briefly available 1999–2001 on the web as ThèseNet; it was withdrawn from service when superseded by SUDOC.

53. Jean Gribenski, *Thèses de doctorat en langue française relatives à la musique: Bibliographie commentée = French Language Dissertations in Music: An Annotated Bibliography*, RILM Retrospectives 2 (New York: Pendragon, 1979).

54. Fichier central des thèses (FCT), Université de Paris X, 200 avenue de la république, FD92001 Nanterre Cedex, France. Fax: 01 40 97 73 60. A detailed description (in French only) of the file and its management is at the FCT website: www.fct.u-paris10.fr.

55. *Hochschulschriften 1945–1997* (Frankfurt: Buchhändler-Vereinigung, 1998), CD-ROM.

56. Deutsche Bibliothek, http://dbf-opac.ddb.de/index_e.htm.

57. *Bibliographie Darstellende Kunst und Musik: Deutschsprachige Hochschulschriften und Veröffentlichungen ausserhalb des Buchhandels 1966–1980*, 3 vols., ed. by Margareth Wolf (Munich; New York: Saur, 1991). Richard Schaal, *Verzeichnis deutschsprachiger musikwissenschaftlicher Dissertationen 1861–1960*, Musikwissenschaftliche Arbeiten 19 (Kassel: Bärenreiter, 1963); and his *Verzeichnis deutschsprachiger musikwissenschaftlicher Dissertationen 1961–1970, mit Ergänzungen zum Verzeichnis 1861–1960*, Musikwissenschaftliche Arbeiten 25 (Kassel: Bärenreiter, 1974).

58. Dissertationsmeldestelle der Gesellschaft der Musikforschung, http://musikwiss.uni-muenster.de.

59. TESEO, www.mcu.es/TESEO/teseo.html.

60. An exception is the Australian Digital Theses Program, established in 1998–1999 by seven Australian universities as a way of distributing electronic versions of theses on the web, and now open to all Australian universities. About this program, see http://adt.caul.edu.au. About electronic theses and dissertations in general, see below.

61. "Dissertations," in Vincent Duckles and Ida Reed, *Music Reference and Research Materials: An Annotated Bibliography*, 5th ed. (New York: Schirmer Books, 1997), 188–91. Michael M. Reynolds, "Music," in *Guide to Theses and Dissertations: An International Bibliography of Bibliographies*, rev. and enl. ed. (Phoenix, AZ: Oryx Press, 1985), 119–23.

62. *The Directory of Music Research Libraries*, Rita Benton, general ed., International Inventory of Musical Sources, ser. C (Kassel: Bärenreiter, 1979– ; preliminary edition of vols. 1–3, Iowa City: University of Iowa, 1967–1972); see the bibliography for contents of individual volumes. *The Directory of University Libraries in Europe* (London: Europa, 2000). *The World of Learning* (London: Allen & Unwin, 1947–).

Notes (continued)

63. Center for Research Libraries, 6050 S. Kenwood Ave., Chicago, IL 60637-2804, www.crl.uchicago.edu.

64. Choose the "Search Collection Databases" link on the center's home page, then "Dissertations Database." At the end of 2003, a search of the database using only the term "music" in the subject field returned 149 titles.

65. Edward A. Fox, John L. Eaton, Gail McMillan, Neill A. Kipp, Laura Weiss, Emilio Arce, and Scott Guyer, "National Digital Library of Theses and Dissertations: A Scalable and Sustainable Approach to Unlock University Resources," *D-Lib Magazine* (September 1996), www.dlib.org/dlib/september96/theses/09fox.html.

66. For full description and links to members, and to browse the NDLTD union catalog, go to www.ndltd.org.

67. "Guide to Electronic Theses and Dissertations," http://etdguide.org.

68. For a brief history of ETDs as of 2003, and a discussion of some of the issues related to access, see Yale Fineman, "Electronic Theses and Dissertations," *portal: Libraries and the Academy* 3, no. 2 (April 2003): 219–27, http://muse.jhu.edu/journals/portal_libraries_and_the_academy/toc/pla3.2.html; and Fineman, "Electronic Theses and Dissertations in Music," *Notes* 60 (2004): 893–907.

GLOSSARY

This glossary defines terms and abbreviations that are frequently encountered in music publishers' literature, that are printed on their publications, and that are used in music bibliographies and catalogs. Foreign-language as well as English terms are included. Words accompanied by an asterisk are defined within this glossary. Some definitions have been adapted from other sources, including Suzanne E. Thorin and Carole Franklin Vidali, *The Acquisition and Cataloging of Music and Sound Recordings: A Glossary*, MLA Technical Reports No. 11 (Canton, MA: Music Library Association, 1984); Meredith Moon, "Glossary of Terms," in *Rules for Full Cataloging,* comp. by Virginia Cunningham, Code international de catalogage de la musique 3 (Frankfurt; New York: C. F. Peters, 1971), 73–85; Stanley Boorman, "Glossary," in *Music Printing and Publishing,* ed. by D. W. Krummel and Stanley Sadie, The Norton/Grove Handbooks in Music (New York: W. W. Norton, 1990), 489–550; and Jan LaRue and Jeanette B. Holland, "Biblioprotocol: With a Brief Glossary of Terms Often Needed in Austrian and German Music Libraries," *Notes* 42 (1985): 29–35. For the English equivalents of musical terms in six other languages, see *Terminorum musicae index septem linguis redactus = Polyglot Dictionary of Musical Terms: English, German, French, Italian, Spanish, Hungarian, Russian,* 2nd ed., ed. by Horst Leuchtmann (Budapest: Akadémiai Kiadó, for the International Association of Music Libraries, and the International Musicological Society, 1980).

Abhandlung: *Ger.* Treatise, essay.

Abteilung (Abt.): *Ger.* Section, unit, subgroup; used to identify a subdivision in some published sets and series emanating from German-language countries.

accompaniment (acc.): The musical background that is provided for a principal *part or parts, such as the piano or other instrument(s) played with a solo vocalist or instrumentalist.

adaptateur: *Fre.* *Arranger.

adaptation: A musical work that is a distinct alteration of all or part of another work. It paraphrases or varies melodies or fragments of the original work, and can incorporate new material. *See also* **arrangement.**

alquiler: *Spa.* Rental.

Alt: *Ger.* Alto, or low voice.

Anhang: *Ger.* Supplement, appendix.

Anmerkung: *Ger.* Annotation, comment.

archi: *Ita. pl.* *Strings.

arrangement (arr.): (1) A musical work rewritten for a different medium of performance than that for which it was originally intended. (2) A simplified version of a work for the original medium of performance. Arrangements may be written by the original composer, or by another. *See also* **adaptation.**

arranger (arr.): Strictly, one who creates an *arrangement. Often used loosely for one who makes any kind of modification.

audiocassette: A permanently encased *audiotape that winds from reel to reel. *See also* **reel-to-reel.**

audiotape: A sound recording on magnetic tape.

Aufdruck: *Ger.* Imprint.

Aufführungsmaterial: *Ger.* Performance material, *parts.

Auflage (Aufl.): *Ger.* *Issue.

Aufzeichnung: *Ger.* Recording.

Ausgabe (Ausg.): *Ger.* *Edition.

ausgewählte (ausg.): *Ger. adj.* Selected

Auswahl: *Ger.* Selection.

B: *Ger.* B-flat (pitch or key signature). *See also* **H.**

band: (1) An instrumental group comprised principally of *woodwinds, *brasses, and *percussion instruments. (2) A section of one side of a *long playing sound disc; may contain a single work or a part of a work. (3) *Ger.* **(Bd.)** Volume.

bajo continuo: *Spa. See* **basso continuo.**

basse continue: *Fre. See* **basso continuo.**

basso continuo (b.c.): *Eng.* and *Ita.*; **basse continue** *Fre.*; **bajo continuo** *Spa.*; **Generalbaß** *Ger.* A shorthand method used ca. 1600–1750 of notating an accompanying part with the bass notes only, and figures indicating the intervals and chords to be played above the bass line; normally performed by two instrumentalists (a keyboard or plucked instrument playing the bass line and harmonies, and a sustaining bass instrument doubling the bass line), and in modern editions usually requiring two separate printed *parts. Also known as thoroughbass, figured bass.

batterie: *Fre.* *Percussion.

b.c.: Abbreviation for *basso continuo.

Bd.: *Ger.* Abbreviation for *Band (volume).

Bearbeiter (Bearb.): *Ger.* Arranger, reviser.

Bearbeitung (Bearb.): *Ger.* Arrangement, adaptation.

Begleitung (Begl.): *Ger.* Accompaniment.

Beiheft: *Ger.* Supplement.

Bestellnummer (Best.-Nr.): *Ger.* *Publisher's number.

Bestellung: *Ger.* Order (merchandise).

Bildtonträger: *Ger.* Music video recording.

Bläser: *Ger. pl.* Players of *winds, the wind section.

Bläsinstrumente: *Ger. pl.* *Wind instruments.

Blechblasinstrumente: *Ger. pl.* *Brasses.

book: *See* **libretto.**

bootleg: An illegal recording of material not available commercially; bootlegs usually contain live performances or unreleased recording-studio outtakes. *See also* **pirate**.

brasses: (1) Instruments, whether made of brass or other material, on which sound is produced by vibration of the lips. (2) Colloquial designation for the brass section of the orchestra, of a brass quintet, a brass quartet, etc., including generally the French horn, trumpet, trombone, and tuba.

cahier: *Fre.* A small volume or booklet.

camera: *Ita.* Chamber, as in *musica da camera* (*chamber music).

canto: *Ita.* Singing, song.

cassette: *See* **audiocassette** and **videocassette**.

catalog: *See* **current catalog, deep catalog,** and **recent catalog.**

chamber music: Music for two or more solo performers, each performer playing a separate *part; generally understood to exclude vocal music, music for a single performer, and music for ten or more performers.

chamber orchestra: *See* **orchestra.**

chanson: *Fre.* Song.

chant: (1) *Fre.* Singing, song. (2) *Eng.* General designation for monophonic liturgical music similar to plainsong.

chœur: *Fre.* *Chorus, choir.

Chor: *Ger.* *Chorus, choir.

choral octavo: *See* **octavo.**

chord diagrams: Frames of lines that simulate the strings and frets of a *plucked instrument, with dots showing placement of the fingers thereon. Usually used in conjunction with *chord symbols, and often with conventional two-stave piano notation as well. Common in editions of popular music.

chord notation: *Chord diagrams and *chord symbols used together.

chord symbols: Abbreviated descriptions of chords, consisting usually of pitch names with qualifiers to indicate minor, diminished, augmented, seventh-chords, etc., similar to the abbreviations used in *basso continuo. Common in editions of popular music. Usually used in conjunction with *chord diagrams, and often with conventional two-stave piano notation.

Chorpartitur: *Ger.* *Chorus score.

chorus: A large vocal ensemble, usually one not connected with a church.

chorus part: For a vocal work that contains chorus, an edition that contains only the music that the chorus sings, each chorus line printed as a separate *part, i.e., a separate part for sopranos, a separate part for altos, etc.

chorus score: For a vocal work that contains chorus, an edition that contains only the music that the chorus sings, printed in *score format, without an accompaniment unless it is in the form of a piano reduction.

clarinet quintet (quartet): Sometimes used imprecisely to refer to a clarinet soloist with four (or three) accompanying string instruments; may also refer to an ensemble of five (or four) members of the clarinet family.

close score: An edition of vocal music with all vocal parts printed on two staves, as hymns; the vocal equivalent of an instrumental condensed score.

collected edition, collected works: An edition of a composer's works that strives to be complete and authentic. Usually does not include separate *parts. Typically published in multiple volumes over an extended period of time.

commercial recording: A sound recording produced for retail sale.

condensed score: An edition of instrumental music with the principal instrumental parts printed on a minimum number of staves, usually two to four, with exact instrumentation shown by verbal indications among the staves; common in band music editions; the instrumental equivalent of a vocal *close score. Also called *particella*, "short score."

conductor's score: A *score of the complete music of a work, of sufficient size to be read by a conductor when placed on the conductor's music stand during rehearsal and performance. Sometimes called a "full score," though, strictly speaking, *miniature scores are also "full" in that they contain the complete music of a work.

continuo: *See* **basso continuo**.

cordes: *Fre. pl.* *Strings.

cotage: *Fre.* Used for both *plate number and *publisher's number.

critical edition: *See* **definitive edition**.

cuerdas: *Spa. pl.* *Strings.

cuivres: *Fre. pl.* *Brasses.

current catalog: In the recording industry, recordings in release for less than 18 months. *See also* **deep catalog** and **recent catalog**.

cutouts: (1) Discontinued or overstock recordings sold in bulk to record retailers for resale at reduced prices; items are "cut out" (the container is defaced, usually with a hole or a notch) to prevent retailers from selling them at full value, or returning them to the *labels for credit. (2) Promotional releases ("promos"), marked in the same way as the above or with a "not for sale" stamp or label, distributed to reviewers, retailers, and radio stations for advertising purposes.

cycle: A group of related compositions intended as a musical entity; usually performed, published, and recorded together in the order specified by the composer; common in song literature.

deep catalog: In the recording industry, recordings in release for more than three years. *See also* **current catalog** and **recent catalog**.

definitive edition: An edition of a work or works that the publisher and editor(s) claim to be authentic and true to the intentions of the composer(s); sometimes includes historical and analytical notes that evaluate and interpret the surviving manuscripts and early printed sources. *Collected editions and *historical editions are usually definitive editions. Extracts from definitive editions are sometimes published in different formats as *practical editions.

deleted: Out of print (recording).

Denkmal (*pl.* **Denkmäler**): *Ger.* Monument (of music). *See* **historical edition**.

Dirigierpartitur: *Ger.* *Conductor's score.

discography: A list of sound recordings, often including descriptions of their contents, performance data, publisher numbers, or similar information.

disque numérique: *Fre.* Digital disc, compact disc.

disque optique numérique: *Fre.* Digital optical disc, CD-ROM.

dur: *Ger.* Major (key), as in A-dur (A major).

DVD-A: Abbreviation for *DVD-Audio.

DVD-Audio (DVD-A): A digital audio recording format on 4¾ inch discs providing very high quality surround sound, plus additional features such as images, video, and limited interactivity, that are not available on conventional compact discs; for optimum sound, must be played on DVD-Audio players; most DVD-Audio discs can be played on DVD-Video players; not playable on compact-disc players. *See also* **Super Audio CD.**

edition: (1) A work prepared for publication. (2) All the copies of a work produced from the same plates, setting of type, or master copy, and distributed by a particular publisher; variations in binding, title page wording, and other secondary features do not alone constitute a new edition. *See also* **issue.**

édition pratique: *Fre.* *Practical edition.

8⁰: Abbreviation for *octavo.

8vo: Abbreviation for *octavo.

enrigstrement: *Fre.* Recording.

entgültige Ausgabe: *Ger.* *Definitive edition.

Erscheinungsdatum: *Ger.* Publication date.

Erstausgabe: *Ger.* First edition.

Erstdruck: *Ger.* First printing.

Erste Auflage: *Ger.* First printing.

excerpt: A portion of a complete musical work (e.g., an aria from an opera, a movement of a sonata) that is published or performed separately.

extrait: *Fre.* *Excerpt.

facsimile: Strictly, a reproduction of an original manuscript or edition that is true in every respect, including size and color; used loosely for editions that may vary in size and color from the originals, and that may be "touched up" to remove apparent imperfections, or to redraw images that are faint in the originals.

Fassung: *Ger.* Version.

fiati: *Ita. pl.* *Winds.

figured bass: *See* **basso continuo**.

folio (f., fol.): (1) A printed collection of music featuring (usually) popular songs composed by, or associated with, a particular performer or musical group (a "personality folio" or "celebrity folio"), a particular album release (a "matching folio"), a particular topic (a "concept folio"), or featuring songs by different songwriters, popularized by different artists (a "mixed folio"). (2) A leaf of a volume that is numbered on only one side (the recto), and referenced usually in the form "fols. 15r–16v," i.e., folio 15 recto through folio 16 verso. (3) In bibliographic contexts, a volume in which the original printed sheets have been folded only once to form its consituent leaves.

4⁰: Abbreviation for *quarto.

4to: Abbreviation for *quarto.

Führer: *Ger.* Guidebook.

full score: *See* **conductor's score**.

gebunden (geb.): *Ger.* Bound.

Generalbaß: *Ger. See* **basso continuo**.

gesamt: *Ger.* Complete, as in *Gesamtaufnahme* (complete recording), *Gesamtausgabe* (complete edition, *collected edition).

H: *Ger.* B-natural (pitch or key). *See also* **B**.

Harmoniemusik: *Ger.* Music for *wind instruments, music for *band.

Heft: *Ger.* Small book, part, number.

herausgeben, herausgegeben (hrsg., hg.): *Ger.* Edited.

Herausgeber (Hrsg., Hg.): *Ger.* Editor.

historical edition, historical set: A collection of works by multiple composers illustrating the musical style of a given period or aspect of music history, or national or cultural group; usually does not include separate *parts; typically published in multiple volumes over an extended period of time; often called a "monument" of music (the equivalent German term *Denkmal* is commonly used by English speakers).

hohe Stimme: *Ger.* High voice, as a soprano (female) or tenor (male).

Holzblasinstrumente: *Ger. pl.* *Woodwinds.

horn quintet (quartet): Sometimes used imprecisely to refer to a French horn soloist with four (or three) accompanying string instruments; may also refer to an ensemble of five (or four) horns.

International Standard Music Number (ISMN): A four-part ten-character standard type of *publisher number for printed music that identifies an edition uniquely; begins with "M," followed by a numerical identifier for the publisher, a numerical identifier for the publisher's edition, and finally a checkdigit.

ISMN: Abbreviation for *International Standard Music Number.

issue: All the copies of an *edition that are prepared under the same printing arrangement, and whose production details are intended to be uniform. *See also* **edition.**

Kammer: *Ger.* Chamber, as in *Kammermusik* (*chamber music), *Kammerorchester* (chamber *orchestra).

Klavierauszug: *Ger.* *Piano reduction.

Klavierpartitur: *Ger.* (1) A *piano score. (2) A *performance score for piano.

Kreis: *Ger.* *Cycle, as in *Liederkreis* (song cycle).

kritische Berichte: *Ger.* Critical commentary printed as a supplement to an *edition; may be printed separately or bound with the music.

Künster: *Ger.* Artist, performer.

label: In popular usage, the name or trademark of a company that publishes sound recordings.

laser disc: A 12-inch disc holding analog video signals and digital audio signals that are read by a laser; also called "videodisc." Not to be confused with DVD or CD-ROM, 4¾-inch discs which also are read by a laser.

Leihmaterial: *Ger.* Rental material.

libretto: The literary text of an extended vocal work such as an opera or musical comedy; not generally used for choral works; may be published as part of the music edition, apart from the music, or in a booklet that accompanies a recording. In a musical comedy, the scenario and spoken dialogue are sometimes referred to as its "book," and the texts of the songs as its *lyrics.

Lied (*pl.* **Lieder**): *Ger.* Song.

livre: *Fre.* Volume.

livret: *Fre.* *Libretto.

location: *Fre.* Rental.

long playing sound disc (LP): An analog sound disc, usually 12 inches (30 cm) in diameter, to be played at 33⅓ revolutions per minute (rpm).

LP: Abbreviation for *long playing sound disc.

lyric(s): The text of a song, particularly a popular song, including those in musical comedies.

material (*Spa.*), **materiale** (*Ita.*), **matériel** (*Fre.*): All of the *parts required by instrumentalists and vocalists to perform a musical work.

mehrstimmig: *Ger.* Multivoice, multipart.

metales: *Spa. pl.* *Brasses.

Mietmaterial: *Ger.* Rental material.

miniature score (m.s.): A *score of the complete music of a work, reduced in size for study purposes rather than for performing or conducting. Also called "study score," "pocket score."

mittlere Stimme: *Ger.* Medium voice, as a mezzo-soprano (female) or baritone (male).

moll: *Ger.* Minor (key), as in G-moll (G minor).

monument: *See* **historical edition**.

movement: A complete section of a symphony, sonata, etc., usually of a character and tempo distinct from other sections of the work, and sometimes with its own title. When separately published or performed, a movement is considered an *excerpt.

m.s.: Abbreviation for *miniature score.

noleggio: *Ita.* Rental.

noncommercial recording: A sound recording produced usually in a limited number of copies for nonretail distribution. Also called "private recording."

oboe quintet (quartet): Sometimes used imprecisely to refer to an oboe soloist with four (or three) accompanying string instruments; may also refer to an ensemble of five (or four) members of the oboe family.

octavo (8⁰, 8vo): Used to define the format of a book in which a sheet of paper, after printing, is folded three times to produce eight leaves or sixteen pages per gathering; used loosely to indicate the approximate size of a printed edition (ca. 10½ x 7½ inches, or 27 x 19 cm) resulting from such folding. In music publishing, "choral octavo" is often used to refer to editions of choral music of this approximate size, but no longer indicates the number of resulting pages (i.e., sixteen) in a gathering.

œuvre (œuv.): *Fre.* A (musical) work. *See also* **opus number**.

opera (op. *pl.* **opere):** *Ita.* A (musical) work. *See also* **opus number**.

Operntext: *Ger.* *Libretto.

opus (op.; *pl.* **opera):** *Lat.* A (musical) work. The *collected edition of a composer's works is sometimes titled or called the *Opera omnia* (all the works). *See also* **opus number**.

opus number (op.): A number assigned to a musical work by its composer or publisher often to indicate the work's chronological place in the composer's total output. Not all composers use opus numbers; on editions of works by those who do, "opus" (or "op.") or its equivalent in another language—*œuvre* (*Fre.*), *opera* (*Ita.*), *Werk* (*Ger.*)—may be used to identify the work being published.

Opuszahl: *Ger.* *Opus number.

Orchesterbesetzung: *Ger.* Orchestration, instrumentation.

orchestra: A large performing ensemble of bowed *strings with more than one performer to a *part, to which *winds and *percussion may be added as required for the musical work being performed; also known as a "full orchestra," "symphony orchestra"; since the mid-19th century, has normally meant an ensemble of about 100 instruments led by a conductor. A "string orchestra" does not include winds. A "chamber orchestra" is a small orchestra of about twenty-five players; most orchestras before about 1800 were of this size.

organ-vocal score: *See* **vocal score.**

ottoni: *Ita. pl.* *Brasses.

part: (1) The music for any one voice or instrument that contributes to the texture of a musical work. (2) The visual representation, commonly printed or written, of (usually) one such part for use by (usually) one performer. (3) Abbreviation for *partition*, *Partitur*, or *partitura* (*score).

partbooks: The manuscript or printed *parts for fifteenth- and sixteenth-century polyphonic music.

particella: *Fre., Ger., Ita., Spa.* Short score. *See* **condensed score.**

partition de poche: *Fre.* Pocket score, *miniature score.

partition (part.): *Fre.* *Score.

partitura (part.): *Ita.* *Score.

Partitur (Part.): *Ger.* *Score.

percussion: (1) Instruments that are sounded by shaking or by striking one object with another. (2) The percussion section of a performing ensemble.

performance score: A full *score intended for use in place of a *part during performance. In *chamber music that includes piano, the pianist normally plays from a performance score, while the other players use separate parts. Rhythmically complex chamber-music works sometimes use this format for all the players. Also known as a "playing score."

piano quartet: (1) Music written for violin, viola, cello, and piano. (2) An ensemble made up of these instruments.

piano quintet: (1) Music written for *string quartet and piano. (2) An ensemble made up of these instruments.

piano reduction: An edition in which most of the *parts (usually the instrumental parts of an *orchestra) are arranged for a piano; used to accompany vocalists or instrumental soloist(s) in rehearsal; sometimes used for a *piano score.

piano score: An orchestral score reduced to a version for piano, on two staves. *See also* **piano reduction**.

piano trio: (1) Music written for violin, cello, and piano. (2) An ensemble made up of these instruments.

piano-vocal score: *See* **vocal score**.

pirate: An illegal copy of an existing commercially released recording; it usually is as accurate a duplication of the existing recording as possible, as the intent is to deceive the buyer. *See also* **bootleg**.

plate number (pl. no.): A number assigned by a publisher or engraver, printed at the bottom of each page of music, and sometimes on the title page as well; may include letters as well as numbers. *See also* **publisher's number**.

Plattennummer: *Ger.* *Plate number.

playing score: *See* **performance score**.

plucked instruments: Instruments on which sound is produced by pulling and releasing stretched cords with the fingers or a pick.

pocket score: *See* **miniature score**.

practical edition: An *edition intended for performance rather than study, and which therefore omits extensive historical and critical notes in favor of editorial suggestions for performance, such as fingerings, phrasings, and dynamics. Such editions sometimes are reissues in a different format of works from a *definitive edition.

praktische Ausgabe: *Ger.* *Practical edition.

private recording: *See* **noncommercial recording**.

promos: *See* **cutouts**.

publisher's number (pub. no.): A number assigned by a publisher, and printed on the cover, title page, and/or first page of music of a score; may include letters as well as numbers. *See also* **plate number** and **International Standard Music Number**.

quarto (4°, 4to): A volume in which the original printed sheets have been folded twice to form its consituent leaves, thus giving pages one-quarter the size of the sheet.

realization: In editions of music that use *basso continuo, a *part for the keyboard or other chordal instrument that has the bass notes and figures of the original converted by the editor to fully notated harmonies, rhythms, embellishments, etc.

recent catalog: In the recording industry, albums in release for more than 18 months, but less than 36 months, except for jazz and classical, which count as recent catalog after 12 months. *See also* **current catalog** and **deep catalog**.

reel-to-reel: Relating to or utilizing magnetic tape that requires threading on an exposed take-up reel. *See also* **audiocassette**, **videocassette**.

registrazione: *Ita.* Recording.

Reihe: *Ger.* Series.

reissue: The releasing of a work subsequent to the original release, usually by a publisher other than the original one. *See also* **rerelease**.

release: A sound recording issued (published) generally for the first time.

release date: The publication date of a sound recording.

rerelease: A second or subsequent release of a sound recording by its original publisher. *See also* **reissue**.

reversgebunden (reversgeb.): *Ger.* Rental.

Revisionsbericht: *Ger.* Editor's report, editor's notes.

SACD: Abbreviation for *Super Audio CD.

Sammlung: *Ger.* Collection.

sämtliche Werke: *Ger.* *Collected edition.

Satz: *Ger.* (1) *Movement. (2) Setting, composition.

Schallplatte: *Ger.* Sound disc.

Schlagzeug: *Ger.* *Percussion.

score: (1) A visual representation of a musical work, usually printed or written, in which all of the two or more *parts of an ensemble that are supposed to be heard simultaneously are aligned vertically, each part on a separate staff. The placement of each part in the score—the "score order"—is normally arranged beginning at the top with *woodwinds, then *brasses, *percussion, *plucked instruments, voices, and *strings; within each instrumental group the instruments are placed from the top according to tessitura, from high to low; solo instruments in concertos are placed above the strings. *See also* **chorus score, close score, condensed score, conductor's score, miniature score, vocal score.** (2) In casual use, all music editions are sometimes referred to as scores, as distinguished from writings about music, and recordings.

score order: *See* **score.**

set of parts: The complete number of instrumental and/or vocal *parts required to perform a musical work. In catalogs of orchestral music, the term usually means one copy of each musical part, including only one of each string part, though some publishers and vendors sell orchestral music in "sets" with a predetermined number of multiple string parts.

sheet music: (1) Unbound songs, piano pieces, etc., of up to eight pages of printed music, the usual printed format for popular songs up until the late twentieth century. (2) Sometimes used imprecisely to refer to any kind of printed music, as distinguished from recorded music.

short score: *See* **condensed score.**

Signatur: *Ger.* Call number, shelfmark.

Sonderreihe: *Ger.* Separate series, supplementary series.

Spielpartitur: *Ger.* *Performance score.

Stimme: *Ger.* Voice, *part.

Streicher: *Ger. pl.* *Strings.

string orchestra: *See* **orchestra**.

string quartet: (1) Music written for two violins, viola, and cello. (2) An ensemble made up of these instruments.

string trio: (1) Music written for violin, viola, and cello. (2) An ensemble made up of these instruments.

strings: (1) Instruments on which sound is produced by vibration of taut cords; usually reserved for instruments of the violin family (violin, viola, cello, double bass). (2) Colloquial designation for the stringed section of the orchestra, of a string trio, a string quartet, etc.

Stück: *Ger.* Piece (of music).

Studienpartitur: *Ger.* Study score, *miniature score.

study score: *See* **miniature score**.

Super Audio CD (SACD): A digital recording format on 4¾ inch discs providing very high quality audio and optional surround sound; requires a SACD player, though some SACD discs are hybrids that include a CD audio layer that will play on conventional CD players, albeit at CD quality; conventional CDs can be played on SACD players. *See also* **DVD-Audio**.

Taschenpartitur: *Ger.* *Miniature score.

Teil (T. or **Tl.):** *Ger.* A section or component of a published set or series.

Textbuch: *Ger.* *Libretto.

thematic catalog: A listing of a composer's works, arranged chronologically or by types of compositions, with the opening musical theme of each work or movement given in musical notation. The compiler of a thematic catalog may devise a unique numbering system for the composer's works (e.g., "K." numbers assigned to the works of Wolfgang Amadeus Mozart by Ludwig Koechel, the compiler of the thematic catalog of Mozart's compositions); these numbers often are used in catalogs and bibliographies, and on published editions to identify precisely the work(s) in the editions.

thoroughbass: *See* **basso continuo**.

tiefe Stimme: *Ger.* Low voice, as a contralto (usually female) or bass (male).

Tonaufzeichnung: *Ger.* Sound recording.

Tonband: *Ger.* Tape.

Tonträger: *Ger.* Sound recording.

transposition: The rewriting of a composition at a higher or lower pitch than that specified by the composer; commonly used for multiple *editions of songs (e.g., high, medium, and low voice editions) to facilitate performance by singers with differing voice ranges.

trio sonata: A type of *chamber music of the baroque era, written in three *parts (two upper parts of similar range, plus a *basso continuo part); normally performed by four instrumentalists, and modern editions normally include four printed parts.

Übersetzung: *Ger.* Translation.

Übertragung: *Ger.* *Transcription, *arrangement.

unaccompanied (unacc.): Vocal or solo instrumental works, other than solo piano, intended to be performed without accompanying instruments.

Urtext: *Ger.* Literally, original text. First used in the late nineteenth century for editions claimed to be free of editorial intervention, such as added tempo and dynamic markings, fingerings, etc.; used since the mid-twentieth century by some publishers to mean a *definitive edition. The term now is disparaged by scholars because of its commercialization, and because "Urtext" editions no longer present composers' original texts, but editors' reconstructions of them. See James Grier, "Editing," *Grove Music Online*, www.grovemusic.com, at I: "Historical Attitudes."

vents: *Fre. pl.* *Winds.

Verlag, Verleger (Verl.): *Ger.* Publisher.

Verlagsnummer: *Ger.* (1) *Publisher's number. (2) Numerical part of an *International Standard Music Number that identifies the publisher of a given music edition.

videocassette: A permanently encased *videotape that winds from reel to reel. *See also* **reel-to-reel**.

videodisc: *See* **laser disc**.

videotape: A video recording on magnetic tape.

vocal score (v.s.): For a chorus and/or solo voice(s) work with instrumental accompaniment other than a keyboard, an edition that includes all music for the voice(s), printed in score format, with instrumental accompaniment reduced for a keyboard. Sometimes called "piano-vocal score," or "organ-vocal score." Not used for a work originally written for voice(s) with a keyboard accompaniment.

Werk: *Ger.* A (musical) work. *See also* **opus number**.

Werkgruppe (Wg.): *Ger.* Literally, work group; used in some *collected editions emanating from German-language publishers to identify a subdivision by type of composition (e.g. orchestral works, dramatic works, etc.).

Werkzahl: *Ger.* *Opus number.

wind quintet: (1) Music written for flute, oboe, clarinet, horn, and bassoon. (2) An ensemble made up of these instruments; also called "woodwind quintet," even though the horn is a member of the brass family of instruments.

winds: The *brasses and *woodwinds collectively.

woodwind quintet: *See* **wind quintet**.

woodwinds: (1) Instruments, whether made of wood or metal, on which sound is produced by vibration of a reed, or by air passing across a fixed obstruction. (2) Colloquial designation for the woodwind section of the orchestra, or the instruments of a woodwind quartet, a woodwind trio, etc., generally including the flute and piccolo, oboe and English horn, clarinet and bass clarinet, saxophone, bassoon and contrabassoon.

Zyklus: *Ger.* *Cycle.

SELECTED BIBLIOGRAPHY

Contents

Music Acquisitions Resources

    Manuals of Music Librarianship   197
    Journals of Music Librarianship   198
    Music Editing, Publishing, and Library Acquisitions   199
    Directories of Music and General Libraries   200
    Directories of Publishers, Record Labels, and Vendors   202
    Music-in-Print   203
    National Bibliographies of Music   205

General Acquisitions Resources

    Acquisitions Manuals   208
    Monographic Series   209
    Bibliographies   211
    Journals   212
    Books-in-Print   212

Music Acquisitions Resources

Manuals of Music Librarianship

These manuals are listed for general and historical information. They contain little that is relevant to music acquisitons practices in U.S. libraries in the twenty-first century.

Bradley, Carol June, ed. *Manual of Music Librarianship.* Ann Arbor, MI: MLA, 1966.

————. *Reader in Music Librarianship.* Reader Series in Library and Information Science. Washington, DC: Microcard Editions Books, 1973.

Bryant, E. T., and Guy A. Marco. *Music Librarianship: A Practical Guide.* 2nd ed. Metuchen, NJ: Scarecrow, 1985.

Dorfmüller, Kurt, and Markus Müller-Benedict. *Musik in Bibliotheken: Materialien, Sammlungstypen, musikbibliothekarische Praxis.* Elemente des Buch- und Bibliothekswesens 15. Wiesbaden, Germany: L. Reichert, 1997.

Griscom, Richard, ed., with Amanda Maple, assistant ed. *Music Librarianship at the Turn of the Century.* Music Library Association Technical Reports 27. Lanham, MD: Scarecrow Press, 2000. Also published as a special issue of *Notes* 56, no. 3 (March 2000).

Jones, Malcolm. *Music Librarianship.* Outlines of Modern Librarianship. London: Clive Bingley; New York: K. G. Saur, 1979.

Ledsham, Ian. *The Comprehensive Guide to Music Librarianship: A Self Study Guide for Music Librarianship.* 2 vols., readings pack, and CD-ROM. Aberystwyth: Open Learning Unit, University of Wales, Llanbadarn Campus, 2000. Supporting website, www.aber. ac.uk/olu/muslib/.

Mann, Alfred, ed. *Modern Music Librarianship: Essays in Honor of Ruth Watanabe.* Festschrift Series 8. Stuyvesant, NY: Pendragon; Kassel: Bärenreiter, 1989.

Journals of Music Librarianship

Brio: Journal of the United Kingdom Branch of the International Association of Music Libraries. London: IAML, UK Branch, 1964– .

Crescendo: Bulletin of the International Association of Music Libraries (New Zealand Branch). Auckland: IAML, New Zealand Branch, 1983– .

Fontes artis musicae. Kassel, Germany: Bärenreiter; International Association of Music Libraries, Archives, and Documentation Centres, 1954– .

Music Reference Services Quarterly. Binghamton, NY: Haworth, 1992– .

Notes: The Quarterly Journal of the Music Library Association. Philadelphia, etc.: MLA, ser. 1, 1934–1942; ser. 2, 1943– .

Music Editing, Publishing, and Library Acquisitions

Balk, Leo F. "The Publisher and the Music Librarian." In *Music Librarianship in America*, ed. by Michael Ochs, 55–59. Cambridge, MA: Eda Kuhn Loeb Music Library, Harvard University, 1991. Originally published in the *Harvard Library Bulletin*, n.s., vol. 2, no. 1 (1991).

Broido, Arnold. "Music Publishing in America." In *Reflections on American Music: The Twentieth Century and the New Millennium; A Collection of Essays Presented in Honor of the College Music Society*, ed. by James R. Heintze and Michael Saffle, 69–80. CMS Monographs and Bibliographies in American Music 16. New York: Pendragon Press, 2000.

Brown, Peter Bennett. *Ordering and Claiming Music Materials: Tips from a Dealer*. Front Music Publications 4. Beverly Hills, CA: Theodore Front Musical Literature, 1981.

Caldwell, John. *Editing Early Music*. Oxford: Clarendon Press, 1985.

Chartier, Richard. "Afterword: Music in Print." In *Music and the Culture of Print*, ed. by Kate Van Orden, 325–41. Critical and Cultural Musicology 1. New York: Garland, 2000.

Emery, Walter. *Editions and Musicians: A Survey of the Duties of Practical Musicians and Editors towards the Classics*. London: Novello, 1957.

Fidler, Linda. "The Acquisition of Out-of-Print Music." In *Out-of-Print and Special Collection Materials: Acquisition and Purchasing Options*, ed. by Judith Overmeier, 5–15. New York: Haworth, 2002; published simultaneously as no. 27 of *Acquisitions Librarian* (2002).

Grier, James. *The Critical Editing of Music: History, Method, and Practice*. Cambridge: Cambridge University Press, 1996.

An Introduction to Music Publishing: A Tour through the Music Publishing Operations Involved in Transforming the Composer's Manuscript into a Printed Publication and Its Dissemination to the Student and the Performer. New York: C. F. Peters, 1981.

Krasilovsky, M. William, and Sidney Schemel, with contributions by John M. Gross. *This Business of Music: The Definitive Guide to the Music Industry*. 9th ed. New York: Billboard Books, 2003; companion website: www.thisbusinessofmusic.info.

Krummel, D. W., comp. *Guide for Dating Early Published Music: A Manual of Bibliographical Practices*. Hackensack, NJ: Joseph Boonin, for the International Association of Music Libraries, Commission for Bibliographical Research, 1974.

————. *The Literature of Music Bibliography: An Account of the Writings on the History of Music Printing and Publishing.* Fallen Leaf Reference Books in Music 21. Berkeley, CA: Fallen Leaf Press, 1992.

Krummel, D. W., and Stanley Sadie, eds. *Music Printing and Publishing.* Norton/Grove Handbooks in Music. New York: W. W. Norton, 1990.

Lenneberg, Hans. *On the Publishing and Dissemination of Music, 1500–1850.* Hillsdale, NY: Pendragon, 2003.

Lubrano, John, and Jude Lubrano. "The Antiquarian Music Market." *Notes* 53 (2000): 641–47; reprinted in *Music Librarianship at the Turn of the Century*, ed. by Richard Griscom, 79–85. Music Library Association Technical Reports 27. Lanham, MD: Scarecrow Press, 2000.

Ochs, Michael. "What Music Scholars Should Know about Publishers." *Notes* 59 (2002): 288–300.

Otto Harrassowitz (firm). *European Music Scores Approval Plan and Form Selections Program.* Wiesbaden, Germany: Harrassowitz, 1999; also at www.harrassowitz.de/sp/emsapp.htm.

Short, Brad. "Prices of Music Monographs and Scores as Reflected in *Notes.*" Annual column published since 1994 in the December issues of the Music Library Association's journal *Notes.*

Sturm, George. "Music Publishing." *Notes* 53 (2000): 628–34; reprinted in *Music Librarianship at the Turn of the Century*, ed. by Richard Griscom, 66–77. Music Library Association Technical Reports 27. Lanham, MD: Scarecrow Press, 2000.

Theodore Front Musical Literature (firm) *Blanket/Approval Plan for European and American Music Scores.* Van Nuys, CA: Front, ca. 1990; also at http://books.tfront.com/music/approval.htm.

Thorin, Suzanne E., and Carole Franklin Vidali. *The Acquisition and Cataloging of Music and Sound Recordings: A Glossary.* Music Library Association Technical Reports 11. Canton, MA: Music Library Association, 1984.

Directories of Music and General Libraries

Benedetti, Amadeo. *Gli archivi sonori: Fonoteche, nastroteche e biblioteche musicali in Italia.* Genoa: Erga Edizioni, 2002.

Benton, Rita, general ed. *Directory of Music Research Libraries.* International Inventory of Musical Sources, ser. C. Kassel, Germany: Bärenreiter, 1979– . 1. Canada and the United States. 2. Austria, Belgium, Switzerland, Germany, Denmark, Spain (2nd ed.). 3, pt.

1. France, Finland, United Kingdom, Ireland, Luxemburg, Norway, Netherlands, Portugal, Sweden (2nd ed.). 3, pt. 2. Forthcoming. 4. Australia, Israel, Japan, New Zealand. 5. Czechoslovakia, Hungary, Poland, Yugoslavia. Preliminary edition of vols. 1–3 published Iowa City: University of Iowa, 1967–1972: 1. Canada and the United States. 2. Austria, Belgium, Switzerland, Federal Republic of Germany, German Democratic Republic, Denmark, Ireland, Great Britain, Luxemburg, Norway, Netherlands, Sweden, Finland. 3. Spain, France, Italy, Portugal.

Conference of European National Libraries (CENL). Gabriel: The Gateway to Europe's National Libraries, www.bl.uk/gabriel.

The Directory of University Libraries in Europe. London: Europa, 2000.

European Music Directory. Munich: K. G. Saur, 1999– .

Harden, Sheila, and Robert Harden. Public Libraries of Europe, http://dspace.dial.pipex.com/town/square/ac940/eurolib.html.

Hausfater, Dominique, Marie-Gabrielle Soret, and Christiane David. *Répertoire des bibliothèques et institutions françaises conservant des collections musicales.* Paris: Association internationale des bibliothèques, archives, et centres de documentation musicaux (AIBM), Groupe français, 2001.

International Association of Music Information Centres. IAMIC Members, www.iamic.net/members/index.html.

International Federation of Library Associations and Institutions. Web Accessible National and Major Libraries, www.ifla.org/II/natlibs.htm.

Internationale Vereinigung der Musikbibliotheken, Musikarchive und Musikdokumentationszentren (IVMB), Gruppe Bundesrepublik Deutschland e.V., Deutsches Bibliotheksinstitut (DBI). *Handbuch der Musikbibliotheken in Deutschland: Öffentliche und wissenschaftliche Musikbibliotheken sowie Spezialsammlungen mit musikbibliothek-arischen Beständen.* 2nd ed. Berlin: Deutschesbibliotheksinstitut, 1998.

LibDex: The Library Index, www.libdex.com.

Libraries Online, www.libraries-online.com.

Moroni, Gabriele, ed. *La musica negli archivi e nelle bibliotheche delle Marche: Primo censimento dei fondi musicali.* Fondi storici nelle biblioteche marchigiane 4. N.p.: Associazione marchigiana per la ricerca e valorizzazione delle fonti musicali, 1996.

Musiker, Reuben, ed. *Directory of South African Music Libraries.* Johannesburg: South African Music Libraries Association, 1993.

Penney, Barbara, ed. *Music in British Libraries: A Directory of Resources.* 4th ed. London: Library Association, 1992.

Poroila, Heikki, ed. *Directory of Music Libraries in Finland 1993 = Suomalaisten musiikkikirjastojen hakemisto 1993.* Suomen musiikkikirjastoyhdistyksen julkaisusarja 36. Helsinki: Suomen musiikkikirjastoyhdistys, 1993; updated version on the web at www. kaapeli.fi/%7Emusakir/engdir/index.htm.

Prokopowicz, Maria, Andrzej Spóz, and Włodzimierz Pigła, eds. *Biblioteki i zbiory muzyczne w Polsce = Guide to Polish Music Libraries and Collections.* Nauka-dykaktyka-praktyka 30. Warsaw: Wydawn. SBP, 1998.

Ulrich, Paul S., ed. SIBMAS International Directory of Performing Arts Collections and Institutions, La société internationale des bibliothèques et des musées des arts du spectacle, www.theatrelibrary.org/sibmas/idpac/index.html.

University of California at Berkeley, Digital Library Sun SITE. Libweb: Library Servers via WWW, http://sunsite.berkeley.edu/Libweb.

University of Queensland Library. National Library Catalogues Worldwide, www.library.uq.edu.au/natlibs.

The World of Learning. London: Allen & Unwin, 1947– .

Directories of Publishers, Record Labels, and Vendors

Allrecordlabels.com, http://allrecordlabels.com.

International ISMN Agency. *Music Publishers' International ISMN Directory.* Munich: K. G. Saur; Berlin: International ISMN Agency, 1995– .

International Record Review, Directory of Record Company Website Addresses, www.recordreview.co.uk.

Music Directory Canada. Toronto: CM Books, 1982– .

Music Publishers' Association. MPA Directory of Music Publishers, www.mpa.org/agency/pal.html.

Musical America: International Directory of the Performing Arts. Great Barrington, MA: ABC Leisure Magazines, 1974– ; web version, MusicalAmerica.com: The Business Source for the Performing Arts, www.musicalamerica.com.

Record Labels on the Web, www.rlabels.com.

Retail Print Music Dealers Association. RPMDA Directory, www. printmusic.org/directory.htm.

Music-in-Print

Listed here are volumes published in the Music-in-Print Series (Philadelphia: Musicdata, 1974–1999). Some volumes are available in paperback reprints from the series' current publisher, emusicquest; some categories are available on CD-ROM; many are available by subscription as searchable online databases. For current availability, see the emusicquest website: www.emusicquest.com. Within each category listed alphabetically below, the component volumes are arranged chronologically.

Classical Guitar Music in Print. Ed. by Mijndert Jape. Vol. 7 of series. 1989.

———. *1998 Supplement.* Ed. by Donald T. Reese. Vol. 7s of series. 1998.

Choral Music in Print. 2 vols. Ed. by Thomas R. Nardone, James H. Nye, and Mark Resnick. Vols. 1 (sacred) and 2 (secular) of series. 1974. Continued by separate sacred and secular series.

———. *Master Index 1991.* Vol. chx of series. 1991.

Classical Vocal Music in Print. Ed. by Thomas R. Nardone. Vol. 4 of series. 1976.

———. *1985 Supplement.* Ed. by Gary S. Eslinger and F. Mark Daugherty. Vol. 4s of series. 1986.

———. *1995 Supplement.* Ed. by F. Mark Daugherty. Vol. 4t of series. 1995.

———. *Master Index 1995.* Vol. 4x of series. 1995.

Music in Print Annual Supplement. 1979–1986.

Music in Print Master Composer Index 1988. Vol. xc of series. 1989.

———. *1995.* 2 vols. Vol. xc [rev.] of series. 1995.

———. *1999.* 2 vols. Vol. xc [rev.] of series. 1998.

Music in Print Master Title Index 1988. Vol. xt of series. 1990.

———. *1995.* Vol. xt [rev.] of series. 1995.

———. *1999.* Vol. xt [rev.] of series. 1999.

Orchestral Music in Print. Ed. by Margaret K. Farish. Vol. 5 of series. 1979.

———. *1983 Supplement.* Ed. by Margaret K. Farish. Vol. 5s of series. 1983.

———. *1994 Supplement.* Ed. by Margaret K. Farish. Vol. 5t of series. 1994.

———. *Master Index 1994.* Vol. 5x of series. 1994.

———. *1999 Supplement.* Ed. by Robert W. Cho, F. Mark Daugherty, and Frank James Staneck. Vol. 5u of series. 1999.

———. *Master Index 1999.* Vol. 5x [rev.] of series. 1999.

Organ Music in Print. Ed. by Thomas R. Nardone. Vol. 3 of series. 1975.

———. 2nd ed. Ed. by Walter A. Frankel and Nancy K. Nardone. Vol. 3 [rev.] of series. 1984.

———. *1990 Supplement.* Ed. by F. Mark Daugherty. Vol. 3s of series 1990.

———. *1997 Supplement.* Ed. by Robert W. Cho. Vol. 3t of series. 1997.

———. *Master Index 1997.* Vol. 3x of series. 1997.

Sacred Choral Music in Print: 1981 Supplement. Ed. by Nancy K. Nardone. Vol. 1 supp. of series. 1981.

Sacred Choral Music in Print. 2nd ed. Ed. by Gary S. Eslinger and F. Mark Daugherty. Vol. 1 [rev.] of series. 1985.

———. *Arranger Index.* Vol. 1c of series. 1987.

———. *1988 Supplement.* Ed. by Susan H. Simon. Vol. 1s of series. 1988.

———. *1992 Supplement.* Ed. by F. Mark Daugherty and Susan H. Simon. Vol. 1t of series. 1992.

———. *Master Index 1992.* Vol. 1x of series. 1992.

———. *Master Index 1996.* Vol. 1x of series. 1996.

Secular Choral Music in Print: 1982 Supplement. Ed. by Nancy K. Nardone. Vol. 2 supp. of series. 1982.

Secular Choral Music in Print. 2nd ed. 2 vols. Ed. by F. Mark Daugherty and Susan H. Simon. Vol. 2 [rev.] of series. 1987.

———. *Arranger Index.* Vol. 2c of series. 1987.

———. *1991 Supplement.* Ed. by F. Mark Daugherty and Susan H. Simon. Vol. 2s of series. 1991.

———. *Master Index 1993.* Vol. 2x of series. 1993.

———. *1993 Supplement.* Ed. by F. Mark Daugherty and Susan H. Simon. Vol. 2t of series. 1993.

———. *1996 Supplement.* Ed. by Robert W. Cho. Vol. 2u of series. 1996.

———. *Master Index 1996.* Vol. 2x of series. 1996.

String Music in Print: 1984 Supplement. Ed. by Margaret K. Farish. Vol. 6s of series. 1984. The original volumes were published out of the series: Margaret K. Farish, *String Music In Print* (New York: R. R. Bowker, 1965), and supplement (1968); 2nd ed. (1973); reprint of 2nd ed. (Philadelphia: Musicdata, 1980).

———. *1998 Supplement.* Ed. by Robert W. Cho, Donald T. Reese, and Frank James Staneck. 1998.

Woodwind Music in Print. Ed. by Harry B. Peters. Vol. 8 of series. 1997.

National Bibliographies of Music

Austria

Österreichische Bibliographie. Reihe A, Verzeichnis der öster-reichischen Neuerscheinungen. Sonderheft— praktische Musik. Vienna: Österreichische Nationalbibliothek, 1992– . Printed music. Annual. Since 2003, available on the web as a component of Österreichische Bibliographie: OeB-online, http://bibliographie. onb.ac.at/biblio.

Belgium

Bibliographie de Belgique: Supplément musique = Belgische Biblio-grafie: Supplement Muziek. Brussels: Koninklijke Bibliotheek Al-bert 1, 1982– . Printed music. Annual. Since 1997, published only on CD-ROM and the web. Accessible through the Royal Library of Belgium website (www.kbr.be), where one can choose the "Cata-logues connectés" link to search online either the library's catalog, the most recent twelve months of the *Bibliographie de Belgique* (books), or the *Supplément musique.*

Canada

Canadiana. Ottawa: National Library of Canada, 1951– . Music books, scores, recordings integrated in Dewey class 780 in the printed version. Print ceased 1991, continued by monthly microfiche edi-tion (1980–), and CD-ROM versions (1998–). All entries are added to the continually updated National Library of Canada AMICUS database, available online at http://amicus.nlc-bnc.ca/ aaweb/amilogine.htm.

Czech Republic

Ceská Národní Bibliografie: Hudebniny = Czech National Bibliogra-phy: Printed Music. Prague: Národní Bibliografie Ceské Repub-liky, 1995– . Annual. Continuation of *Národní Bibliografie Ceské Republiky: Hudebniny* (1995), *Bibliografický Katalog CSFR.: Ceské Hudebniny, Gramofonové Desky a Kompaktní Disky* (1989–1992), and earlier variants. Published quarterly since 1997 only on CD-ROM.

———. *Zvukové Dokumenty = Czech National Bibliography: Sound Recordings.* Prague: Národní Knihovna Ceské Republiky, 1996– . Annual. Continues *Národní Bibliografie Ceské Republiky: Zvukové*

Dokumenty (1995), and earlier variants. Published quarterly since 1997 only on CD-ROM.

Denmark

Dansk Musikfortegnelse = Danish National Bibliography of Music. Copenhagen: Musikhandlerforeningen, 1934– . Printed music. Annual. Publisher varies.

France

Bibliographie nationale française: Documents sonores, audiovisuels et multimédias. Paris: Bibliothèque nationale, 1996– . CD-ROM. Sound and video recordings. Printed music was included in the print editions of the French national bibliography between 1946 and 2000. The most recent version appeared thrice yearly as *Bibliographie nationale française. Musique: Bibliographie établie par la Bibliothèque nationale à partir des documents déposés au titre du dépot légal* (Paris: Bibliothèque nationale, 1992–2000). Publication in printed format ceased when the book and series components of the bibliography were first offered online in 2000 at http://bibliographienationale.bnf.fr. The *Musique* component resumed publication in 2004 at the same web location with a cumulation for 2003, and thrice-yearly updates thereafter.

Germany

Deutsche Nationalbibliographie und Bibliographie der im Ausland erschienenen deutschsprachigen veröffentlichungen. Reihe M, Musikalien und Musikschriften monatliches Verzeichnis. Bearbeiter und Herausgeber, Die Deutsche Bibliothek. Frankfurt am Main: Buchhändler-Vereinigung, 1991– . Monthly. Scores and books about music. Continues *Deutsche Musikbibliographie,* ed. by Deutsche Bücherei, Leipzig (Leipzig: F. Hofmeisters Musikverlag, 1944–1990).
———. *Reihe T, Musiktonträger monatliches Verzeichnis.* Berabeiter und Herausgeber, Die Deutsche Bibliothek. Frankfurt am Main: Buchhändler-Vereinigung, 1991– . Monthly. Sound recordings.

Hungary

Magyar nemzeti bibliográfia: Zeneművek bibliográfiája. Budapest: Or-szágos Széchényi Könyvtár, 1977– . Annual. Scores and sound re-cordings.

Norway

Nornoter: Norske Notetrykk = Norwegian National Bibliography of Printed Music. Oslo: National Library of Norway, www.nb.no/baser/nornoter. Music scores published in Norway since 1981, and some older. Online database continues and supersedes annual *Norsk Musikkfortegnelse: Notetryk = Norwegian National Bibliography of Printed Music* (Oslo: Universitetsbibliotek I Oslo, 1994–1997), and earlier versions.

Romania

Bibliografia nationala româna: Note muzicale, discuri, casete. Bucha-rest: Biblioteca nationala a României, 1992– . Quarterly. Continues *Bibliografia României: Note muzicale, discuri, casete.* Printed mu-sic, compact discs, audiocassettes.

Russia

Notnaia letopis'. Moscow: Izd-vo "Kniga," 1967– . Quarterly. Contin-ues *Letopis' Muzykal'noi literatury.*

Spain

Bibliografia musical española: BIME. Madrid: Asociación Española de Documentación Musical, 1997– . Biennial. Continues the annual *Bibliografia española: Música impresa* (Madrid: Ministerio de Cultura, Biblioteca Nacional, 1995–1997), and its predecessor *Su-plemento de musica impresa* (1990–1995). Printed music.

Switzerland

Das Schweizer Buch: Bibliographisches Bulletin der Schweizerischen Landesbibliothek, Bern = Le livre suisse: Bulletin bibliographique de la Bibliothèque nationale suisse, Berne = Il libro svizzero: Bolletino bibliografico della Biblioteca nazionale svizzera, Berna. No. 16, *Musica practica.* Bern: Schweizerischen Buchhändler- und Verlagervereins, 1943– . Twenty-four issues per year. No. 16 each year (late August) is devoted to music, and cumulates a year's worth of entries for printed music.

United Kingdom

The British Catalogue of Music. London: British Library Bibliographic Services Division, 1957– . Printed music. Semiannual, with annual cumulations.

General Acquisitions Resources

Acquisitions Manuals

Anderson, Rick. *Buying and Contracting for Resources and Services: A How-to-Do-It Manual for Librarians.* How-to-Do-It Manuals for Librarians 125. New York: Neal-Schuman, 2004.

Chapman, Liz. *Managing Acquisitions in Library and Information Services.* 2nd ed. London: Library Association, 2001. First edition published 1989 as *Buying Books for Libraries.*

Drury, F. K. W. *Order Work for Libraries.* Chicago: ALA, 1930.

Eaglen, Audrey. *Buying Books: A How-to-Do-It Manual for Librarians.* 2nd ed. How-to-Do-It Manuals for Librarians 99. New York: Neal-Schuman, 2000.

Ford, Stephen. *The Acquisition of Library Materials.* Rev. ed. Chicago: ALA, 1978.

Johnson, Peggy, and Bonnie MacEwan, eds. *Virtually Yours: Models for Managing Electronic Resources and Services.* ALCTS Papers on Library Technical Services and Collections 8. Chicago: ALA, 1999.

Melcher, David. *Melcher on Acquisitions.* Chicago: ALA, 1971.

Schmidt, Karen A., ed. *Understanding the Business of Library Acquisitions.* 2nd ed. Chicago: ALA, 1999.

Scholtz, James C. *Video Acquisitions and Cataloging: A Handbook.* The Greenwood Library Management Collection. Westport, CT: Greenwood Press, 1995.

Wilkinson, Frances C., and Linda K. Lewis. *The Complete Guide to Acquisitions Management.* Library and Information Science Text Series. Westport, CT: Libraries Unlimited, 2003.

Woods, William E., ed. *Library Acquisition Procedures circa 1985.* Evergreen Park, IL: Woods Library Publications, 2002. A collection of procedures manuals from thirteen libraries.

Monographic Series

Acquisitions Guidelines. Chicago: ALA, 1973– .

1. American Library Association, Bookdealer-Library Relations Committee. *Guidelines for Handling Library Orders for In-Print Monographic Publications.* 1973.

2. Association for Library Collections and Technical Services, Serials Section. *Guidelines for Handling Library Orders for Serials and Periodicals.* 1974; 2nd ed., 1992.

3. American Library Association, Bookdealer-Library Relations Committee. *Guidelines for Handling Library Orders for Microforms.* 1977.

4. ———. *Guidelines for Handling Library Orders for In-Print Monographic Publications.* 2nd ed. 1984.

5. American Library Association, Collection Management and Development Committee. *Guide to Performance Evaluation of Library Materials Vendors.* 1988.

6. *Statistics for Managing Library Acquisitions.* Edited by Eileen D. Hardy for the Association for Library Collections & Technical Services, Acquisitions Committee. 1989.

7. Association for Library Collections & Technical Services, Serials Section. *Guidelines for Handling Library Orders for Serials and Periodicals.* 2nd ed. 1992.

8. Marsha J. Hamilton. *Guide to Preservation in Acquisition Processing.* For the Association for Library Collections & Technical Services, Acquisition of Library Materials Section. 1993.

9. Stephen Bosch, Patricia Promis, and Chris Sugnet. *Guide to Selecting and Acquiring CD-ROMS, Software and Other Electronic Publications.* 1994.

10. Association for Library Collections & Technical Services, Serials Section Acquisitions Committee. *Guide to Performance Evaluation of Serials Vendors.* 1997.

11. Susan C. Flood. *Guide to Managing Approval Plans.* 1998.

The Acquisitions Librarian. New York: Haworth Press, 1989– .

1. *Automated Acquisitions: Issues for the Present and Future.* Edited by Amy Dykeman and Bill Katz. 1989.

2. *The Acquisitions Budget.* Edited by Bill Katz. 1989.

3. *Legal and Ethical Issues in Acquisitions.* Edited by Katina Strauch and Bruce Strauch. 1990.

4. *Operational Costs in Acquisitions.* Edited by James R. Coffey. 1990.

5. *Vendors and Library Acquisitions.* Edited by Bill Katz. 1991.

6. *Evaluating Acquisitions and Collection Management.* Edited by Pamela S. Cenzer and Cynthia I. Gozzi. 1991.

7. *Collection Assessment: A Look at the RLG Conspectus.* Edited by Richard J. Wood and Katina Strauch.

8. *Popular Culture and Acquisitions.* Edited by Allen Ellis. 1992.

9/10. *Multicultural Acquisitions.* Guest Editor Karen Parrish; Edited   by Bill Katz. 1993. Double volume.

11. *A.V. in Public and School Libraries: Selections and Policy Issues.* Edited by Margaret J. Hughes. 1994.

12. *Management and Organization of the Acquisitions Department.* Edited by Twyla Racz and Rosina Tammany. 1994.

13/14. *New Automation Technology for Acquisitions and Collection Development.* Edited by Rosann Bazirjian. 1995. Double volume.

15. *Current Legal Issues in Publishing.* Edited by A. Bruce Strauch. 1996.

16. *Approval Plans: Issues and Innovations.* Edited by John H. Sandy. 1996.

17/18. *Acquisitions and Collection Development in the Humanities.* Edited by Irene Owens. 1997. Double volume.

19. *Fiction Acquisition/Fiction Management: Education and Training.* Edited by Georgine N. Olson. 1998.

20. *Public Library Collection Development in the Information Age.* Edited by Annabel K. Stephens. 1998.

21. *Periodical Acquisitions and the Internet.* Edited by Nancy Slight-Gibney. 1998.

22. *Gifts and Exchanges: Problems, Frustrations—and Triumphs.* Edited by Catherine Denning. 1999.

23. *The Internet and Acquisitions: Sources and Resources for Development.* Edited by Mary E. Timmons. 2000.

24. Not published.

25. *Readers, Reading, and Librarians.* Edited by William A. Katz. 2001.

26. *Publishing and the Law: Current Legal Issues.* Edited by Bruce A. Strauch. 2001.

27. *Out-of-Print and Special Collection Materials: Acquisitions and Purchasing Options.* Edited by Judith A. Overmeier. 2002.

Bibliographies

Association for Library Collections & Technical Services, "ALCTS Publications Acquisitions Bibliography," 4th ed., ed. by Barbara Hall (2002). www.ala.org/ala/alctscontent/alctspubsbucket/web-publications/alctsacquisitions/selectedbibliogr/acquisitions.htm.

German, Lisa B. "A Closer World: A Review of Acquisitions Literature: 1992." *LRTS* 37 (1993): 255–60.

Hudson, Judith A., and Geraldene Walker. "The Year's Work in Technical Services Research: 1986." *LRTS* 31 (1987): 275–86.

Jasper, Richard P. "Challenge, Change, and Confidence: The Literature of Acquisitions: 1991." *LRTS* 36 (1992): 263–75.

Schenck, William Z. "The Year's Work in Acquisitions and Collection Development: 1988." *LRTS* 34 (1990): 326–37.

Schmidt, Karen A. "Acquisitions." In *Guide to Technical Services Resources*, ed. by Peggy Johnson, 27–44. Chicago: ALA, 1994.

———. "Acquisitions." *New Directions in Technical Services*, 28–45. Chicago: ALA, 1997.

———. "Buying Good Pennyworths? A Review of the Literature of Acquisitions in the Eighties." *LRTS* 30 (1986): 333–40.

———. "Please, Sir, I Want Some More: A Review of the Literature of Acquisitions: 1990." *LRTS* 35 (1991): 245–54.

Simpson, Charles W. "Technical Services Research: 1988–1991." *LRTS* 36 (1992): 383–408.

Vickery, Jim. "Acquisitions." *Collection Management* 22 (1997): 101–86.

Journals

ACQNET: The Acquisitions Librarians Electronic Network (1990–2000). Archives available at www.infomotions.com/serials/acqnet. Continues 2000– as an electronic discussion list: subscription is by e-mail message "subscribe acqnet-l [your name]" to listproc@list-proc.appstate.edu.

The Acquisitions Librarian. New York: Haworth Press, 1989– . Irregular. Each issue is also published as a monograph in the series of the same title.

Against the Grain: Linking Publishers, Vendors, and Librarians. Charleston, SC: Against the Grain, 1989– . Bimonthly. Subscriptions c/o Katina Strauch, Citadel Station, Charleston, SC 29409. Tables of contents of each issue beginning with vol. 6 (1994) with brief abstracts can be found on the web at www.against-the-grain. com.

Collection Management. New York: Haworth Press, 1976– . Quarterly.

Library Acquisitions: Practice and Theory. New York: Pergamon Press, 1977–1998. Quarterly. Continued by the following title.

Library Collections, Acquisitions, & Technical Services: LCATS. New York: Pergamon Press, 1999– . Quarterly. Continues the preceding title.

Library Resources & Technical Services. Chicago: ALCTS, 1957– . Quarterly.

Books-in-Print

Australia

Australian Books in Print. Melbourne: D. W. Thorpe, 1967– . Annual. See also the international listings.

Canada

Canadian Books in Print: Author and Title Index. Toronto: University of Toronto Press, 1975– . Annual. Intended to bridge the gap between *Books in Print* (see United States) and *Whitaker's Books in Print* (see United Kingdom). See also the international listings.

France

Les livres disponibles = *French Books in Print.* Paris: Cercle de la Librairie, 1977– . Annual. Formed by the merger of *Le catalogue de l'édition français* (Paris: VPC Livres; Port Washington, NY: Paris Publications, 1973–1976); and *Répertoire des livres de langue française disponibles* (Paris: France-Exansion, 1972–1976).

German-Language Areas

Verzeichnis lieferbarer Bücher: VLB. Frankfurt: Verlag der Buchhändler-Vereinigung; Munich-Pullach: Vertrieb Auslieferung, Verlag Dokumentation Saur KG, 1971– . Annual. Also available on the web and on CD-ROM.

Italian-Language Areas

Associazione italiana editori. *Cataloge dei libri in commercio: Libri e opere multimediali: Autori [Titoli. Soggetti].* Milan: Editrice bibliografica; Ann Arbor, MI: dist. by R. R. Bowker, 1976– . Annual. Also available on CD-ROM.

Portugal

Livros disponiveis. Lisbon: Associação portuguesa dos editores e livreiros, 1987– . Annual.

Spain and Latin America

Libros en venta en América Latina y España: LEV. San Juan, PR: NISC Puerto Rico, 1997– . Annual. Continues *Libros en venta en Hispanoamérica y España* (New York: R. R. Bowker, 1964–93). Contains books in the Spanish language whatever the country of origin. Also available on CD-ROM, which adds out-of-print titles omitted from the print edition; available as well through subscription to the NISC search service BiblioLine.

United Kingdom

Whitaker's Books in Print. London: J. Whitaker & Sons, 1988– . Annual. Whitaker is the ISBN agency for the United Kingdom. Continues *British Books in Print* (London: J. Whitaker & Sons, 1965–1987). See also the international listings.

United States

Books in Print. New York: R. R. Bowker, 1948– . Annual. Bowker is the ISBN and ISMN agency for the United States. Also available by subscription on the web and on CD-ROM. See also the international listings below.

International

Bowker/Whitaker Global Books in Print Plus. CD-ROM. New Providence, NJ: Bowker Electronic Publishing, 1994– . Contains *Books in Print*; *Subject Guide to Books in Print*; *Books in Print Supplement*; *Forthcoming Books in Print*; *Paperbound Books in Print*; *Children's Books in Print*; *Subject Guide to Children's Books in Print*; *Publishers, Distributors, and Wholesalers of the United States*; *Whitaker's Books in Print*; *International Books in Print*; *Australian Books in Print*; *New Zealand Books in Print*; and, in cooperation with Canadian Telebook Agency, titles representing Canadian publishers. A web version also is available by subscription from Bowker: *Globalbooksinprint.com* (2001–).

Guide to Microforms in Print. Microform Review Publications. Munich; New York: K. G. Saur, 1978–. Annual. Publisher varies.

International Books in Print. Munich; New York: K. G. Saur; distributed by Gale Research, 1979–. Annual. Includes English-language titles published outside the United States and the United Kingdom.

INDEX

AAA Music Hunter, 76

AACR2R, 92n5

AB Bookman's Weekly, 139, 148n9

Abebooks, 141

ACQflashes, 3

ACQNET, 3, 7nn4–5

The Acquisition and Cataloging of Music and Sound Recordings (Thorin, Vidali), 6, 9nn23–24

The Acquisition of Library Materials (Ford), 2

"The Acquisition of Library Microforms" (Sullivan), 172n21

"The Acquisition of Out-of-Print Music" (Fidler), 147n2

"Acquisitions: College Library" (Gerboth), 8n11

acquisitions: definition, 1–2; literature of (general), 2–3; literature of (music), 4–6; organization of work, 4; training for, 1, 6n1

Acquisitions Guidelines (series), 2

The Acquisitions Librarian, 3

The Acquisitions Librarians Electronic Network. *See* ACQNET

"Acquisitions: Public Library" (Millen), 8n11

AcqWeb, 3, 100

Adam Matthew Publications (microfilms), 155

AddAll Used and Out-of-Print, 141

Adkins, Cecil, *Doctoral Dissertations in Musicology*, 160, 173n32

Against the Grain, 3

Aissing, Alena, "Cyrillic Transliteration and Its Users," 92n6

ALA: Collection Management and Development Committee, *Guide to Performance Evaluation of Library Materials Vendors*, 78n9; Filing Committee, *ALA Filing Rules*, 91n3; publications, 6n2

ALA–LC Romanization Tables (Barry), 92n5

ALCTS. *See* Association of Library Collections and Technical Services

Alibris, 141, 145

Alix, Yves, *Musique en bibliothèque*, 7n8

Allen, Nancy, *Humanities and the Library*, 9n21

Allrecordlabels.com (directory), 108

Amazon: 77, 106–7; corporate accounts, 77, 106

Ambassador Book Service, 67, 78n7

American Library Association. *See* ALA

"American Music Librarianship: An Overview in the Eighties" (Watanabe), 8n9

"American Music Libraries and Librarianship: Challenges for the Nineties" (Davidson), 8n9

AMICUS Web (union catalog), 98, 174n35

Andante.com: "Music in Print," 103; "Recordings in Print," 109

Anglo-American Cagaloguing Rules, 2nd ed. (AACR2R), 92n5

ANRT. *See* Atelier national de reproduction des thèses

Antiquarian Booksellers' Association of America, 137, 147n6

antiquarian: catalogs, 134; definition, 134, 147n3; directory, 137–38, 147n5; reasons to acquire, 134; services, 136–37. *See also* secondhand

approval plans: Association for Research Libraries survey, 131n12–32n12; contemporary composers lists, 126–27, 129–30, 132nn16–17; management reports, 128; monetary commitments, 132n13; monitoring, 130; printed music, 124–28; profiles, 125–28; reasons to use, 124; recorded music, 129–30; reissues, 130; returns, 124, 132n14; standard repertoire, 125–26, 129; vendors, 124–27, 128, 129, 132n15

A-R Editions, copyright sharing policy, 67, 77n5

Arneson, Arne J., "Microformats and the Music Library: A Bibliographic-Use Survey of Recent Trends," 172n18

Association for Research Libraries, *Evolution and Status of Approval Plans*, 131n12–32n12

Association of Library Collections and Technical Services (ALCTS), 3

Atelier national de reproduction des thèses (ANRT), 166–67, 175n49–51; *Catalogue des thèses reproduites*, 175n50

Australian Digital Theses Program, 176n60

"Authority Control: An Overview" (Tillett), 111n1

"Automation Requirements for Music Materials" (Music Library Association), 131n10

AV Source. *See* Compact Disc Source/AV Source

Baker & Taylor, 67, 78n7

Balay, Robert, *Guide to Reference Books*, 174n43

band music, 24

bar code numbers, types used on music products, 55–58. *See also* European Article Number (EAN); Universal Product Code (UPC)

Barnes & Noble (retailer), 67, 77, 107; corporate accounts, 77

Barry, Randall K., *ALA–LC Romanization Tables*, 92n5

Basart, Ann P., *Writing about Music*, 30n12

BBC Music Magazine, 112n18–13n18

Bel Canto Books, 135

Benton, Rita, *The Directory of Music Research Libraries*, 169, 176n62

Berkshire Record Outlet (cutouts), 145

Berman, Marsha. *See* Marsha Berman Musical Literature

The Best of MOUG (Weidow), 85, 92n8

Bibliofind, 141

Bibliographie Darstellende Kunst und Musik (Wolf), 167, 176n57

bibliographies of acquisitions, 3

Bielefelder Katalog Jazz, 106, 112n12

Bielefelder Katalog Klassik, 106, 112n12

Bilboard, 46n4

Billboard International Buyer's Guide, 40

Binding and Care of Printed Music (Carli), 30n14

binding: need for in libraries, 17–18, 30n13; types of, 17–19, 30n14

Blackley, Christi Birch, "An Overview of Orchestra Librarianship,"

8–9n20

Blackwell's Book Services, 72; secondhand searching, 139; standing orders, 71, 72, 78n11

Blackwell's Music Shop, 72, 78n11

Bonner Katalog, rental information in, 26, 31n21

"Book Buying in a University Music Library" (Duckles), 5

Book Industry Advisory Committee, *Machine-Readable Coding Guidelines for the U.S. Book Industry*, 61n10

"Book Vendor Records in the OCLC Database" (Shedenhelm, Burk), 78–79n13

book vendors: availability of recordings from, 67; nonavailability of printed music from, 67

Bookfinder, 141

Bookland EAN (European Article Number), 57

books about music: prices, 111n8; reviews, 30nn11–12

Books On Demand (reprints), 145

Boorman, Stanley, "Printing and Publishing of Music," 28n1

Borders Books and Music (retailer), 67, 77, 107; corporate accounts, 77, 106, 107

The Bowker Annual: Library and Book Trade Almanac, 60n4, 61n10

Boyer, Calvin James, *The Doctoral Dissertation as an Information Source*, 173n27

Bradley, Carol June, *Manual of Music Librarianship*, 4, 8n11; *Reader in Music Librarianship*, 5, 8nn12–16

British Thesis Service, 164, 175n44

Brookhaven Press (microfilms), 155–56

Broude Brothers Limited, 70

Brown, Peter B., *Ordering and Claiming Music Materials*, 6,

9n22

Bryant, E. T., *Music Librarianship*, 7n7

Building a Superior Band Library (Intravaia), 8n20

Burk, Bartley A., "Book Vendor Records in the OCLC Database," 78–79n13

Bush, S. H., "Undue Dominance of the Dissertation in Training for the Doctorate," 173n25

Buying Books (Eaglen), 2, 78n9, 130n1

"Buying Discs on the Internet" (Ritter), 112n16

BuyUsed.co.uk, 145–46

Byrne, Frank, *Practical Guide to the Music Library*, 8n20, 30n18

Byron Hoyt Music (database), 102

Canadian Theses 1947–1960 and supplements, 174n35

Canadian Theses Service, 174n35

Carli, Alice, *Binding and Care of Printed Music*, 30n14

Casalini Libri, 71–72; catalog numbers of, 59; MARC records available from, 72, 74; MARC records in OCLC WorldCat and the RLG Union Catalog, 78nn12–13, 102–3

"Cataloging and Treatment of Theses, Dissertations, and ETDs" (Hoover, Wolverton), 173n26

Cataloging-in-Publication (CIP) program, 96, 111n3

"Cataloging Theses and Dissertations: An Annotated Bibliography" (Hoover), 173n26

Catalogue collectif de France (CCFR, union catalog), 98

Catalogue des thèses reproduites, 175n50

Catrice, Anne, *Guide d'acquisition de la musique imprimée*, 7n8

CCFR (union catalog), 98

CD Now, 107
CD Sheet Music (reprints), 143–44
CDtrackdown (secondhand searching), 146
Census Catalogue of Manuscript Sources of Polyphonic Music, 1400–1550, 150, 171n7
Center for Research Libraries, 169, 176n63
choral music formats, 23–24
Church Music Publishers Association, 29n7
Clark, Christine, viii, 29n9, 132n18
ClassicalNet: "Classical Music Commercial Sites," 112n15; "Recording Labels and Distributors," 108
Classical Vocal Reprints, 144
Coleman, Mark, *Playback: From the Victrola to MP3*, 45n1
Collection Management, 3
Compact Disc Source/AV Source: 76; approval plans, 129–30
Compact Disc World, 76
The Complete Guide to Acquisitions Management (Wilkinson, Lewis), 2
composers' complete editions, volume hierarchy in, 117
Comprehensive Guide to Music Librarianship (Ledsham), 5, 8n18
compulsory licensing. *See* copyright; recorded music; on-demand publication
Conference of European National Libraries (CENL), 97
Consortium of University Research Libraries (CURL), 98
Cook Music Library, Indiana University, "Music Publishers," 100
Coover, James G., "Selection Policies for a University Music Library," 5
COPAC (union catalog), 98, 164
copyright: compulsory licensing in recorded music, 86–87, 92n9,

93n10, 130, 132n19; copying exceptions for libraries, 20; fair use, 67, 78n6; public domain, 148n14; recorded music, 92–93nn9–10, 93n12; video acquisitions and reproduction, 47n16, 47n20; video performance rights, 44
Couch, Nena, *Humanities and the Library*, 9n21
Coutts Library Services (secondhand searching), 139
Cox, Lisa. *See* Lisa Cox Music
CURL Online Public Access Catalog (COPAC, union catalog), 98
currency conversion, 69, 75
custom print editions. *See* on-demand publication
cutouts. *See* Berkshire Record Outlet
"Cyrillic Transliteration and Its Users" (Aissing), 92n6

Dan Fog Musikantikvariat, 137
Davidson, Donald, *Theses and Dissertations as Information Sources*, 173n28
Davidson, Mary Wallace, viii; "American Music Libraries and Librarianship: Challenges for the Nineties," 8n9
Dawson, H. P., "The Ordering and Supply of Sheet Music," 5, 8n10
DDM-Online, 160–61, 173n31
"Default Record Displays in Web-Based Catalogs" (Timmons), 61n9
Describing Music Materials (Smiraglia, Pavlovsky), 92n7
desiderata lists, 139–40
Deutscher Musikverleger-Verband, 100
Deutsches Musikgeschichtliches Archiv (DMA), 153, 154, 171n12; catalog, 154, 171n12
diacritics, 83–84
Diapason: Catalogue général, 112n12

Dickinson, Alis, *Doctoral Dissertations in Musicology*, 160, 173n32
difficulty levels. *See* grade levels of printed music
Digital Image Working Group of the Western States Digital Standards Group, 148n12
Digital Video Disc. *See* DVD
Digital Virtual Disc. *See* DVD
The Directory of Music Research Libraries (Benton), 169, 176n62
Directory of University Libraries in Europe, 169, 176n62
Dirty Linen Folk & World Music, "Record Company Addresses," 108
"Dissertations: A New Approach to Acquisitions" (Lopez), 173n29
dissertations and theses, 159–70; Australia and New Zealand, 168, 176n50; borrowing, 169; in Center for Research Libraries, 169, 176n63; continental Europe, 164–68; copyright issues, 162; databases, 160–62, 163, 167–68; in DDM-Online, 160–61; electronic, 163, 169–70, 176n60; in European libraries, 165; European publication and deposit requirements, 164–65, 176n57; formats available, 163; France, 166–67; Germany, 167–68; guides to, 174n43; in progress, 160, 167–68, 176n54, 176n58; musical examples in, 162; in ProQuest Digital Dissertations, 161–63; publication, 160, 164–66, 173n29; in *RILM Abstracts*, 161; Spain, 168, 176n59; terminology for, 159, 173n28; titles, 163, 174n42; treatment in libraries, 159, 160, 173n26, 173n30; from UMI Dissertation Services, 66; the United Kingdom and Ireland, 164; the United States and Canada, 161–64, 174n35; verifying, 160–61

Dissertationsmeldestelle der Gesellschaft der Musikforschung (DMS), 167–68, 176n58
DocThèses, 175n52
The Doctoral Dissertation as an Information Source (Boyer), 173n27
"The Doctoral Dissertation: Boon or Bane?" (Phelps), 173n25
Doctoral Dissertations in Musicology (Adkins, Dickinson), 160, 173n32
Doctoral Dissertations in Musicology-Online (DDM-Online), 160–61, 173n31
Dooley, Rosemary. *See* Rosemary Dooley Secondhand Books on Music
Dove, Jack, *Music Libraries*, 7n7
Dover Publications (reprints), 144
Drüner, Michael. *See* Musikantiquariat Dr. Ulrich Drüner
Duchin, Douglas, "Trials and Tribulations: Out-of-Print 101," 147n7
Duckles, Vincent: "Book Buying in a University Music Library," 5; *Music Reference and Research Materials*, 151, 168, 171n8, 176n61
Duhon, Bryant, "Technology-Proof Archival," 173n24
DVD, 41, 110; region codes, 42–43. *See also* laser disc; video recordings
DVD Planet, 110

Eaglen, Audrey, *Buying Books*, 2, 78n9, 130n1
Educational Music Service, 70; music-in-print database, 70, 102; orchestral music from, 23
Edwin F. Kalmus: orchestral music, 23; reprints, 144
ejazzlines.com, 104
electronic theses and dissertations (ETDs), 169–70
"Electronic Theses and Dissertations" (Fineman), 177n68
"Electronic Theses and Dissertations

in Music" (Fineman), 177n68
Elibron Classics (reprints), 144
Elliott M. Katt Books on the Performing Arts, 135
emusicquest: The Music-in-Print Series: 103; reviewed, 110n7
Erasmus. *See* Librairie Erasmus
Erasmushaus Musik (antiquarian), 137
ETDs. *See* electronic theses and dissertations
European Article Number (EAN) on printed music, 56–57
Evolution and Status of Approval Plans (ARL), 131n12–32n12

Facets Multi-Media, 110
facsimile editions. *See* OMI—Old Manuscripts and Incunabula
Fair, Judy H, *Microform Management in Special Libraries*, 172n18
Falconer, Joan O., "A Handguide to Do-It-Yourself Music Binding," 30n13
Fichier central des thèses, 176n54
Fidler, Linda, "The Acquisition of Out-of-Print Music," 147n2
Films for the Humanities & Sciences, 110
Fineman, Yale: "Electronic Theses and Dissertations," 177n68; "Electronic Theses and Dissertations in Music," 177n68
Fischer, Harald. *See* Harald Fischer Verlag
Fog, Dan. *See* Dan Fog Musikantikvariat
Folter, Siegrun H, "Library Restriction on the Use of Microfilm Copies," 171n5
Ford, Stephen, *The Acquisition of Library Matierials*, 2
Fox, Edward A., et al., "National Digital Library of Theses and Dissertations," 177n65
Fox, Lisa, *Preservation Microfilming*, 172n17, 172n23–73n23
Frakowski, Marlena, "The Survey of Miniature Scores Deterioration in the Indiana University School of Music Library," 147n1
Front, Theodore. *See* Theodore Front Musical Literature

Gabriel, The Gateway to Europe's National Libraries, 97
Gallini. *See* Libreria musicale Gallini
Gary Thal Music, 76
Gasaway, Lolly, "When U.S. Works Pass into the Public Domain," 148n14
GEMM, Global Electronic Music Marketplace, 146
GEMMvideos, 146
Gerboth, Walter, "Acquisitions: College Library," 8n11
German Music Publishers Association, 100
Global Electronic Music Marketplace, 14
grade levels of printed music, 1
Gramophone Classical Catalogue, 112n12
Gramophone, "Gramofile," 109
Gribenski, Jean, *Thèses de doctorat en langue française relatives à la musique*, 167, 176n53
Griscom, Richard, *Music Librarianship at the Turn of the Century*, 8n9, 29n6
Gronow, Pekka, *An International History of the Recording Industry*, 45n1
Gross, John M., *This Business of Music*, 28n2
Grove Music Online, 28n1
Guerrieri, *Guide d'acquisition de la musique imprimée*, 7n8
Guide d'acquisition de la musique imprimée (Lancelin, Catrice, Guirrieri), 7n8
Guide for Dating Early Published

Music (Krummel), 60n2
Guide to Microforms in Print, 157, 172n19
"Guide to Electronic Theses and Dissertations," 170, 177n67
Guide to Performance Evaluation of Library Materials Vendors (ALA), 78n9
Guide to Reference Books (Balay), 174n43
Guide to Theses and Dissertations (Reynolds), 168, 174n43, 176n61
Guitar Gallery, 104

H & B Recordings Direct, 76
Hall, Barbara, "A Selected Bibliography for Library Acquisitions," 3
Hamm, Charles, "The Musicological Archive for Renaissance Manuscript Studies," 172n15
"A Handguide to Do-It-Yourself Music Binding" (Falconer), 30n13
Handman, Gary P., *Video Collection Development in Multi-Type Libraries*, 47n20
Harald Fischer Verlag (microfilms), 156
Harrassowitz, Otto. *See* Otto Harrassowitz
Hill Monastic Manuscript Library (HMML), 153, 154, 171n13
Hill, Richard S., *Music and Libraries*, 7n9; [editorial on acquiring microfilms from Europe], 171n3
Hochschulschriften 1945–1997 (CD-ROM), 167, 176n55
Höflich, Jürgen. *See* Musikproduktion Jürgen Höflich
Hoover, Lona: "Cataloging and Treatment of Theses, Dissertations, and ETDs," 173n26; "Cataloging Theses and Dissertations: An Annotated Bibliography," 173n26
Hoyt, Byron. *See* Byron Hoyt Music

Humanities and the Library (Couch, Allen), 9n21

Iberbook International, 72–73; MARC records available from, 73, 74; MARC records in OCLC WorldCat and the RLG Union Catalog, 78nn12–13, 102–3
ICCU (union catalog), 9
IDC Publishers (microfilms), 156
Index to Theses . . . of Great Britain and Ireland, 164, 175n45
International Bibliography of Printed Music, Music Manuscripts, and Recordings (CD-ROM), 111n2
International Federation of Library Associations and Institutions (IFLA), Web Accessible National and Major Libraries, 97
International Federation of the Phonographic Industry, 46n7
International History of the Recording Industry (Gronow, Saunio), 45n1
International League of Antiquarian Booksellers, 137, 147n6
International Record Review, "Record Company Addresses," 108
International Standard Book Number. *See* ISBN; ISBN-13
International Standard Music Number. *See* ISMN
International Standard Serials Number. *See* ISSN
Internet retailers. *See* web retailers
Intravaia, Lawrence J., *Building a Superior Band Library*, 8n20
ISBN, 60n4; conversion to European Article Number, 56–57; declining supply of, 58–59; format of, 52–53; in MARC records, 55; on printed music, 53, 67
ISBN-13, 58–59; conversion to in 2007, 59; equivalent to Bookland EAN, 59

Isham Memorial Library at Harvard University, 154, 172n14

ISMN, 60n6, 61n7; acceptance of, 54; administration of, 54, 61n7; conversion to European Article Number, 56–57; false use of, 60n5; format of, 53; in MARC records, 54, 55, 61n9; printing on purchase orders, 54–55; publishers' numbers as elements of, 53–54; *Users' Manual*, 61n6

"ISMN: The International Standard Music Number" (Walravens), 60n6

ISSN: administration of, 54, 61nn7–8; format of, 54; in MARC records 54–55

Istituto centrale per il catalogo unico delle biblioteche Italiane (ICCU, union catalog), 98

J. & J. Lubrano Music Antiquarians, 137

J. B. Muns Fine Arts Books, 135

J. W. Pepper & Son, 70; approval plans, 124–28; catalog numbers, 59; database, 102

Jeffery, Peter, "Music Manuscripts on Microfilm in the Hill Monastic Manuscript Library," 171n13

Jones, Malcolm, *Music Librarianship*, 5, 8n17

Jones, R. Mahlon. *See* R. Mahlon Jones Books & Scores

JRH Media Services, 76

just-in-time publication. *See* on-demand publication

Kalmus, Edwin F. *See* Edwin F. Kalmus

Katt, Elliott M. *See* Elliott M. Katt Books on the Performing Arts

Katz, Bill, *Vendors and Library Acquisitions*, 78n9

Keller, Barbara, "Subject Content through Title," 174n42

Keller, Michael A., "Music," in *Selection of Library Materials in the Humanities, Social Sciences, and Sciences*, 5, 9n21, 29n10

Kellerman, L. Suzanne, "Out-of-Print Digital Scanning," 148n11

Kellman, Herbert, "The Musicological Archive for Renaissance Manuscript Studies," 172n15

King, Robert. *See* Robert King Music Sales

Krasilovsky, M. William, *This Business of Music*, 28n2

Kreider, J. Evan, "Austrian Graduals, Antiphoners, and Noted Missals on Microfilm in the Hill Monastic Manuscript Library," 171n13–72n13

Krieger, Lee A., "OP Scanning: An Acquisitions and Preservation Solution," 148n11

Krummel, D. W., *Guide for Dating Early Published Music*, 60n2; *Music Printing and Publishing*, 29n4, 60n3; "Observations on Library Acquisitions of Music," 5; "Printing and Publishing of Music," 28n1, 29n6

Kuik, Paul van. *See* Paul van Kuik Antiquarian Music

Kultur International Films, 110

labels. *See* recorded music

Lancelin, Michèle, *Guide d'acquisition de la musique imprimée*, 7n8

large-ensemble music. *See* band music; choral music formats; orchestral music

laser discs, 43. *See also* DVD; video recordings

LeBlanc, Albert, *Organizing the Instrumental Music Library*, 8n20

Ledsham, Ian, *Comprehensive Guide to Music Librarianship*, 5, 8n18

Leiserson, Anna Belle, AcqWeb, 3

Lenneberg, Hans: *On the Publishing and Dissemination of Music, 1500–1850*, 28n1, 30n17; "Problems in the International Exchange of Microfilm," 171n4

Lewis, Linda, *Complete Guide to Acquisitions Management*, 2

Librairie Erasmus, 72–73

Library Acquisitions: Practice and Theory, 2

Library Bookseller, 139, 148n10

Library Collections, Acquisitions, & Technical Services, 2

Library of Congress: authorities file, 91n4, 111n4; film archive, 154

"Library Requisition for Out-of-Print Copyrighted Music" (Music Publishers' Association of the United States), 148n16

Library Resources & Technical Services, 3

"Library Restriction on the Use of Microfilm Copies" (Folter), 171n5

Libreria musicale Gallini (antiquarian), 137

Lisa Cox Music (antiquarian), 138

Lopez, Manuel D., "Dissertations: A New Approach to Acquisitions," 173n29

Lubrano, J. & J. *See* J. & J. Lubrano Music Antiquarians

Luck's Music Library, 71; orchestral music, 23

MAchine-Readable Cataloging. *See* MARC, definition of; MARC records

Machine-Readable Coding Guidelines for the U.S. Book Industry, 61n11

Major Orchestra Librarians' Association (MOLA), "The Orchestra Librarian," 30n18

Mann, Alfred, *Modern Music Librarianship*, 8n9

Manual of Music Librarianship (Bradley), 4, 8n11

Maple, Amanda, *Music Librarianship at the Turn of the Century*, 8n9, 29n6

MARC records: contributed by vendors to OCLC WorldCat and the RLG Union Catalog, 74–75, 102–3; 022 field for ISSN; 024 field as nondefault display, 61n9; 028 field as nondefault display, 61n9; 028 field for music publishers' and plate numbers, 51; fields for purchase orders, 131n10; harvested from vendor databases, 74–75; vendor record problems, 74–75

MARC, definition of, 30n20–31n20

Marco, Guy A., *Music Librarianship*, 7n7

Marks, B. R., "The Ordering and Supply of Sheet Music," 5, 8n10

Marsha Berman Musical Literature, 135

Martin Silver Musical Literature, 136

Masters Music Publications (reprints), 144

Matthew, Adam. *See* Adam Matthew Publications

Maxwell, Robert L., *Maxwell's Guide to Authority Work*, 91n4

Maxwell's Guide to Authority Work (Maxwell), 91n4

McClellan, William M., "Microformated Music Indexes," 172n18

McColvin, Lionel, *Music Libraries*, 7n7

Melcher, David, *Melcher on Acquisitions*, 2

Melcher on Acquisitions (Melcher), 2

microfilms, 150–59; archives, 153–55; availability from Europe, 149–50, 171nn2–5; compared to other media, 158–59, 173n24;

film types, 158, 172n23–73n23; handling costs, 158; longevity, 158–57, 173n24; ordering from libraries, 152–53; ordering from publishers, 157–58; published, 155–58; publishers, 155–57; quality control, 155, 172n17; restrictions on use, 150, 153, 171n5; scholars use, 149; standards, 172n22; terminology in this manual, 170n1; verification, 150–52

Microform & Imaging Review, 172n20

"Microform Developments Related to Acquisitions" (Sullivan), 172n21

Microform Management in Special Libraries (Fair), 172n18

"Microform Publishing: Alive and Well in the Electronic Age" (William), 173n24

"Microformated Music Indexes" (McClellan), 172n18

"Microformats and the Music Library: A Bibliographic-Use Survey of Recent Trends" (Arneson), 172n18

Midwest Library Service (second-hand searching), 139

Mikrokosmos, 146

Millen, Irene, "Acquisitions: Public Library," 8n11

Milligan, Stuart, "Music and Other Performing Arts Serials Available in Microform and Reprint Editions," 172n18

MLA. *See* Music Library Association

MLA-L, viii, 30n15

Modern Music Librarianship, 8n9

Montagnana Books, 136

Morrow, Jean, viii

MPA. *See* Music Publishers' Association of the United States

Multicultural Media, 76

Muns, J. B., *See* J. B. Muns Fine Arts Books

Munstedt, Peter, viii

Music and Libraries (Hill), 7n9

"Music and Other Performing Arts Serials Available in Microform and Reprint Editions" (Milligan), 172n18

music information centers: directory of, 66; publications of, 66

Music Librarianship at the Turn of the Century (Griscom and Maple), 8n9, 29n6

Music Librarianship (Bryant, Marco), 7n7

Music Librarianship in America (Ochs), 8n9

Music Librarianship in the United Kingdom (Turbet), 5, 8n19

Music Librarianship (Jones), 5, 8n17

Music Libraries (McColvin, Reeves, Dove), 7n7

Music Library Association: "Automation Requirements for Music Materials," 131n10. *See also* MLA-L

"The Music Library in the College of the Future" (Orne), 7n9

Music Library Service Company: 76, 107; corporate accounts, 106, 107

"Music Literature and Its Dealers" (Wright), 8n10

"Music Manuscripts on Microfilm in the Hill Monastic Manuscript Library" (Jeffery), 171n13

Music OCLC Users Group (MOUG). See *The Best of MOUG*

Music Printing and Publishing (Krummel, Sadie), 29n4, 60n3

Music Publishers' Association [of the United Kingdom], 100

Music Publishers' Association of the United States (MPA): directory of publishers, 15–16, 28, 30n19, 100; "Library Requisition for Out-of-Print Copyrighted Music," 148n16; mission and membership, 29n7

Music Publishers' International ISMN Directory, 28, 60n6

"Music Publishing" (Sturm), 29n6

Music Reference and Research Materials (Duckles, Reed), 151, 168, 171n8, 176n61

"Music Research in Italian Libraries" (Rubsamen), 171n2

Music Selection Sources on the WWW (Seaberg), 146

Musica Bona, 104

Musica Virtual Choral Library: database, 104; publishers list, 100

MusicalAmerica.com, "Industry Links," 100, 108. *See also Musical America International Directory*

Musical America International Directory, 40, 108. *See also* MusicalAmerica.com

Musical Heritage Society, 76–77

The Music-in-Print Series (emusicquest), 103

Musicological Archive for Renaissance Manuscript Studies at the University of Illinois at Champaign-Urbana, 154, 172n15

Musikantiquariat Dr. Michael Raab, 138

Musikantiquariat Dr. Ulrich Drüner, 138

Musikantiquariat Hans Schneider, 138

Musik-Antiquariat Heiner Rekeszus, 138

Musikproduktion Jürgen Höflich, 144

Musique en bibliothèque (Alix, Pierret), 7n8

National Authority File (NAF), 84, 91n4

national bibliographies of music: as selection tools, 99; as verification tools, 99

"National Digital Library of Theses and Dissertations" (Fox), 177n65

national library catalogs: directories, 97; as verification tools, 97

National Library Catalogues Worldwide (University of Queensland), 97

National Music Publishers' Association (NMPA): mission and membership, 29n7; International Survey of Music Publishing Revenues, 28n3

National Television Standards Committee. *See* NTSC video format

Networked Digital Library of Theses and Dissertations (NDLTD), 170, 177nn65–66

NMPA. *See* National Music Publishers' Association

Northern Lights Internet Solutions, "Publishers' Catalogs: Sheet Music," 100

Notes: image scanning requirements for authors, 148n13; price indexes in, 111; as reviewing source, 17

NTSC video format, 41–42

"Observations on Library Acquisitions of Music" (Krummel), 5

Ochs, Michael: *Music Librarianship in America*, 8n9; "What Music Scholars Should Know about Publishers," 30n11

OCLC, definition of, 30n20

OCLC WorldCat: CIP records in, 96; definition of, 30n20, 37; rental music in, 26, 27; searching in, 59–60, 89; vendor MARC records in, 74–75, 78nn12–13, 96, 102–3; as verification tool, 96–97

OMI—Old Manuscripts and Incunabula, 71; facsimile editions from, 70, 71

on-demand publication: of printed music, 16, 18–19, 27; of recorded music, 38–39

On the Publishing and Dissemination of Music, 1500–1850 (Lenneberg), 28n1, 30n17

Online Computer Library Center. *See* OCLC; OCLC WorldCat

online retailers. *See* web retailers

"OP Scanning: An Acquisitions and Preservation Solution" (Krieger), 148n11

The Opera Box, 136

"The Orchestra Librarian" (Major Orchestra Librarians' Association), 30n18

orchestra librarianship, 8n20–9n20, 30n18

orchestral music: definition of sets for, 22–23; description in catalogs, 21–23; ordering parts for, 22–23; vendors of, 23

order requests, organizing, 115–18

Ordering and Claiming Music Materials (Brown), 6, 9n22

"The Ordering and Supply of Sheet Music" (Dawson, Marks), 5, 8n10

ordering process, goals of, 115

orders: approval plan, 124–30; firm, 116; secondhand, 134–35; standing, 116–18; subscription, 117–18; types, 116–18

Organizing the Instrumental Music Library (LeBlanc), 8n20

Orne, Jerrold, "The Music Library in the College of the Future," 7n9

Otto Harrassowitz, 5, 29n9, 71, 72, 73, 78n10, 105; approval plans, 124–28; catalog numbers of, 59; MARC records available from, 73, 74; MARC records in OCLC WorldCat and the RLG Union Catalog, 78nn12–13, 102–3; secondhand searching, 139; web resources provided, 130n2–31n2

out-of-print. *See* secondhand

"Out-of-Print Digital Scanning" (Kellerman), 148n11

"An Overview of Orchestra Librarianship" (Blackley), 8–9n20

PAL video format, 41–42

Parnassus Records, 146

parts: library circulation of, 30n15; replacement of lost, 19–20, 30n16

Paul van Kuik Antiquarian Music, 138

Pavlovsky, Taras, *Describing Music Materials*, 92n7

Pepper, J. W. *See* J. W. Pepper & Son

Phase Alternation Line. *See* PAL video format

Phelps, Roger P., "The Doctoral Dissertation" 173n25

Phillips, Don, *A Selected Bibliography of Music Librarianship*, 4, 8n10

Phonolog (recorded music trade catalog), 106, 112nn13–14

photocopying: copyright implications, 20, 142–43, 148nn15–16; for replacement, 20, 141–43

Pierret, Gilles, *Musique en bibliothèque*, 7n8

plate numbers: definition and original purpose of, 50–51; in MARC records, 51–52; as publishers' numbers, 50

Playback: From the Victrola to MP3 (Coleman), 45n1

Practical Guide to the Music Library (Byrne), 8n20, 30n18

preorder searching: 81–93; authority control, importance of, 95; collections of printed music, 89; diacritics, 83–84; multiple editions, 86–89, 90–91; musical training required, 81, 91n1; pitfalls, 82–91; publishers' numbers, 90; purposes, 81; reissues of recorded music, 88–89; spelling of names and titles, 82–85; transliterations, 84, 92nn5–6 preorder verification, 95–113, 150–52; authority control, importance of, 95; national library catalogs, 97; prices, 97, 105; specialty databases, 104; union catalogs, 98, 150; vendor databases, 102–3

prepublication offers, 66

Preservation Microfilming (Fox), 172n17

"Prices of Music Monographs and Scores as Reflected in *Notes*" (Short), 111n8

Primary Source Microfilm, 156, 157

printed music: approval plans, 124–28; in bookstores, 67, 78n8; collections published, 89; deterioration, 133, 147n1; directories of publishers, 15–16, 28, 30n19, 100; domestic distribution, 14; formats, 86, 120–21; hierarchy in composers' collected editions, 117; ineligible for CIP, 96; international distribution, 15–16, 29n8, 123, 131n5; ISBN used on, 53; MARC records in vendor databases, 74; on-demand publication, 16, 18–19, 27; in periodicals, 117–18; persistence in print, 16; prices, 105, 111n8, 131n5; publishers' catalogs, 99–101; quantity of output, 17–18, 29n4, 29n9; reprints, 143–45; reviews, 17, 29n10, 30n12; types of publishers, 12–14, 16–17, 143–45; unobtainable from book vendors, 67; variant editions, 87–88, 120; vendors, 70–73

"Printing and Publishing of Music" (Boorman, Selfridge-Field, Krummel), 28n1

"Problems in the International Exchange of Microfilm" (Lenneberg), 171n4

Professional Media Services, 77

ProQuest: Digital Dissertations database, 161–63; microfilms (nondissertation), 156; UMI Books On Demand (reprints), 145

publishers: functions of, 11–12, 29n5; limited discounts to libraries, 64; ordering direct from, 64, 65–67; reprint, 143–45; returns policies of, 65, 77n3. *See also* printed music; recorded music

The Publishers' International ISBN Directoryy, 60n4

publishers' numbers: 49–61; formats of, 50, 56, 57, 58; internal production numbers, 52; in MARC records, 51–52; multiples used, 50, 56, 57; on purchase orders, 55, 122; reasons to use in acquisitions, 49; reuse in ISMNs, 53–54; reuse of, 49, 60n1; searching by, 59–60, 90. *See also* ISBN; ISMN; ISSN

publishing: association of term with printing, 11; international nature of, 15–16, 82; sources of income from, 11, 28n3. *See also* publishers; printed music; recorded music

purchase orders: edition specifications, 120; format specifications, 120–21; information to include, 119–23; performance media specifications, 121–22; preparation of, 119–20; publishers' numbers, 122; uniform titles, 122; vendor assignments, 118–19; vendors' catalog numbers, 123

purchase requests, forms for, 81–82

Puvill Libros, 72, 73; MARC records available from, 73, 74; MARC records in OCLC WorldCat and the RLG Union Catalog, 78nn12–13, 102–3

R. Mahlon Jones Books & Scores, 136

Raab, Michael. *See* Musikantiquariat Dr. Michael Raab

Reader in Music Librarianship (Bradley), 5, 8nn12–16

Rebman, Elisabeth, "Music," in *Humanities and the Library*, 9n21
Recital Publications (reprints), 144
The Record Collector (secondhand searching), 146
Record Labels on the Web, 108
recorded music: approval plans, 129–30; compulsory licensing, 86, 92–93nn9–10; copyright in, 93n12; cutouts, 145; directories of publishers, 40, 108–9; history of, 33–34, 45n1; independent labels, 35–36; industry volatility, 36, 46nn3–4; ineligible for CIP, 96; international distribution, 37–38, 112n17; longevity in print, 38, 46n8; major labels, 34–34; on-demand publication, 38–39; in periodical publications, 117–18; prices, 109–10, 113nn18–19; private labels, 36–37; quantity of output, 38–39; reissues, 88–89, 130; reviews, 39, 46nn12–13, 89; secondhand, 145–46
Recording Industry Sourcebook, 40
R.E.D. Classical Catalogue, 106, 112n12
Reed, Ida, *Music Reference and Research Materials*, 151, 168, 171n8, 176n61
Reeves, Harold, *Music Libraries*, 7n7
Rekeszus, Heiner. *See* Musik-Antiquariat Heiner Rekeszus
rental music: in *Bonner Katalog*, 26, 31n21; described in publishers' catalogs, 26–27; early history of, 24; fees for, 25; foreign-language terms for, 26; in OCLC WorldCat and the RLG Union Catalog, 26, 27; procedures for renting, 25; purchase of, 27, 77n4; reasons to rent, 24–25
Répertoire international des sources musicales. See RISM
replacement parts. *See* parts
reprints, 143–45

Research Libraries Group Union Catalog. *See* RLG Union Catalog
Retail Print Music Dealers Association, 71
Reynolds, Michael M., *Guide to Theses and Dissertations*, 168, 174n43, 176n61
Rhinebeck Records, 77
RILM Abstracts of Music Literature: dissertations in, 161; publication formats available, 173n34
RISM, 150, 171n6; sigla used, 151–52, 171n9
Ritter, Steven, "Buying Discs on the Internet," 112n16
RLG, definition of, 30n20
RLG Union Catalog: CIP records in, 96; definition of, 30n20, 37; music records published on CD-ROM, 111n2; rental music in, 26, 27; searching in, 59–60, 89; vendor MARC records in, 74–75, 78nn12–13, 96, 102–3; as verification tool, 96–97
Robert King Music Sales, 104
Rosemary Dooley Secondhand Books on Music, 136
Rubsamen, Walter, "Music Research in Italian Libraries," 171n2

Sadie, Stanley, *Music Printing and Publishing*, 29n4, 60n3
Saffady, William, "Stability, Care, and Handling of Microforms, Magnetic Media, and Optical Disks," 172n23–73n23
sales offers: clearance, 66; microform "gaps," 66; prepublication, 66
Saunio, Ilpo, *International History of the Recording Industry*, 45n1
scanning (digital) 141–42, 148nn11–13. *See also* photocopying
Schaal, Richard: *Verzeichnis deutschsprachiger musikwissenschaftlicher Dissertationen 1861–1960*, 167, 176n57; *Verzeichnis*

deutschsprachiger musikwissen-schaftlicher Dissertationen 1961–1970, 167, 176n57

Schmidt, Karen, *Understanding the Business of Library Acquisitions*, 2, 78n9

Schneider, Hans. *See* Musikanti-quariat Hans Schneider

Scholtz, James C., *Video Acquisitions and Cataloging*, 47n20

Schwann catalogs, 105–6, 112nn10–11

Seaberg, Anna, Music Selection Sources on the WWW, 146

searching. *See* preorder searching

SECAM video format, 42

secondhand, 133–48; catalogs, 135; definition, 134, 147n3; directory of dealers, 135–36, 147n5; orders, 66–67; reasons to acquire, 133; recordings, 145–46; searching, 139–40, 141, 146, 147nn7–8; terms used, 147n4; web sources, 140–41, 145–46. *See also* antiquarian

"A Selected Bibliography for Library Acquisitions" (Hall), 3

A Selected Bibliography of Music Librarianship (Phillips), 4

Selection of Library Materials in the Humanities, Social Sciences, and Sciences, 5, 9n21

"Selection Policies for a University Music Library" (Coover), 5

self-publishing, 16, 65

Selfridge-Field, Eleanor, "Printing and Publishing of Music," 28n1

séquential couleur avec mémoire. See SECAM video format

Shar Music, 104

Shedenhelm, Laura D., "Book Vendor Records in the OCLC Database," 78n13–79n13

Shemel, Sidney, *This Business of Music*, 28n2

Sheppard's Book Dealers in North America, 147n5, 147n8

Short, Brad, "Prices of Music Monographs and Scores as Reflected in *Notes*," 111n8

Sibley Library, 155, 156

Silver, Martin. *See* Martin Silver Musical Literature

Smiraglia, Richard P., *Describing Music Materials*, 92n7

Society of Professional Audio Recording Studios. *See* SPARS codes

society publications, 65–66

Sommer, Susan, "Toscanini Memorial Archives," 172n16

sound recordings. *See* recorded music

SPARS codes, 40–41

"Stability, Care, and Handling of Microforms, Magnetic Media, and Optical Disks" (Saffady), 172–73n23

standard numbers. *See* ISBN; ISBN-13; ISMN; ISSN

"Stop the Dissertation!" (Williams), 173n25

Sturm, George, "Music Publishing," 29n6

"Subject Content through Title" (Keller), 174n42

SUDOC, 98; dissertations in, 167, 175n52

Sullivan, Robert C.: "The Acquisition of Library Microforms," 172n21; "Microform Developments Related to Acquisitions," 172n21

"The Survey of Miniature Scores Deterioration in the Indiana University School of Music Library" (Frakowski), 147n1

système universitaire de documentation (SUDOC, union catalog), 98

"Technology-Proof Archival" (Duhon), 173n24

TESEO, 168, 176n59

Thal, Gary. *See* Gary Thal Music

Theodore Front Musical Liberature,

6, 29n9, 71, 75–76, 136; approval plans, 124–28, 132n18; database, 102

theses. *See* dissertations and theses

Theses and Dissertations as Information Sources (Davidson), 173n28

Thèses canadiennes, 1947–1960 and supplements, 174n35

This Business of Music (Krasilovsky, Shemel, Gross), 28n2

Thor Power Tool Company v. Commissioner of Internal Revenue, 134

Thorin, Suzanne E., *The Acquisition and Cataloging of Music and Sound Recordings*, 6, 9nn23–24

Tillett, Barbara B., "Authority Control: An Overview," 111n1

Timmons, Traci E., "Default Record Displays in Web-Based Catalogs," 61n9

titles of musical works, variations in, 85

Toscanini Memorial Archives (Library at Lincoln Center), 154–55, 172n16; "Toscanini Memorial Archives" (Sommer), 172n1

Touzot Librairie Internationale: MARC records available from, 74; MARC records in OCLC World-Cat and the RLG Union Catalog, 78nn12–13, 111n6

Tower Records, 107

translations of titles, 85

transliteration of non-Roman alphabets, 84, 92nn5–6

Travis & Emery, 136

"Trials and Tribulations: Out-of-Print 101" (Duchin, Wagner), 147n7

Turbet, Richard, *Music Librarianship in the United Kingdom*, 5, 8n19

UMI Books On Demand (reprints), 145

UMI Dissertation Services: Bibliographies available from, 163; DATRIXDirect, 163; Dissertations ASAP, 163–64; participating institutions, 161–62, 174n36–39; prices of products, 163, 174n41

Understanding the Business of Library Acquisitions (Schmidt), 2, 78n9

"Undue Dominance of the Dissertation in Training for the Doctorate" (Bush), 173n25

uniform titles, 85, 92nn7–8; automation requirements for, 131n10; on purchase orders, 122

union catalogs: directories, 98; as verification tools, 98, 150

Universal Product Code (UPC), use on published recordings, 55–56, 74

University Microfilms International. *See* UMI Dissertation Services

University Music Editions, 155, 156

University of Queensland, National Library Catalogues Worldwide, 97

VAI Audio, 110

van Kuik, Paul. *See* Paul van Kuik Antiquarian Music

vendor assignment, criteria for, 118–19

vendors: catalog numbers, 59, 123; criteria for selection and evaluation of, 68–69, 78n9; discounts from publishers, 64, 77n2; discounts to libraries, 64; MARC records in OCLC WorldCat and the RLG Union Catalog, 74–75, 78nn12–13, 102–3; reasons to use, 63–64; specialities of, 69; terms used for, 77n1

Vendors and Library Acquisitions (Katz), 78n9

vendors of printed music, 70–75; catalog numbers of, 59; databases as verification tools, 102–3; directory, 70–71, 72–73; price limits for, 105; prices charged by domestic vs. foreign, 69, 75, 78n10; orchestral music, 23

vendors of recorded music: 75–77; backorder policies, 75; directory, 76–77

vendors of video recordings, 110

verification. *See* preorder verification

Verzeichnis deutschsprachiger musikwissenschaftlicher Dissertationen 1861–1960, 1961–1970 (Schaal), 167, 176n57

VHS, 46–47n14, 110; international standards, 41–42. *See also* video recordings

Vidali, Carole Franklin, *The Acquisition and Cataloging of Music and Sound Recordings*, 6, 9nn23–24

Video Acquisitions and Cataloging (Scholtz), 47n20

Video Artists International, 110

Video Collection Development in Multi-Type Libraries (Handman), 47n20

video home system. *See* VHS

video recordings: formats, 41–43, 46–47n14; international recording standards, 41–42, 47nn15–16, 119; performance rights in libraries, 43–45, 47nn17–18, 48n24; prices, 109, vendors, 110. *See also* DVD; laser discs; VHS

Videolog, 106, 112n14

Wagner, Celia Scher, "Trials and Tribulations: Out-of-Print 101," 147n7

Walravens, Hartmut, "ISMN: The International Standare Music Number," 60n6

want lists, 139–40

Watanabe, Ruth, "American Music Librarianship: An Overview in the Eighties," 8n9

Web Accessible National and Major Libraries (International Federation of Library Associations and Institutions), 97

web retailers, 106–8, 112n15; directory, 112n15

Weidow, Judy, *The Best of MOUG*, 85, 92n8

Western States Digital Standards Group, *Digital Imaging Best Practices*, 148n12

"What Music Scholars Should Know about Publishers" (Ochs), 77n3, 30n11

"When U.S. Works Pass into the Public Domain" (Gasaway), 148n14

Wilkinson, Frances, *Complete Guide to Acquisitions Management*, 2

William, Norman H., "Microform Publishing," 173n24

Williams, David C., "Stop the Dissertation!" 173n25

Wolf, Margareth, *Bibliographie Darstellende Kunst und Musik*, 167, 176n57

Wolverton, Robert E., "Cataloging and Treatment of Theses, Dissertations, and ETDs," 173n26

World Microfilms, 156–57

World Music Central, "Record Labels," 109

The World of Learning, 169, 176n62

Wright, Gordon B., "Music Literature and Its Dealers," 8n10

Writing about Music (Basart), 30n12

Wurlitzer-Bruck (antiquarian), 138

Yankee Music Search (secondhand searching), 146

ABOUT THE AUTHOR

R. Michael Fling is the bibliographer and acquisitions librarian for the William & Gayle Cook Music Library of Indiana University. He received his M.A. in musicology and M.L.S. from the University of Iowa. As a member of the Music Library Association he has served as editor of the MLA Technical Reports Series and the MLA Index and Bibliography Series. His bibliography *Musical Memorials for Musicians: A Guide to Selected Compositions* was published in the latter series in 2001.